200 SELECTED FILM CLASSICS
FOR CHILDREN OF ALL AGES

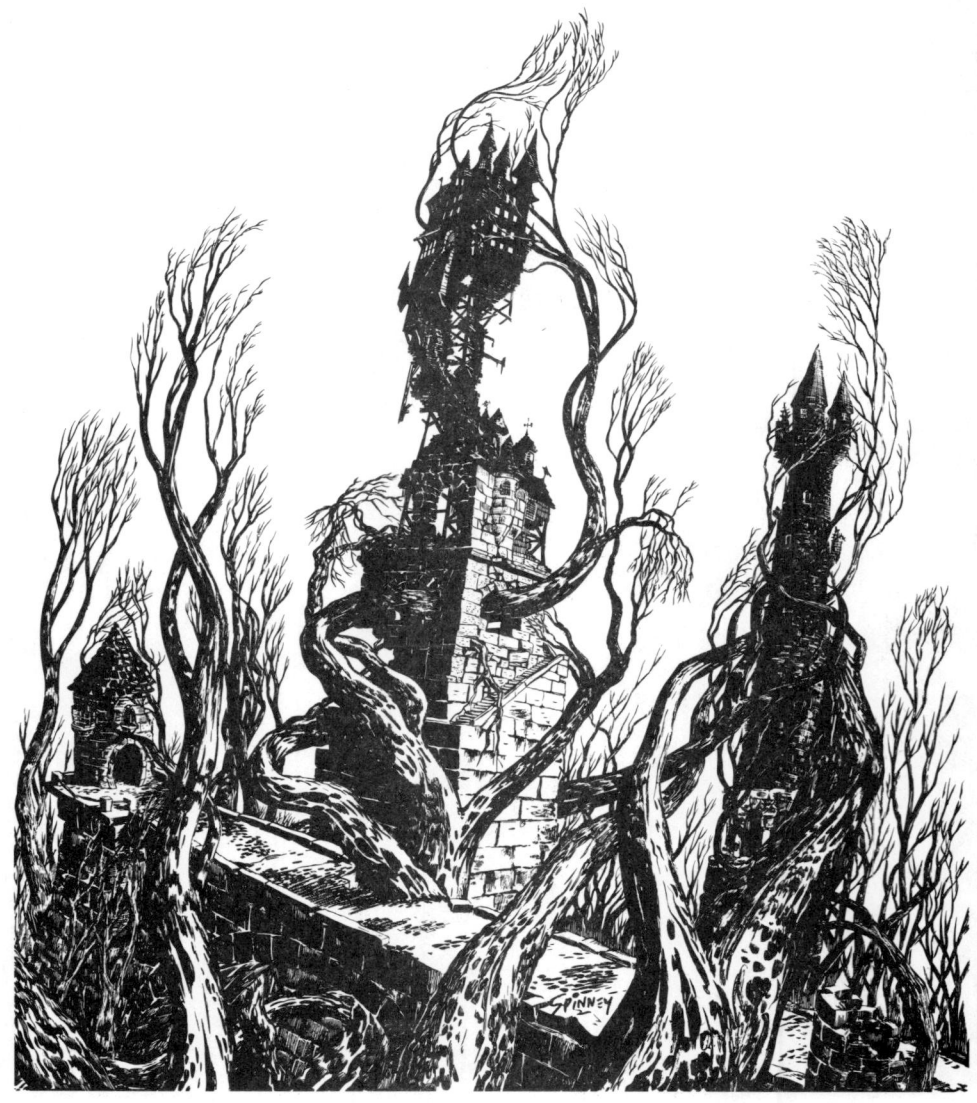
Teetering Tower by Caroll Spinney. Published with permission of the artist.

200 SELECTED FILM CLASSICS
FOR CHILDREN OF ALL AGES
WHERE TO OBTAIN THEM AND HOW TO USE THEM

By

PHILLIP J. SLEEMAN

Director
University Center for Instructional Media & Technology
Professor
University of Connecticut
Storrs, Connecticut

BERNARD QUEENAN

Director
Media Center
Concordia University
Montreal, Quebec
Canada

and

FRANCELIA BUTLER

Professor
Department of English
University of Connecticut
Storrs, Connecticut

CHARLES C THOMAS • PUBLISHER
Springfield • Illinois • U.S.A.

Published and Distributed Throughout the World by
CHARLES C THOMAS • PUBLISHER
2600 South First Street
Springfield, Illinois 62717

This book is protected by copyright. No part of it
may be reproduced in any manner without written
permission from the publisher.

© *1984 by* CHARLES C THOMAS • PUBLISHER
ISBN 0-398-04869-X
Library of Congress Catalog Card Number: 83-4988

With THOMAS BOOKS *careful attention is given to all details of manufacturing and design. It is the Publisher's desire to present books that are satisfactory as to their physical qualities and artistic possibilities and appropriate for their particular use.* THOMAS BOOKS *will be true to those laws of quality that assure a good name and good will.*

Printed in the United States of America
Q-R-3

Library of Congress Cataloging in Publication Data
Sleeman, Phillip J.
  200 selected film classics for children of all ages.

  Includes index.
  1. Children's films — Catalogs. 2. Children's films — History and criticism. I. Queenan, Bernard. II. Butler, Francelia, 1913-   . III. Title. IV. Title: Two hundred selected film classics for children of all ages.
PN1998.S66   1984   011'.37   83-4988
ISBN 0-398-04869-X

PREFACE

THIS book is designed to fill a pressing need for information on developing film programs of works that have endured, as film and literary classics, for the past fifty years and that have extended the life experiences of children and adults.

Whether preparing a film program for television networks, universities or colleges, public schools, public and school libraries, community groups, or professional personnel, organizers of programs are currently significantly perplexed about where to find information and program formats. In media centers and libraries they are confronted with a bewildering collection of feature film catalogs that generally give little inkling of film quality. An obvious extension of this basic information is to expand scholarly expertise to include the study of children and the media. It is expected that this book will be heavily in demand by people in church groups, school groups, and PTA groups and by individuals who are looking for healthy, wholesome entertainment to provide children in church basements or school halls, in homes on rainy weekends, or during a heavy North American winter.

The academic world, which is interested in children's literature and would like to substantiate and strengthen courses on children's cinema, will find this volume extremely helpful. The parent who is interested in organizing neighborhood groups might wish to show children films to expand their world and/or to give them quality entertainment. The intent of this book is to narrow the field to selected film classics and produce a resource useful for the educational, entertainment, and leisure markets. Attention is paid not only to the quality of films but, equally important, to the corresponding literary quality of the books on which the films are based.

This book is designed (1) to be preselective — to include only quality combinations of books and films; (2) to be comprehensive — to bring together information on suggested film programs, addresses of distributors, and related information for rental; (3) to provide a selection of over 200 book/film combinations from which to plan a program; and (4) to offer films in a variety of classifications, i.e., adventure, cartoon animation, children (as central characters), comedy, crime (illegal actions, their detection and exposure), documentary, drama, family (featuring family relationships), fantasy, history (re-creation of a period, recent or remote), horror, musical, nature, religious, romantic, science fiction (including futurism), sea (ships, voyages, action on the high seas), war, and westerns.

This book looks to the future. The information on books and films will be equally helpful regardless of the form of media presentation, whether book, film, videotape, or videodisk. What is important is, as stated previously, to extend life experiences through the classics.

GUIDELINES FOR BOOK USE

YOU have in your hands an invaluable resource for the selection, scheduling, and programming of worthwhile viewing materials for the young.

In the following pages, full details are listed of over 200 quality feature films, selected from the best production output of the last fifty years.

Each film is derived from a literary original, available in English and still in print, that has become by design or usage a regular feature of the reading fare for young people.

The majority of the titles shown are available in 16 mm sound-film format and therefore are suitable for projection to nontheatrical audiences anywhere that a standard projector can be used. Where indicators are not listed of distribution agencies, the films are available in 35 mm format only.

The authors hope that you share their concern for the development of informed and critical standards in viewing, as well as in reading.

A judicious combination of film showings and guided reading projects chosen from these materials will further that aim. This document is not intended as an end — merely a beginning!

ACKNOWLEDGMENTS

FOR substantive research and writing in connection with the literary classics and films listed in this critical anthology, we wish to express our indebtedness to Mr. Richard Wayne Rotert. Additionally, we wish to acknowledge the personal and professional advice and assistance of Ms. Etta Bishop, Assistant to the Director, University Center for Instructional Media and Technology, The University of Connecticut, and Ms. Marian Rollin, University Librarian, Head of Audio-Visual and Microtexts for the University of Connecticut Library, who was generous with her time and her professional suggestions. Furthermore, our special thanks to Walt Disney Productions for their cooperative efforts in providing photographs for this publication.

CONTENTS

Page

Preface v
Guidelines for Book Use vii

Section I
A PHILOSOPHY

Chapter
1. THE PHILOSOPHY OF FILM CLASSICS FOR CHILDREN OF ALL AGES 5

Section II
SPECIAL APPLICATION

2. FILM CLASSICS FOR GRADE KINDERGARTEN THROUGH GRADE 6 13
3. FILM CLASSICS FOR JUNIOR HIGH AND HIGH SCHOOL 18
4. FILM CLASSICS FOR YOUNG AND YOUNG-AT-HEART ADULTS (FROM COLLEGE AGE ON) 25
5. FILM CLASSICS FOR LIBRARIES 31
6. TELEVISION: BROADCAST AND CABLECAST 35

Section III
FILM INDICATORS

7. FILM INDICATORS FOR FILM CLASSICS 41

Section IV
FILM LISTINGS

8. 209 FILM CLASSICS 49

Section V
FILM RENTAL INFORMATION

9. GENERAL FILM RENTAL INFORMATION 257

Section VI
FILM DISTRIBUTORS

10. DIRECTORY OF FILM COMPANIES AND DISTRIBUTORS 267

Section VII
HOW TO USE AND CARE FOR FILMS

11. FILM CARE AND PROJECTION GUIDES 285

Section VIII
INDEX

Author Index 293

200 SELECTED FILM CLASSICS FOR CHILDREN OF ALL AGES

© Walt Disney Productions

SECTION I
A PHILOSOPHY

CHAPTER 1

THE PHILOSOPHY OF FILM CLASSICS FOR CHILDREN OF ALL AGES

THE extension of life experience through selected film classics is so important for children and youth that all persons with special knowledge of the problem should cooperate in making such films available. Reading a book in conjunction with seeing a film of the book reinforces any message the book may have and develops discrimination and literary taste. After hearing his father read *Charlotte's Web* to him, one small boy was taken to see the film.

"And what do you think of the film?" his father asked.

"It was OK," the boy replied. "But the book was better." From such humble beginnings, all literary critics emerge.

Because of the present threat of a world holocaust, many people, including many youths, see no purpose in perfecting the life of man and woman and their relations to other human beings. Such an attitude is not new. Socrates was teaching during chaotic political conditions in Athens, which, in fact, ended in the destruction of the Athenian Empire. Yet, he continued to teach those around him through questions and answers to help youth to develop as perfect plants and, in the words of his pupil Plato, to reach the idea of the Good.

Generally speaking, the film programs currently dished out to children may seem to be psychologically sound, but they reek of materialism and are often unimaginative and shallow. Messages beamed at children are chaotic. In attempts to arrive at truth, truth is lost.

To remedy this distressing situation, two courses of action are suggested. The first is to encourage the filming of the traditional folktales of every culture and of every ethnic group. Bruno Bettelheim, the famous Freudian psychologist, has pointed out "the uses of enchantment" in his best-selling volume of that title. Enchantment through folktales is not only useful but extremely entertaining, and film versions of quality should enter the media. Some unimaginative psychologists oppose this action on the grounds that the tales are sexist and violent. This opposition has prevented the tales from entering the media. The truth is that the tales are all things in life — sexist and nonsexist, violent and nonviolent — but this is not the point.

Children see instances of real sexism and real violence on television all the time. In the folktales, all these unfortunate aspects of life become part of the whole and are transformed in the process. The ultimate endings tell us that in spite of tribulations, there is usually a final justice, that we will "live happily ever after," if not in this world, then in the next. For this reason, folktales, unlike newspaper stories or TV dramas, which often have disturbing loose ends, give us, in the words of Bettelheim, "consolation and hope."

James Hillman, a top Jungian psychologist who gave the Terry lectures at Yale following such distinguished men as Dewey, Erich Fromm, and Jung himself, shares Bettelheim's point of view about the wholesomeness of folktales. Hillman says that adults are "adulterated" people and that they can only be restored by being "restoried." He urges his patients to try the prescription of reading a few folktales every night. He has been doing this for thirty years and says he does not know how it works, but it helps them. The practice helps to bring the jigsaw pieces of their minds together. Similarly, he recommends that children be acquainted with folktales as preventive psychotherapy. The tales are the inheritance we have from our ancestors, emotional wisdom conveyed symbolically.

Telling folktales to children, however, narrows the possibilities of such therapy. Children who need this exposure most are generally in families too poor, too disturbed because of lack of work, or too busy from overwork to read or tell the tales. One of the author's students made a survey of the childhood exposure to folktales of criminals in a large penitentiary. Not one had been told stories or read to. The authors have questioned abused children and discovered a similar deprivation prevails.

A desperate need exists, then, for talented film writers to turn their attention to the wonderful material in the thousands of folktales of every ethnic group. The plots are similar to those of contemporary novels, but the old tales have been emotionally polished so that disturbing loose ends are eliminated. Far from fixing images, filmed stories would be transformed by the viewer's own subtle concept of what characters were like or what transpired.

The second need in children's film programs is realizable now, that is, to select from old books that have stood the test of time and that have been made into good films, programs of ten or twelve that would be appealing and wholesome for each age group: grades K through 6, preteen and early teen, and young adults. (All age groups might enjoy the films, however, for they would be authentic translations of human experience.)

For small children, since they relate instinctively to animals, a series of films are suggested in which animals play a leading role: *Bambi* (a deer), *Dumbo* (an elephant), *Charlotte's Web* (a spider — and there are other denizens of the barnyard as well in the film), *Hansel and Gretel* (whom birds help), *Heidi* (with the goats on the mountain), *The Jungle Book* (in which there are several animals, including wolves and monkeys), *King of the Grizzlies* (a big bear of the American West), *Lassie Come Home* (a collie dog), *One Hundred and One Dalmations* (more dogs), and *Swiss Family Robinson* (various animals).

For children a little older, adventure stories are suggested. These children have moved from the crib to the playpen, to the rooms at home, to the yard, and to the street. They are now ready to extend their experience still further. Films that might appeal to them include *The Adventures of Huckleberry Finn, Around the World in Eighty Days, The Call of the Wild, Christopher Columbus, David Copperfield, The Deerslayer, King Richard and the Crusaders, Kon-Tiki, Little Women,* and *Treasure Island.* (In *Little Women* travel is inward rather than in miles.)

The theme of inward travel would govern the selection of films for still older human beings — college age and above — the young and the young-at-heart. This third film program would begin with *Gulliver's Travels*, an eighteenth-century political satire as contemporary as when it was written, if thoughtful viewers compare it with current situations in Washington and elsewhere. This could be followed by two films that demonstrate the cruelty of prejudice — *The Hunchback of Notre Dame* and *Ivanhoe* — though, of course, there is much more to both stories. The dramatic portrayal of medieval history in *Ivanhoe* would stimulate interest in that period. *Jonathan Livingston Seagull* explores the struggle for human perfection. *Madame Curie* furnishes an ideal role model — and a woman as the model. The *Knights of the Round Table* not only gives a dramatic glimpse into the Old English period but demonstrates the importance of loyalty. *Oliver Twist* has much to say about child abuse, a subject of widespread attention only in recent times. *A Tale of Two Cities* reveals an ugly aspect of human personality that must be guarded against — *Scheudenfreude*, or joy in the misfortune of others. Besides giving a romanticized picture of life in seventeenth-century France, which is bound to stimulate interest in that period, *The Three Musketeers* depicts the devious personalities of the cardinal and of the elegant but vixenish Milady, a totally inauthentic personality in terms of the philosophy of Martin Heidegger.

Finally, the program could climax with the showing of *Moby Dick*, which not only explores the depths of the ocean but the depths of human revenge and depravation.

The reader may think of other films that would be good for little children which would also expand the imaginations of older children and would trigger mind and soul searching among young adults and older people. The preceding lists are only meant to furnish directions. All of them are eligible for deletions and expansions.

The mass media are expanding and will continue to expand, but the nature of the material offered demands more deep and serious attention than it has thus far received.

© Walt Disney Productions

SECTION II
SPECIAL APPLICATION

CHAPTER 2

FILM CLASSICS FOR GRADE KINDERGARTEN THROUGH GRADE 6

THOUGH the following program is designed for grades K through 6, many children as young as three would enjoy participating, and many adults would enjoy it, too. Children relate instinctively to animals, so their own "wisdom of heart" will help to carry them along through this extension of their experience. Ten films would be shown in the program. After showing each film, a workshop would be held in which various activities would be planned to extend the imaginative contemplation of the film just shown. The films selected combine story, attractive pictures, movement, and easily understood dialogue, but other films from the manual could be substituted at the teacher's discretion. The following workshop activities are only suggestions, and teachers may have original ideas that they would prefer to work out with the class.

Day 1. *Bambi* (film, 69 minutes. See Section IV for alphabetical listing of films.)

Day 2. Can you tell the story of Bambi?
What kind of animal was Bambi?
Can you draw Bambi?
What do deer eat?
Where do they live?
Who were Bambi's friends?
Can you draw Thumper the rabbit and Flower the skunk?
What does Bambi do when he is frightened?

What color is his tail when he flips it up?
What does the rabbit do?
What does the skunk do?
How did the animals help Bambi?
(A field trip to a zoo or children's museum might be fun.)

Day 1. *Charlotte's Web* (film, 94 minutes)
Day 2. How did Charlotte help Wilbur?
What words did she write for him?
Let's write these words.
How many legs does a spider have?
Can you draw a spider?
What is a web?
Where does a web come from?
Can you draw a web?
How many children did Charlotte have? (514) Can you count them?
What other animals were in the barnyard?
Can you draw a pig? A sheep? A goose? A rat?
Do you know the noises a pig, a sheep, and a goose make?
Let's pretend we are in a barnyard and we are talking animal talk to each other. What parts do you want to play?

Day 1. *Dumbo* (film, 64 minutes)
Day 2. What kind of animal was Dumbo?
Can you draw an elephant?
What is the elephant's trunk for?
What does an elephant eat?
Who was Dumbo's best friend?
Can you draw a mouse?
Have you ever been to a circus?
Why did the circus animals laugh at Dumbo?
The animals do tricks in the circus ring. What animal would you like to be? Let's be animals in a circus and march around the room.
Do you know what country Dumbo's family came from? (Show pictures of Africa from *The National Geographic*, a geography book, or a wildlife magazine.)

Day 1. *Hansel and Gretel* (film, 75 minutes)

Film Classics for Grade Kindergarten Through Grade 6   15

Day 2. What was the witch's house made of? (If a kitchen is available, have the children help make a large batch of gingerbread — a mix can be used — but let them each cut out a small gingerbread house.)

Gingerbread contains ginger, a spice. Do you know what a spice is?

(If there is a recess, play a game of tag in which one child in a witch hat chases the others. Whoever gets caught becomes the witch.)

Birds helped Hansel and Gretel find their way home. (Bring in a supply of straight reeds or slender branches. Tie strings to one end.) Now draw, color, and cut out some pretty birds, and we will staple them to the other end of these strings. You can then skip and "fly" the birds around the outside part of the room or fly them in the yard during recess.

Now we will make a bird scrapbook of feathers. When you go home, look for feathers and bring them in. We will make a book of all kinds of feathers — neck feathers, which are small and very soft; breast feathers, which are soft, too; wing feathers, which are strong and straight or curved; and tail feathers. Try to get feathers of various colors from robins, cardinals, bluejays, and sparrows. Perhaps you would like to make your own bird scrapbook.

Day 1. *Heidi* (film)
Day 2. Do you know what a mountain is?
What makes a mountain?
Draw Heidi and her grandfather and Peter, the goatherd.
What did Heidi eat in her grandfather's house?
What is bread made of?
What is cheese made of?
Can you draw a goat?
Do you know where Switzerland is? (Show its position on a globe and show pictures of the country.)
Let's make up our own story about Heidi. Does anyone want to play Heidi? Peter? the grandfather? the goat? The rest of you can be the people in the village.

Day 1. *The Jungle Book* (film, 115 minutes)
Day 2. (Try to get a record of wolf howls.)
Are wolves bad or good? (They are just animals trying to live.)
What animals that you know are related to wolves? (Dogs.)
What is a mongoose? What do they look like? (Long, small, skinny, pointed faces, bushy tails. Found in India and Africa, but not in the United States. They live in holes of various kinds.)
Where is India? (Show on a globe and show still pictures of the country.) The author, Rudyard Kipling, once lived in India.
What happened to Mowgli?
Where do monkeys stay most of the time? (Trees). What do they look like? Can you draw a monkey? A camel?

Day 1. *King of the Grizzlies* (film, 93 minutes)
Day 2. Where do grizzlies live? (American West)
Do you know what hibernation is?
Do you know what an Indian is? (Show still pictures from a library of various tribes.)
Are there Indians where you live?
Who was in this country first? We or the Indians?
There are many kinds of bears. (Show still pictures from a geography book, wildlife book, or *National Geographic*.)

Day 1. *Lassie Come Home* (film, 88 minutes)
Day 2. Do you have a dog? What kind is it?
What kind of dog is Lassie?
(Show pictures of all the various kinds of dogs, as shown in a children's encyclopedia.)
Act out the story of Lassie. You can pretend that its long journey was around your room.

Day 1. *One Hundred and One Dalmations* (film, 79 minutes)
Day 2. What does a Dalmation look like? (Short white hair, black or dark-brown spots. Developed in Yugoslavia several hundred years ago. Used in fire departments and as a circus dog, but mainly as a good pet.)

Can you tell the story of the film?
(A field trip to a dog show or a pet shop might be fun at this point.)

Day 1. *Swiss Family Robinson* (film, 128 minutes)

Day 2. Cut out the top of a large cardboard box. Pretend it is an island. Make figures of the people and animals in the story and tie them to long strings. Drop them through the top of the box (holding onto the strings) and act out the play in your own words.

Do you know any other stories about people living on islands?

There are *Island of the Blue Dolphins, Robinson Crusoe, Treasure Island*, where people lived for awhile, hiding from pirates, and many other stories about islands. (The class might read a shortened version of *Robinson Crusoe*, that is, the older children, or the teacher might tell or read it to the little ones.)

CHAPTER 3

FILM CLASSICS FOR JUNIOR HIGH AND HIGH SCHOOL

As human experience expands beyond the playpen, the home, the yard, the street, and the school, new places appear on the horizon that preteen or early teenagers are eager to explore. For this reason, adventure stories of quality are appealing. The best are often based on literary classics, so young readers can either read the book in the original or in some instances a simplified version and compare it with the film. Interesting discussions can develop out of such comparisons. This is important in an age increasingly occupied with the media. Of interest are why the screenwriter cut certain portions of the book, why s/he highlighted certain parts, and so on. In this way, much can be learned about societal strictures, things a writer can say that a film writer cannot say. This dual approach also helps children learn about the technique of writing stories and screenplays for an expanding market.

Through film, the content of the book — the psychology of the characters as portrayed through their actions, the nature of strange environments, as well as other periods of time — can be further explored and understood. Films can motivate nonfictional studies of psychology, sociology, geography, and history.

A film program for students in the upper grades or high school might include ten films: *Adventures of Huckleberry Finn, Around the World in Eighty Days, Call of the Wild, Christopher Columbus, David Copperfield, The Deerslayer, King Richard and the Crusaders, Kon-Tiki, Little*

Women, and *Treasure Island*. (Other films, of course, could be substituted at the discretion of the leader.)

Day 1. Before seeing the film today, read Mark Twain's *Huckleberry Finn*.

Day 2. What differences did you notice between the book and the film?
Why do you suppose the scenario writer or director made these changes?
About how old was Huck Finn in this story?
How would Huck's life change if he were living it now?
What does the river symbolize? The land?
Discuss Huck's battle with his conscience over turning Jim in to the authorities.
On whose side was Mark Twain? How do you know?

Day 1. Before seeing the film, read Jules Verne's *Around the World in Eighty Days*. (*Note to teacher:* Reading lists might be given to students the previous spring so that books could be read during summer vacation.)

Day 2. This story was published in 1873. What changes might Jules Verne make in telling the story if he were to rewrite it now?
Get a list from a futurist group of predictions of what will happen in the next 100 years. Or, projecting future changes on your own, write a science fiction story — a short one of perhaps six pages, typed, double spaced, imagining life at a future time.
To understand better what science fiction is, read a few stories from the magazine, *Fantasy and Science Fiction*, or some other science fiction magazine.

Day 1. *Call of the Wild*. If possible, read the book before seeing the film.

Day 2. Jack London, the author of *The Call of the Wild*, lived his novels. He was greatly influenced by Karl Marx and by Darwin. (The pet dog in the Yukon who becomes leader of a wolf pack is an example of Darwinian survival.) London himself took part in the Klondike gold rush.
Can you make an outline of the plot of this novel? Does it

parallel that of the film? (To make the plot outline, include the following five major sections: (a) How does the book begin? (b) Do you notice a major conflict that must be resolved? (c) What keeps the story moving ahead? That is, do problems arise that lead to other problems, and so on, so that you are eager to see how it all comes out? (d) At what point do things become the most exciting? (e) When do the problems begin to be solved? (f) How does it all end? That is, include the five Cs: Commencement, Conflict, Carrying force (or motivation), Climax, and the Conclusion. After these major section headings of your outline, you can put the specific subpoints that relate to them. In this way, you will have some idea about how to plot an exciting novel.

Day 1. See the film *Christopher Columbus*.

Day 2. After looking in a biography or history, discuss how the filmmaker fleshed out the story of Columbus. Some historians now believe that several other men discovered the New World before Columbus. In this connection, be prepared to discuss such books as Cyrus Hoy's *Before Columbus* (Brandeis University). You might also want to read Jesse Stuart's novel about the Melungeons in Northeast Tennessee or factual accounts of other groups believed to have been here before Columbus.

Day 1. See the film *David Cooperfield*.

Day 2. If possible, read one of the many biographical accounts of the author, Charles Dickens. These accounts are particularly important in connection with this novel and film, as the story contains much autobiography. Dickens had a hard life as a boy. His father went to prison for debt, and Dickens had to work in a blacking factory and experienced the seamy side of London street life.

If you were writing an imaginary (fictional) account of your own life, do you have exciting experiences that you could use in the story? You might try writing a short story in which you changed the place and the names but used some of your own experiences.

Day 1. See the film *The Deerslayer*.
Day 2. If possible, read the book on which this film is based. The author, James Fenimore Cooper, turned his experiences as a seaman and wanderer in the woods of upper New York State in the early nineteenth century into exciting novels, some of the best of which were about Indians.

What was the political and social status of Indians at the period when *The Deerslayer* was written? What is it now?

In an encyclopedia or book about Indians, look up the major tribes of Indians and their customs. Which live in the far West? In the Midwest? In the South? In the Northeast? Which lived in wigwams? Which in tepees? Groups of students might be asked to research and discuss Indians in particular areas. The Wampanoag Nation, Narragansett tribe, for example, celebrated four Thanksgivings: the Maple Sugar Thanksgiving, the Strawberry Thanksgiving, the String Bean Thanksgiving, and the Harvest Thanksgiving, which was taken over by the Pilgrims.

Can anyone tell any Indian legends?

Obtain a record of Indian music. Perhaps someone can do an Indian dance. If there is an Indian museum in the area, students might enjoy visiting it to study Indian artifacts.

Day 1. See the film *King Richard and the Crusaders* (114 minutes).
Day 2. This film is derived from the novel *The Talisman* by Sir Walter Scott, which some more advanced students might like to read.

If one counts the Children's Crusade, there were ten crusades in all between 1095 and 1272, or within about 200 years. This story is about the Third Crusade, in which Richard occupied Acre and later Jaffa, and gained control of Jerusalem and Cyprus for a while. On a map of Israel, find Acre and Jerusalem. Jerusalem has a long political history. What is its status now? Go to a travel agency and try to get pictures of Acre, Jerusalem, and Cyprus. If you know travelers, borrow guidebooks to these places.

Study the history of the crusades in Ernest Barker's *The Crusades* (reprinted 1971) or in some other book. All of the crusades make fascinating reading, especially the tragic Children's Crusade, 1212, led by a visionary French boy. Many hundreds of children, dressed in white, went to the port of Marseilles to beg rides of sea captains to the Holy Land. It was thought that their innocence would persuade the Moslems to give up the country, but they never reached the Holy Land, for the captains sold them into slavery in Africa.

Day 1. See the film *Kon-Tiki* (72 minutes).

Day 2. Some students might want to read Thor Heyerdahl's book on which the film is based.

Where is Polynesia? Ask an anthropologist if s/he thinks the Polynesians could have come from South America. You might also read Heyerdahl's *Sea Routes to Polynesia* (1968). Does his theory sound plausible? Since Heyerdahl made the crossing on a raft from Peru, you might also want to study the history and peoples of Peru. A short study appears in the *Columbia Encyclopedia*. You might also like to read about ancient places in Peru such as Machu Picchu. (See Hiram Bingham, *Lost City of the Incas* [reprinted, 1969].)

Oral reports, pictures, and maps would make the story even more fascinating.

Day 1. *Little Women* (film version starring Katharine Hepburn, 115 minutes).

Day 2. This film affords an excellent opportunity to study the changing sex roles of women. Would Jo be regarded as a "liberated" woman?

How did Louisa May Alcott's life experiences help her build the story (her experiences as a nurse during the Civil War, putting on plays as a child, etc.)

Did the film include the acting out by the girls of *Pilgrim's Progress*? Read the book, of course, to see what the screenwriter chose to highlight, what to eliminate. Do you think his/her choices were correct?

Do you think the actors chosen suited their roles?

In connection with this film showing, you might want to

extend your literary knowledge of the Civil War period. Walt Whitman also served as a hospital nurse during the Civil War and wrote many poems about this experience, which appeared in *Drum Taps* and its sequel *Hospital Visits*. You might want to read some of these poems as well as some of his others, including "Out of the Cradle Endlessly Rocking" and "When Lilacs Last in the Dooryard Bloom'd."

An especially thoughtful article is Anne Hollander's "Reflections on *Little Women*," *Children's Literature*, vol. 9, pp. 28-39, Yale University Press, 1981.

Day 1. *Treasure Island* (96 minutes).

Day 2. The book's author, Robert Louis Stevenson, lived in Edinburgh, Scotland. He married an American, and they "spent a peaceful honeymoon in a deserted miner's cabin on top of Mount St. Helens." (Since then, the eruptions of St. Helens make it the last place to spend a peaceful honeymoon.) The book was originally called *The Sea Cook* and was serialized in a boys' magazine, *Young Folks* (1881-1882).

The story takes place in the mideighteenth century. Various ships were popular then, including the English man-of-war, the pinnace, the topsail schooner, the frigate, and the galleass. What kind of ship was the *Hispaniola*, on which Jim was sailing? What flag did the ship fly? (Union Jack). What flag did the pirates fly? (Jolly Roger). Why did the ship carry lemons? What is a powder horn? You might want to read a book about pirates such as Philip Gosse's *The History of Piracy* (1954) or Juan Cabal's *Piracy and Pirates* (1957). What are "pieces of eight"?

Stevenson does not tell where Treasure Island is, but it is known that he was inspired to write the story after reading Edgar Allen Poe's story "The Gold Bug." That fantasy island lies near Charleston, South Carolina, not far from Savannah, Georgia. Do you know the meaning of "caulk, coxswain, bosun, fathom, figurehead, fo'c'sle, galley, halyards, heave to, keel, knot (nautical mile, or 6,080 feet per hour), lee-side, and log"?

Buried treasure of several pirates is believed still to be found in the Cocos Islands, near the Galapagos Islands and Costa Rica. Two of the pirates who are believed to have hidden gold there are Edward Davis and Benito Benito.

Stevenson wrote other works including the famous *Child's Garden of Verses* and *Dr. Jekyll and Mr. Hyde*, a story based on a real life tavern keeper in Edinburgh, who was a respectable citizen by day and a highwayman by night.

CHAPTER 4

FILM CLASSICS FOR YOUNG AND YOUNG-AT-HEART ADULTS (FROM COLLEGE AGE ON)

THROUGH books and films one can travel not only into other periods and places but also into the human mind. Like books, some films can be appreciated by children on a simple level but are best understood by adults.

The following ten films extend the life experience of adults in many ways: revealing satire of political situations (*Gulliver's Travels*), suggesting the cruelty of prejudice against physical handicaps or ethnic background (*Hunchback of Notre Dame* and *Ivanhoe*), exploring the struggle for human perfectibility (*Jonathan Livingston Seagull*) and portraying an ideal role model (*Madame Curie*), noting the repercussions of disloyalty (*Knights of the Round Table*), the suffering occasioned by child abuse (*Oliver Twist*), the inhumanity sparked by revolution (*Tale of Two Cities*), ultimate justice and the rewards of courage (*Three Musketeers*), and the nature of revenge (*Moby Dick*). Readers and/or viewers are likely to ruminate on what the literary experience adds up to in terms of their own lives.

Day 1. *Gulliver's Travels* (film, 85 minutes).
Day 2. When he wrote this book, Swift had in mind the political situation in the eighteenth century. Discuss the imaginary realms of Lilliput and Brobdingnag, but bring the political satire up to date. Place the happenings in Washington, D.C., for example.

Discuss and give examples of the various kinds of satire, such as irony and sarcasm.

Students who read well should read and make a report on the two books of *Gulliver's Travels* not included in the film: The Floating Island of Laputa and the story of Gulliver's adventures among the Houyhnhnms. Some students might want to obtain a book on scenario writing from the library and try writing a scenario of either of these two stories.

Swift is also satirizing Gulliver. From what point of view, then, is *Gulliver's Travels* told?

Read another of Swift's works, *A Modest Proposal*, and write a similar satire of the arms race. (*A Modest Proposal* is brief.)

Dip into a biography of Swift or read an account in an encyclopedia of his unusual life — his love for the girl Stella and his baby talk to her in the *Journal to Stella* (H. Williams, editor, 1948).

Day 1. *The Hunchback of Notre Dame* (117 minutes).
Day 2. Make a plot outline of the film. How exactly is it introduced? When does the conflict occur? What successive incidents keep the film moving ahead? When do things reach a climax? How long after that does the film end? Does the conclusion satisfy you?

Victor Hugo is one of the most famous of all French writers. Read a selection of another of his works, *Les Misérables*, and note how Jean Valjean is forced into crime through poverty. Interview a sociologist on the relationship between poverty and crime or read an article or book on criminology.

Day 1. *Ivanhoe*.
Day 2. The role of Rebecca. Is she fairly treated?

Discuss the period in which the story takes place, 1190. Twenty years earlier, Sir Thomas à Beckett had been murdered in his own cathedral at Canterbury, and about twenty years later, King John was forced to sign the Magna Carta at Runnymede. What historical relationship does the signing of the Magna Carta have to our own democratic government? Read a brief biography of the author, Sir Walter Scott.

Day 1. *Jonathan Livingston Seagull* (114 minutes).

Day 2. Do you think this story is a classic? How would you define a classic? Will the story still be read 100 years from now? Sea gulls are scavengers. Was the sea gull a good choice as a protagonist?

Jonathan believed that most gulls are bound by chains of thought. Would you volunteer to say what chains bind you? He also believed that boredom, fear, and anger shorten life. Do you agree?

Love, he defines, as seeing the good in everyone. Would you consider this a comprehensive definition?

Day 1. *Madame Curie* (124 minutes).

Day 2. Madame Curie's life might be looked on as a practical application of the philosophy of Jonathan Livingston Seagull, although she lived long before Jonathan's story was written. Hers is a biography rather than a fantasy or novel. How does her life reveal her philosophy?

A general discussion might be held on distinguished women in France, England, and the United States in the nineteenth century. Another woman in France who is fascinating to study is the novelist George Sand.

Day 1. *Knights of the Round Table* (115 minutes).

Day 2. This story takes place in the Old English period, or long before *Ivanhoe*. Many books chronicle the development of the Arthurian legend. One of the clearest accounts may be found in Albert C. Baugh's *The Literary History of England*. The person, however, who brought the story to perfection was Sir Thomas Malory, a knight of the fifteenth century, a rapist, and cattle rustler, who may have died in prison. (See Richard Altick, *The Scholar Adventures*.) Many subsequent accounts of Arthur derive from Malory's telling, including Tennyson's *Idylls of the King*.

Discuss any versions of the Arthurian legend that you may have read and liked and any other film versions you may have seen.

Using Baugh or some other source as a guide, list the major steps in the development of the legend — first in England, then in France, and then its return to England. This legend's history serves as an example of how all legends can be enriched through time and retelling.

Day 1. *Oliver* (musical).

Day 2. If you have read the story *Oliver Twist*, compare the two versions. Which do you prefer?

Read one of the biographical accounts of the author, Charles Dickens. These accounts are important in connection with this novel and film because they reflect some of the boyhood observations of the author. Dickens, whose father went to debtor's prison, had to work in a blacking factory as a boy, and he experienced the rough London street life. Dickens wrote the novel partly to expose workhouses and the Poor Law. He was deeply concerned with societal conditions that breed crime.

Are his characters true to life or caricatures?

Can you discuss his sense of the dramatic?

Can you think of a place now filled with human wretchedness and poverty that might yield a story comparable in quality to *Oliver Twist*? Do you know of any such stories? Have his techniques become dated, or would they still work? Could you write three pages or more, imitating Dicken's style?

Day 1. *Tale of Two Cities* (128 minutes).

Day 2. Also by Dickens, this account of the French Revolution has been criticized as revealing his penchant for melodrama, but the horror is probably a fairly accurate representation of history. The guillotined bodies of Louis XVI and Marie Antoinette still rest in the ground of a small park a short distance behind the Paris Opera, along with the bodies of some 2,000 of their Swiss Guard. People *did* knit as they watched the executions. The last guillotining in Paris occurred in 1939, but the watchers were limited to officials and the news corps.

Seeing this film might lead to a discussion of capital punishment — whether it is ever justified. People are still divided on this subject. Some people believe that there is sentience immediately after death. When Charlotte Corday was beheaded during the French Revolution, she is said to have registered indignation for an instant. This subject, too, is still a matter of debate.

Day 1. *The Three Musketeers* (126 minutes).
Day 2. If you have read the book, you will see that it was greatly shortened in the film version, though the film sticks substantially to the major story theme.

This swashbuckling narrative is by Alexandre Dumas, Sr., whose life was almost as romantic as that of his protagonists in this novel and also in *The Man in the Iron Mask* and *The Count of Monte Cristo*. His background was unusual in that his grandfather was white, his grandmother, black. He was a friend of George Sand and of Charles Dickens (you have seen two films based on Dickens's novels). At the end of his life, Dumas, a gourmet, occupied himself with the writing of a massive cookbook. It is said that on his deathbed, he remarked ironically that he would eventually live through that last book, rather than through the fame of his novels.

Gene Kelly, the dancer, plays the leading role of D'Artagnan in this film. There are at least ten different films of *The Three Musketeers* in English, one of them being a musical comedy, with the Ritz Brothers. Discuss the use of music and dance as adjuncts to film versions of novels. Do you find them helpful or distracting?

Day 1. *Moby Dick* (115 minutes).
Day 2. After reading the book or portions of it, be prepared to discuss what major techniques were used to change the novel into a film. Do you think they were effective? Would you have retained some things and cut others from the book to make a good film?

The ship represents the world. What other symbol for the world have we encountered in a previous film? (The

Round Table).

Discuss the nature of vengeance in psychological or religious terms.

Can you compare the great white whale to a principal object in a lesser film — the great white shark in the film *Jaws*? Do the whale and the shark symbolize the same thing, or is there a difference?

What was the fatal character flaw of Captain Ahab? It was the first of the Seven Deadly Sins, the others being covetousness, lust, anger, gluttony, envy, and sloth. Do you find evidence of the existence of any of the other sins among the characters in the book or in the film?

You might want to read a brief biographical account of Melville to see how his life experience served as source material for his novels. Shorter stories of his that are fascinating reading are "Bartleby" and "Billy Budd." The novel *Pierre* is an interesting psychological study. In fact, his stories generally contain deep explorations into human psychology. You might want to make a psychological comparison of Ishmael, Bartleby, and Billy.

If you are near an old whaling port such as New Bedford or Mystic, several persons might enjoy making a field trip in connection with the film program and look into the terminology used by seamen on a whaler.

CHAPTER 5

FILM CLASSICS FOR LIBRARIES

FILM programs in libraries are at once the broadest in appeal and the most difficult to arrange. Often they must attract both children and the adults who accompany them. They are sometimes followed by art shows or other events that take place in special seasons. They are expected to accomplish something beyond a commercial showing, perhaps to be shown in conjunction with study programs on topics or themes related to the films. More practical instruction may accompany a showing. For instance, children and adults may be given a demonstration on how to use a camera or cameras. They may even be given an opportunity to write a script and re-create in their own way a scene from a film. Beyond this, film showings are sometimes followed by lively discussions of the merits of a film or of the changes that have taken place between the book version and the film version and the reasons for these changes.

Thus, the film showings become a multiple learning process of great potential value. For this reason, it is a mistake to show only shorts designed solely for children. These have their place in limited library programs in connection with preschool children or slightly older children, but there are times when even the youngest children enjoy watching film classics, particularly if their older siblings accompany them.

Many librarians have discovered to their surprise that bright

---

The authors wish to thank Etta Bishop, Elizabeth Moody, and Marian Rollin for their comments on film viewing in school and public libraries, which assisted them in preparing this chapter.

children as young as three will watch an adult movie with rapt attention if they are accompanied by adults. It is difficult to determine what or how much they derive from the experience, but they undoubtedly observe a great deal more than is generally acknowledged. After all, the astounding amount of all learning that these children absorb within a few years is more wondered at than understood. For this reason, any series of movies of quality based on the classics may enrich a child's life experience, no matter how young the child is.

If some children become restless during a film, other activities can be arranged, and these children can be quietly transferred to another room or to a recreation area. Sometimes they may be especially fascinated with one portion of the film and would enjoy drawing pictures of what they have seen and appreciated. They might also want to dance or to act out a portion.

One possibility would be to show only a portion of a film to the young children before the adult showing, then take the children into another room to draw pictures or to act out the episode while the adults continue to watch the film. Selected portions of films such as *Gulliver's Travels*, *Treasure Island*, or *Oliver Twist*, for example, might be chosen and shown to the youngsters. Children could thus be introduced pleasantly to the classics and be tempted to take out simplified versions for home reading.

Librarians agree that film showings tend to increase use of the library. Not only are the books on which the films are based taken out, but visitors see others checking out books and are tempted to follow suit. While in the library, they browse through the collections and find unexpected areas of interest.

Creativity is greatly stimulated by film showings. Children and adults together may want to go on to learn how to operate cameras, write scripts, act out scenes, and have previews and final showings of their own productions made either with videotape or film. Though these procedures are difficult, people are often surprised at how successful their first attempts can be, and in any case, there is a great satisfaction in producing something original. Seldom does any medium enable one to profit so clearly from one's mistakes, for they are clearly visible. For first attempts, the actors need not speak. A narrator can read an episode that the actors interpret.

Adding cameras and videotape is not necessary for a successful school or library film program, however. The story can be acted out without attempting to film it, or activities for older children may be limited simply to discussing the lighting, acting, costumes, scenery, and plot of a film, describing what changes might be made if the viewers were producing it instead of a professional. Since this kind of intellectual exercise sharpens the powers of observation, it is also helpful in developing writing skills.

John T. Short, an executive of Coronet Media, has suggested certain guidelines for a film series for young people, among them (1) listing and discussing key words prior to showing the film; (2) introducing the film, telling people why this particular film is being shown; (3) suggesting certain questions for which the viewers can look for answers in the film; (4) keeping notes on the film — the lighting, the acting, the story, and particularly the reaction of those who saw it, for future reference; these notes should be filed; (5) handing out a prepared bibliography to viewers, including information on the film — the cast, director, date of production, story line — and parallel information on the classic on which it was based — author, title of book, date of publication — with space on the form for viewers to record differences they have noted between the plot development of the book and the film, that is, what is highlighted, what was omitted or downplayed, and which version viewers preferred and why.

Considerable confusion and disagreement exist as to the role the classics should have in a film series. For instance, in an article entitled "Teaching Film," (*Audiovisual Instruction*, September 1977), Steve Ryan writes, "Rather than starting by showing 'classics,' start at the students' level of understanding and interest. Show films that appeal to their tastes, that they can relate to. Introduce the 'classics' later when they have developed their film literacy skills." With this point of view, the authors of this text totally disagree. Many simplified versions of classics exist to which younger library goers can be introduced. They should be conditioned to an interest in the best literature as early as possible. After all, that is why certain books are classics. To give children film shorts, experimental films, or documentaries when they can view at the least segments of films with more depth and human meaning or films based on books with these components is a mistake.

Professor Ryan did give some excellent suggestions on how to involve the viewing audience in a film. Some of the suggestions include the following: Talk about people in the films. "What kind of a character. . . . Why did this character do what he or she did? . . . Are the characters believable. . . . Do you know anyone like that?" Also, "What happens in the film?" (Sure to cause disagreement.) Prove points with reference to "particular scenes or shots or plot sequences." Older students can identify filming techniques (low angle shots, fast editing, dolly shots, etc.) and discuss how these individual shots build up "a particular scene or scenes."

They can also discuss "how a film works on an audience." That is, they can answer such questions as, "What scene had the most effect on you? Why? . . . When watching the film whose side are you on? Why? . . . What techniques does the film use to get us involved in it?" Viewers can also discuss who creates the film: "Who is primarily responsible for the film looking the way it did — the actors, the writer, the producer, the director, the editor?"

Professor Ryan also suggests discussing the work of the actor or actress: "What is the difference between an actor on the screen and someone in real life in a similar situation?" Also, viewers can make comparative judgments with films seen in previous weeks. Finally, an attempt should be made to help a viewer to "relate the experiences and values of a particular film to one's own life."

CHAPTER 6

TELEVISION: BROADCAST AND CABLECAST

MUCH has been researched, written, and discussed relative to the adequacy and quality of television programs for the viewers. Unfortunately, most of these studies are conducted in response to the volume of negative public reaction to the present quality and type of broadcast programming, that is, too much violence, sex, divorce, racial discrimination, and sexism. This even includes the Saturday morning children's television.

Even though the preceding statements are directed primarily at broadcast television, quality programs have been and will continue to be a problem of both broadcast and cablecast television. Broadcast television, by its nature and financial structure is difficult to change; however, with the rapid addition of cable television companies in the United States, the significant interconnections of the companies, both inter- and intrastate, and their transmission and relay by satellite, the pressure for change within the broadcast area is significant.

Cable companies are designed for local rather than national programming and are in serious need of a variety of weekly quality programming to meet the expressed local needs. Fortunately, most cable companies have established program advisory boards, which consist of personnel from local government, school boards, school administrations and teaching staff, and community interest groups, all of which are concerned with and responsible for quality programming and cablecast.

Cable companies, therefore, are a natural medium for the dissemination of selected film classics to the local community, as the typical equipment and presentation problems have been resolved by the installation of a cable system itself.

This book, with the annotated collection of over 200 film classics, is an extremely useful document for both broadcast and cablecast company personnel who are seriously interested in generating quality television programs.

The annotated film listings with their identified descriptions for each film listing are —

- proven classics in both print and film form;
- of the highest scholastic standards, which provide quality reading material with viewing;
- "greats" that have stood the test of time;
- the selections that have received national acceptance and approval by censors, organizations, many concerned citizen groups, parents, and children;
- accepted by educators *at all levels*, as the selections incorporate clear-cut educational values in both the print and the film medium.

The selections and indicators provide suggestions for —

- programming by themes that tie in with social awareness programs, i.e., ecological, religious, racial, Christmas themes;
- comparative study of periods and styles: the fifties, sixties, seventies, and so forth;
- literary study programs and "think" pieces, i.e., film study, treatment, styles, themes, history, and trends, the real versus the imaginary, or distortion;
- retrospectives of authors, producers, directors, actors, and their power to create a definitive version of the story;
- quality viewing materials for use in panel program discussion, and phone-in shows.
- summaries and excerpts from selected films for special programs; notes, themes, and introductory commentaries, e.g., "Wonderful World of Disneyland";
- program selection for nostalgia and in-depth viewing, i.e., ev-

eryone has been a child and most have seen or read *The Wizard of Oz, Pinocchio, Captain Blood, Robin Hood, Bambi, Cinderella,* etc.; see them again and compare the film to the written story; note second experiences at a later age; identify fantasy as a mechanism or escape;
* viewing and role-playing possibilities for the poor reader, special education, handicapped, and gifted child; the social pressures, role stereotypes, values, ideas, issues, heroes, heroines, idols, models, etc.

In summary, this book will be extremely useful to the television program manager and his/her related advisory panel concerned with nationally accepted quality programming. If used properly, the programs will truly provide the viewer with an enjoyable, exciting, and entertaining experience in reading, viewing, and thinking. Indeed, daily life experiences are extended through the classics.

Note: Films generally require permission for use from the film producer or distributor; and therefore, *written permission* should be obtained by the user. It is suggested that the special local interest group (school system, P.T.A., social agency, etc.) request use of the film over cable and restrict it to its specific audience. This will often eliminate or minimize costs or denial of request.

© Walt Disney Productions

SECTION III
FILM INDICATORS

CHAPTER 7

FILM INDICATORS FOR FILM CLASSICS

Film Indicators

Title

The full title is listed, disregarding the definite or the indefinite articles.

Production Center

The corporation, company, studio, or center in which the film originated is shown.

Country of Origin

Usually, productions are from the United States or Great Britain. Some coproductions are included, and in some cases, the reference indicates where production work, rather than shooting, was completed.

Release Date

The year in which the film was issued for distribution is given.

Nominal Running Time

The official quotation is given in minutes of overall running time. (Shortened versions of films are often prepared for special purposes, such as television or repertory theatre showings. Prints supplied by distributors may also be shorter in length than the official figure because of editing of damaged sections or sequences.)

Color/Black and White

Indication given is of the process used in the original production. Black-and-white versions of color originals are frequent and may be equally acceptable.

Producer

The name of the individual producer is quoted, wherever it is known. (The practice of giving name credits to individual producers has varied from company to company, and from time to time.)

Director

The name of the professional who coordinated the talents of performers and technical specialists to realize the finished film is given.

Main Performers

A listing is given of the actors and performers featured in the main credits. Often the sequence is arbitrarily limited in the interests of brevity.

Original Literary Work

An indication is given of the book, story, play, or poem on which the film is based, along with the author.

Story Outline

The story line has been condensed to give an impression of the central plot or theme.

Distribution Agency

Coded indications are shown of agencies or distributors from whom films may be rented. The great majority of films are available in 16-millimeter format and are therefore suitable for presentation anywhere that a standard projector is available. Note that where no coded indicator is shown, the film is available only in 35-millimeter format and requires projection on commercial cinema equipment.

Interest Indicators

Each film has been analyzed for its value in stimulating or developing interest in particular subject areas. Short summaries on each film give a quick composite of the main characteristics it displays.

Genres

Films have been loosely classified into categories that have taken on the status of cinematic genres, or styles. The groupings are general and frequently overlap.

ADVENTURE: Story lines have a strong emphasis on action, emphasizing personal courage, daring, and boldness.

ANIMATION: Characters and settings derive from the artwork of graphics specialists and special technical effects, rather than the contribution of live actors.

CRIME: Story line development centers on wrongdoing, and the detection, pursuit, and bringing to justice of offenders.

FANTASY: Flights of fancy defy the practical laws of everyday life, and imagination pushes reality into the background.

MARINE: The ocean in all its moods is central to the setting and often becomes a featured performer.

MILITARY: The story has some reference to life under arms, in organized formations, in war or peace.

MONSTERS: Strange creatures of known or imaginary background, are re-created as dinosaurs, pterodactyls, giant apes, or as the more sinister manifestations of deviants such as Frankenstein or Dr. Jekyll.

MUSICALS: The cinematic form of opera, with melodious performers, off-screen orchestras, and supporting choirs.

SCIENCE FICTION: The projection into the unknown future of the trends of technology, towards utopia or less optimistic aspects of things to come.

WESTERN: The conventional setting of the American West, with cowboys, cattle, rustlers, and usually the law of the gun.

Treatment

Treatment is the traditional approach to glimpses of the human condition.

COMEDY: Light hearted, inconsequential, with an emphasis on amusement, entertainment, laughter.

DOCUMENTARY: With serious inventions designed to capture and convey an atmosphere of realism and actuality.

DRAMA: Intense, exciting, with larger-than-life emotions. In this book it is extended to include the exaggerated situations of melodrama.

ROMANCE: Featuring a love interest as a central theme and individual relationships between the sexes.

TRAGEDY: Leading to unhappy endings with catastrophe, ruin, and agony the scripted fate of the central characters.

Topics and Themes

Treatments, story lines, and characteristics suggest that the film has relevance in developing thinking and discussion in major study areas or subject groupings.

BIOGRAPHICAL: Offering significant insights into the character, outlook, and behavior of historical personages.

CHILDREN: Featuring nonadults in central or important roles while examining their relationships, aspirations, and problems.

CULTURAL: Treating of other civilizations, life-styles, peoples, philosophies, or social groupings, whether in a historical or a contemporary context.

ECOLOGY: Illustrating the physical environment, nature, the wild, animals in their own habitat.

ETHICS: Illustrates or exemplifies moral or ethical issues, problems of good and evil, conflicts of conscience, the clash of principles.

FAMILY: Featuring relationships and situations involving parents and children.

FEMINISM: Treating or illustrating the status of women and girls, their roles and treatment in social groups.

HISTORICAL: Presenting, accurately or inaccurately, events or atmosphere from periods of the past, whether recent or remote.

RACIAL: Illustrating contacts between individuals or groups in circumstances in which racial background is an issue.

RELIGIOUS: Treating of personages, events, or stories in which religious belief and faith is a factor.

WAR: Illustrating conditions of organized warfare, battles, hostilities, and their effects, whether moral or material.

In the listings that follow, details are given of feature films linked to literary source-materials that are regularly included in reading programs for young people within the age range of the school system. In most cases, the film represents an attempt to present in movie terms the content of the original. In some, the screen scenario has a much looser contact with the basic work, developing concepts, ideas, characters, and situations in terms of the demands of the medium and abandoning the conventions appropriate to the printed page.

Guideline comments have been added on the interest of individual productions, either as filmed adaptations of literary creations, or on their established value as films, reflecting some distinction in content, treatment, or style.

The categories adopted are as follows:

No comment: Details of the film are included for information and record only. The production is not considered to have any particular merit but at least is available as the film version of a published work.

Recommended: The film is considered to contain some values or qualities that give it above-average interest.

Highly recommended: The film is considered to reflect qualities of marked significance and to merit selection for programming.

Very highly recommended: The film has become generally accepted as a screen classic and is therefore in or near the "required viewing" category.

© Walt Disney Productions

SECTION IV
FILM LISTINGS

CHAPTER 8

209 FILM CLASSICS

Note: Films are listed in alphabetical order by film title.

Full Film Title
ABE LINCOLN IN ILLINOIS

Release Date
1939

Production Studio
RKO RADIO

Country of Origin
USA

Running Time (Minutes)
110

Producer
Max Gordon

Director
John Cromwell

Principal Performers
Raymond Massey, Ruth Gordon, Mary Howard, Gene Lockhart, Harvey Stephens, Elizabeth Risdon, Charles Middleton, Dorothy Tree.

Literary Original and Date of Production
ABE LINCOLN IN ILLINOIS (play) 1938

Author and Biographical Dates
Robert E. Sherwood   1896-1955

Codings of 16 mm Distribution Agencies
TIM

Recommended Viewing
Recommended Reading
16 mm Film, B & W

SUMMARIES

THEME INDICATORS
BIOGRAPHICAL
ETHICS
FAMILY
FEMINISM
HISTORICAL
RACIAL
RELIGIOUS
DRAMA
ROMANCE

Literary Original
Awarded a Pulitzer Prize, this play depicts the early domestic and professional life of Abraham Lincoln as storekeeper, postmaster, and politician. The dialogue contains excerpts from speeches and writings from the man who would become the sixteenth president of the United States.

Film Version: **Recommended**
An intelligent and imaginative version of a successful theatrical play, providing inspirational biographical insights into the personality and formative influences shaping the ideals and aspirations of a major historical character.

Full Film Title
ADVENTURES OF HUCKLEBERRY FINN, THE

Release Date
1939

Production Studio
METRO-GOLDWYN-MAYER

Country of Origin
USA

Running Time (Minutes)
91

Producer
Joseph L. Mankiewicz

Director
Richard Thorpe

Principal Performers
Mickey Rooney, William Frawley, Rex Ingram, Lynne Carver, Walter Connolly.

Literary Original and Date of Publication
ADVENTURES OF HUCKLEBERRY FINN, THE   1884

Author and Biographical Dates
Mark Twain (Samuel Langhorne Clemens)   1835-1910

Codings of 16 mm Distribution Agencies
FNC

Recommended Viewing
Recommended Reading
16 mm Film, B & W

SUMMARIES

Literary Original
Huckleberry Finn and Tom Sawyer run away and sail down the Mississippi on a raft. They fall in with a pair of confidence tricksters and have a series of adventures before shaking off their amusing but undesirable companions and making their way back to their families.

THEME INDICATORS
ADVENTURE
CRIME
COMEDY
DRAMA
CHILDREN
CULTURAL
ETHICS
FAMILY
HISTORICAL
RACIAL

Film Version: **Recommended**
An entertaining and lively version of a famous story, with a charismatic performance by the lead juvenile and notably good technical quality.

Full Film Title
ADVENTURES OF HUCKLEBERRY FINN

Release Date
1960

Production Studio
METRO-GOLDWYN-MAYER

Country of Origin
USA

Running Time (Minutes)
107

Director
Michael Curtiz

Principal Performers
Tony Randall, Eddie Hodges, Patty McCormick, Andy Devine, Archie Moore, Judy Canova, Buster Keaton.

Literary Original and Date of Production
ADVENTURES OF HUCKLEBERRY FINN, THE   1884

Author and Biographical Dates
Mark Twain (Samuel Langhorne Clemens)   1835-1910

Recommended Viewing
Recommended Reading
35 mm Film, Color

SUMMARIES

Literary Original
Huckleberry Finn and Tom Sawyer run away and sail down the Mississippi on a raft. They fall in with a pair of confidence tricksters and have a series of adventures before shaking off their amusing but undesirable companions and making their way back to their families.

THEME INDICATORS
ADVENTURE
CRIME
COMEDY
CHILDREN
CULTURAL
ETHICS
FAMILY
HISTORICAL
RACIAL

Film Version
This remake is notable for beautiful outdoor photography filmed in the Sacramento River Valley. The characterization of Huck and the treatment of adventure sequences depart from the intent of the author.

Full Film Title
ADVENTURES OF ROBIN HOOD, THE

Release Date
1938

Production Studio
WARNER

Country of Origin
USA

Running Time (Minutes)
102

Producer
Michael Curtiz/Hal B. Wallis

Director
William Keighley

Principal Performers
Errol Flynn, Olivia de Havilland, Claude Rains, Basil Rathbone, Ian Hunter, Eugene Pallette, Alan Hale, Melville Cooper.

Literary Original
ENGLISH BALLADS, FOLKTALES

Codings of 16 mm Distribution Agencies
UAS

Recommended Viewing

16 mm Film, Color

SUMMARIES

THEME INDICATORS
ADVENTURE
CRIME
COMEDY
DRAMA
ROMANCE
ETHICS
HISTORICAL

Literary Original
The legendary rebel Robin Hood contends with treacherous nobles and the wicked Sheriff of Nottingham to save the throne of England for the absent King Richard. Robin and his followers reside in a forest, and are bowmen renowned for their archery skills and generosity.

Film Version: **Very highly recommended**
A robust, fast-moving and exciting compilation of episodes in the legendary life of the outlaw who robbed the rich to help the poor. Errol Flynn portrays the hero with great athletic bravado, and is backed by a seasoned cast who match his gusto with colorful presentations of medieval stereotypes of bravery and villainy.

Full Film Title
ADVENTURES OF ROBINSON CRUSOE, THE

Release Date
1954

Production Studio
UNITED ARTISTS

Country of Origin
USA

Running Time (Minutes)
100

Director
Luis Bunuel

Principal Performers
Dan O'Herlihy, Jaime Fernandez, Felipe De Alba, Chel Lopez, Jose Chavez.

Literary Original and Date of Production
ROBINSON CRUSOE   1719

Author and Biographical Dates
Daniel Defoe   1660-1731

Codings of 16 mm Distribution Agencies
ALB   MAC

Recommended Viewing
Recommended Reading
16 mm Film, Color

SUMMARIES

THEME INDICATORS
ADVENTURE
MARINE
DRAMA
CULTURAL
ECOLOGY
ETHICS
HISTORICAL
RACIAL
RELIGIOUS

Literary Original
Shipwrecked and alone on a deserted island, an eighteenth-century English sailor at first faces his plight with despair. However, by using the simple resources at his command, he achieves some measure of self-sufficiency and passes beyond the necessities of simple survival to being monarch of all he surveys. After years of solitary life, he encounters another human, whom he names Friday. The pair defend themselves from cannibals, recapture a mutinous ship, and return to England.

Film Version: **Recommended**
Daniel Defoe's classic story is followed step by step, in a powerful evocation of the sense of isolation and frustration felt by the central character. The location photography is splendid, and the sustained solo performance by the featured actor is simple but impressive.

Full Film Title
ADVENTURES OF TOM SAWYER, THE

Release Date
1938

Production Studio
UNITED ARTISTS

Country of Origin
USA

Running Time (Minutes)
91

Producer
David O. Selznick

Director
Norman Taurog

Principal Performers
Tommy Kelly, Walter Brennan, Ann Gillis, May Robson, Victor Jory, Jackie Moran, Spring Byington, Margaret Hamilton, Victor Kilian.

Literary Original and Date of Production
ADVENTURES OF TOM SAWYER, THE   1876

Author and Biographical Dates
Mark Twain (Samuel Clemens)   1835-1910

Codings of 16 mm Distribution Agencies

TIM	ARG	BUC	BUD	CCC	CWF
KER	MAC	MOD	NEW	ROA	SEL
TWF	TWY	VCI	WCF	WEL	WHO

Recommended Viewing
Recommended Reading
16 mm Film, Color

SUMMARIES

THEME INDICATORS
ADVENTURE
CRIME
DRAMA
CHILDREN
ETHICS
FAMILY
HISTORICAL
RACIAL

Literary Original
The setting is a small town along the Mississippi in the mid-1800s. A shrewd youngster, Tom Sawyer, witnesses a murder, which occurs in a moonlit cemetery. Revealing his knowledge during the trial of an innocent man, Tom is pursued by the fugitive murderer, Injun Joe.

Film Version: **Highly recommended**
Excellent casting in lead roles supports the story line, which is faithfully followed. The development of melodramatic situations heightens the entertainment value of the original.

Full Film Title
ALICE IN WONDERLAND

Release Date
1951

Production Studio
RKO Radio Pictures

Country of Origin
USA

Running Time (Minutes)
75

Producer
Walt Disney

Director
Claude Geronimi/Hamilton Luske/Wilfred Jackson

Principal Performers
Animation

Literary Original and Date of Production
Alice's Adventures in Wonderland 1865

Author and Biographical Dates
Lewis Carroll (Charles Lutwidge Dodgson) 1832-1898

Codings of 16 mm Distribution Agencies
AIM   COU   DIS   FNC   NAT   SWA

Recommended Viewing
Recommended Reading
16 mm Film, Color

SUMMARIES

THEME INDICATORS
Animation
Fantasy
Comedy
Drama
Children

Literary Original
In this famous fantasy, a young schoolgirl falls down a rabbit hole and enters a series of fantastic, dreamlike experiences, which contrast with the accepted limitations of the real world. For instance, her size is altered by nibbling at a magic mushroom. She is confronted by unusual creatures such as an arrogant White Rabbit, the Mad Hatter, and a disappearing Cheshire Cat.

Film Version: **Recommended**
In this animation film, the characters of Wonderland are rather reduced in stature by their conversion into terms of modern cartoon personages.

Full Film Title
ALICE'S ADVENTURES IN WONDERLAND

Release Date
1972

Production Studio
TCF/AMERICAN NATIONAL

Country of Origin
Great Britain

Running Time (Minutes)
101

Producer
Michael Stringer

Director
Michael Stringer

Principal Performers
Michael Crawford, Sir Ralph Richardson, Dudley Moore, Peter Sellers, Spike Milligan, Denis Price, Flora Robson, Peter Bull.

Literary Original and Date of Production
ALICE'S ADVENTURES IN WONDERLAND   1865

Author and Biographical Dates
Lewis Carroll (Charles Lutwidge Dodgson)   1832-1898

Codings of 16 mm Distribution Agencies
AIM   BUD   CWF   MAC   VCI   WCF

Recommended Reading
16 mm Film, Color

SUMMARIES

THEME INDICATORS
ANIMATION
FANTASY
COMEDY

Literary Original
In this famous fantasy, a young schoolgirl falls down a rabbit hole and enters a series of fantastic, dreamlike experiences, which contrast with the accepted limitations of the real world. For instance, her size is altered by nibbling at a magic mushroom. She is confronted by unusual creatures such as an arrogant White Rabbit, the Mad Hatter, and a disappearing Cheshire Cat.

Film Version
Live actors in costume and makeup carry the action in a lengthy, slow-paced, and not very convincing interpretation, which fails to convey the fun and lightheartedness that are the essence of a standard children's text.

Full Film Title
ANNE OF GREEN GABLES

Release Date
1934

Production Studio
RKO RADIO PICTURES

Country of Origin
USA

Running Time (Minutes)
79

Producer
Kenneth MacGowan

Director
George Nicholls, Jr.

Principal Performers
Anne Shirley, Tom Brown, O. P. Heggie, Helen Westley, Sara Haden, Charley Grapewin.

Literary Original
ANNE OF GREEN GABLES 1908

Author and Biographical Dates
Lucy Maud Montgomery 1874-1942

Recommended Viewing
Recommended Reading
35 mm Film, B & W

SUMMARIES

THEME INDICATORS
COMEDY
CHILDREN
FAMILY
FEMINISM

Literary Original
Written for a schoolgirl audience, this story has wide appeal. A farmer on Canada's Prince Edward Island requests a boy for adoption from a Nova Scotia institution. The order is inaccurately filled, and a girl, Anne, arrives instead.

Film Version
A routine, straightforward presentation of the content of the classic story, adequate in itself, but lacking any great distinction in acting performance or production values.

Full Film Title
AROUND THE WORLD IN EIGHTY DAYS

Release Date
1957

Production Studio
UNITED ARTISTS CORPORATION

Country of Origin
USA

Running Time (Minutes)
148

Producer
Michael Todd

Director
Michael Anderson

Principal Performers
David Niven, Cantinflas, Shirley MacLaine, Robert Newton, Joe E. Brown, Charles Boyer, Martine Carol, John Carradine, Charles Coburn.

Literary Original and Date of Production
AROUND THE WORLD IN EIGHTY DAYS 1872

Author and Biographical Dates
Jules Verne   1828-1905

Codings of 16 mm Distribution Agencies
UAS

Recommended Viewing
Recommended Reading
16 mm Film, Color

SUMMARIES

THEME INDICATORS
ADVENTURE
MARINE
COMEDY
DRAMA
ROMANCE
CULTURAL
HISTORICAL

Literary Original
As the result of a wager made in a London club, the hero, Phineas Fogg, attempts to circle the globe. He and his valet, Passe-Partout, encounter fantastic adventures and overcome all odds by completing the journey in only eighty days, thereby winning the bet.

Film Version: **Highly recommended**
The humorous potential of the original story line has been exploited for its entertainment value and expanded into a three-hour series of comic episodes featuring a hugh cast of star actors in a colorful, lighthearted, and amusing spectacular.

Full Film Title
AS YOU LIKE IT

Release Date
1936

Production Studio
20TH CENTURY FOX

Country of Origin
Great Britain

Running Time (Minutes)
96

Producer
Joseph Schenk/Paul Czinner

Director
Paul Czinner

Principal Performers
Elizabeth Bergner, Sir Laurence Olivier, Henry Ainley, Leon Quatermaine, Felix Aylmer, Austin Trevor, John Laurie.

Literary Original and Date of Production
AS YOU LIKE IT 1623

Author and Biographical Dates
William Shakespeare 1564-1616

Codings of 16 mm Distribution Agencies

| AIM | BUD | CAL | EMG | IMA | JAN | KPF |
| MAC | MOD | RAD | SEL | TWY | VCI | WCF |

Recommended Viewing
Recommended Reading
16 mm Film, B & W

SUMMARIES

THEME INDICATORS
- COMEDY
- ROMANCE
- CULTURAL
- FEMINISM
- HISTORICAL

Literary Original
When deposed of his estates, an aged duke takes refuge in the forest of Arden. His daughter, Rosalind, also is banished from court and, disguised as a boy, goes to the forest to live the pastoral life. A comedy of errors results in an entanglement of the love stories of two young couples, but everything turns out happily, with the lovers united and the duke restored to his possessions.

Film Version: **Recommended**
In a script adapted for the screen by J.M. Barrie, the author of *Peter Pan*, this production now appears to be rather flat and dated in its acting conventions and techniques but retains some interest and value for its successful flashes of humor and some supporting performances that have been strong enough to resist the passage of time.

Full Film Title
BAMBI

Release Date
1942

Production Studio
RKO RADIO PICTURES

Country of Origin
USA

Running Time (Minutes)
69

Director
Walt Disney

Principal Performers
Animation

Literary Original and Date of Production
BAMBI 1926 (trans. Whittacker Chambers, 1928)

Author and Biographical Dates
Felix Salten 1869-1945

Recommended Viewing

35 mm Film, Color

SUMMARIES

THEME INDICATORS
- **ANIMATION**
- **FANTASY**
- **MUSICAL**
- **COMEDY**
- **CHILDREN**
- **ECOLOGY**
- **FAMILY**

Literary Original
Bambi is a deer whose life history is narrated from newborn fawn to full-grown stag, in episodes featuring his loving parents and other forest inhabitants — squirrels, rabbits, birds, a wicked fox, and even death-dealing man. Bambi survives the hazards of his situation to found his own family.

Film Version: **Very highly recommended**
A masterpiece of technique from the Disney studio team, which has achieved the status of a classic, not only for its splendid visual effects but also for its delicately handled treatment of a story line featuring courage, friendship, and humor as defenses against the hazards involved in growing up from helplessness to self-reliance.

Full Film Title
BEAU GESTE

Release Date
1939

Production Studio
UNIVERSAL

Country of Origin
USA

Running Time (Minutes)
114

Producer
William A. Wellman

Director
William A. Wellman

Principal Performers
Gary Cooper, Robert Preston, Ray Milland, Brian Donlevy, Susan Hayward, J. Carroll Naish, Broderick Crawford, Albert Dekker.

Literary Original and Date of Production
BEAU GESTE   1924

Author and Biographical Dates
Percival Christopher Wren   1885-1941

Codings of 16 mm Distribution Agencies
TWY   UNI

Recommended Viewing
Recommended Reading
16 mm Film, B & W

SUMMARIES

Literary Original

In this best-seller, three Geste brothers enlist in the French Foreign Legion. During their attempt to save a lady's honor in a jewel-theft case, they fall afoul of the brutal Sergeant Markoff. The action culminates in a fierce battle with Arabs in the isolated desert outpost of Fort Zinderneuf, where all the legionnaires are killed.

THEME INDICATORS
ADVENTURE
MILITARY
DRAMA
TRAGEDY
CULTURAL
ETHICS
HISTORICAL
RACIAL
WAR

Film Version: **Recommended**

The period style of this old feature goes well with the dated conventions of the highly colored novel on which it is based. Acting, settings, and general production values remain adequate, and the dramatic pacing still conveys excitement in the development of a standard film adventure story.

Full Film Title
BEAU GESTE

Release Date
1966

Production Studio
UNIVERSAL

Country of Origin
USA

Running Time (Minutes)
105

Producer
Walter Seltzer

Director
Douglas Heyes

Principal Performers
Guy Stockwell, Doug McClure, Telly Savalas, Leslie Nielsen, Leon Gordon, Michael Constantine.

Literary Original and Date of Production
BEAU GESTE   1924

Author and Biographical Dates
Percival Christopher Wren   1885-1941

Codings of 16 mm Distribution Agencies
UNI

Recommended Viewing
Recommended Reading
16 mm Film, Color

SUMMARIES

Literary Original
In this best-seller, three Geste brothers enlist in the French Foreign Legion. During their attempt to save a lady's honor in a jewel-theft case, they fall afoul of the brutal sergeant Markoff. The action culminates in a fierce battle with Arabs in the isolated desert outpost of Fort Zinderneuf, where all the legionnaires are killed.

THEME INDICATORS
ADVENTURE
MILITARY
DRAMA
TRAGEDY
CULTURAL
ETHICS
HISTORICAL
RACIAL
WAR

Film Version
This remake discards much of the simple romanticism of the original in favor of an emphasis on violence and the hardships and brutalities of army life and substitutes a new ending in which the central character is allowed to escape the fate prescribed by his literary creator.

Full Film Title
BEN HUR

Release Date
1959

Production Studio
METRO-GOLDWYN-MAYER

Country of Origin
USA

Running Time (Minutes)
217

Producer
Sam Zimbalist

Director
William Wyler

Principal Performers
Charlton Heston, Jack Hawkins, Stephen Boyd, Haya Harareet, Hugh Griffith, Martha Scott, Sam Jaffe, Cathy O'Donnell, Finlay Currie.

Literary Original and Date of Production
BEN HUR 1880

Author and Biographical Dates
Lew Wallace 1827-1905

Codings of 16 mm Distribution Agencies
FNC

Recommended Viewing
Recommended Reading
16 mm Film, Color

SUMMARIES

THEME INDICATORS
ADVENTURE
DRAMA
CULTURAL
ETHICS
FAMILY
FEMINISM
RACIAL
RELIGIOUS

Literary Original
Falsely accused of the attempted murder of the Roman governor of Palestine, a young Jew, Judah Ben Hur, is sent to the galleys. He escapes from servitude and becomes a Roman officer. In a violent chariot race, Ben Hur defeats his betrayer, Messala, and is finally converted to Christianity.

Film Version: **Highly recommended**
A lavish spectacular costume epic, with rapid and exciting action, and a famous tightly edited chariot race sequence, which conveys sincerely the atmosphere and spirit of the very early days of Christianity in a more lively way than in the pages of the nineteenth-century novel by General Lew Wallace.

Full Film Title
BIG FISHERMAN, THE

Release Date
1959

Production Studio
CENTURION

Country of Origin
USA

Running Time (Minutes)
166

Producer
Rowland V. Lee

Director
Frank Borzage

Principal Performers
Howard Keel, Alexander Scourby, Susan Kohner, John Saxon, Martha Hyer, Herbert Lom, Ray Stricklyn, Beulah Bondi.

Literary Original and Date of Production
BIG FISHERMAN, THE   1948

Author and Biographical Dates
Lloyd Cassell Douglas   1877-1951

Recommended Viewing
Recommended Reading
35 mm Film, Color

SUMMARIES

Literary Original
This best-selling novel is set in the early days of Christianity. The disciple Simon Peter meets an Arab princess, whom he dissuades from her intention of killing her hated stepfather, King Herod.

THEME INDICATORS
ADVENTURE
DRAMA
BIOGRAPHICAL
CULTURAL
ETHICAL
HISTORICAL
RACIAL
RELIGIOUS

Film Version
This film represents a respectfully faithful rendering of a best-selling novel into cinematic format. The overall effect is not a complete success, and the spiritless result is not redeemed by any brilliance in the acting interpretation, or any up-beat message that emerges from the slow development of the central story line.

Full Film Title
BIG RED

Release Date
1962

Production Studio
DISNEY

Country of Origin
USA

Running Time (Minutes)
89

Producer
Winston Hibler

Director
Norman Tokar

Principal Performers
Walter Pidgeon, Gilles Payant, Emile Genest.

Literary Original
BIG RED   1945

Author and Biographical Dates
Jim Kjelgaard   1910-1959

Codings of 16 mm Distribution Agencies
AIM   BUC   CCC   COU   CWF   DIS   FNC   FPC
MAC   MOD   NAT   NEW   ROA   SWA   TFC   TWY

Recommended Viewing

16 mm Film, Color

SUMMARIES

THEME INDICATORS
ADVENTURE
DRAMA

Literary Original
Big Red was a champion Irish Setter. He and Danny, a young trapper who knows more about the wilderness and mutts than he does about thoroughbreds, become friends. Joining forces, they battle a legendary bear, Old Majesty, that threatens to destroy them. The grandeur of the outdoors permeates this moving story of a youngster's love for a dog.

CHILDREN
ECOLOGY
FAMILY

Film Version
A competent but routine version by the Disney studios of a simple out-of-doors adventure tale of the relationship of a boy and his dog, suitable for junior audiences.

Full Film Title
BLACK BEAUTY

Release Date
1971

Production Studio
PARAMOUNT

Country of Origin
Great Britain

Running Time (Minutes)
106

Producer
Peter Andrews/Malcolm B. Hayworth

Director
James Hill

Principal Performers
Mark Lester, Walter Slezak, Peter Lee Lawrence, Patrick Mowrer.

Literary Original and Date of Production
BLACK BEAUTY   1877

Author and Biographical Dates
Anna Sewell   1820-1878

Codings of 16 mm Distribution Agencies
PAR

Recommended Viewing
Recommended Reading
16 mm Film, Color

SUMMARIES

THEME INDICATORS
ADVENTURE
DRAMA
CHILDREN
ECOLOGY
ETHICS
FAMILY

Literary Original
Treated as the autobiography of a horse, this book stresses the need for humane treatment of animals. Beginning life as a favorite in a gentleman's stable, the thoroughbred Black Beauty is separated from little Joe Evans and faces cruelty from a series of inconsiderate owners. Enduring tribulations as a racehorse, circus pony, and gypsy work animal, Black Beauty is finally reunited with Joe.

Film Version: **Recommended**
A straightforward film repetition of the original narrative, slanted to have strong emotional appeal for younger viewers.

Full Film Title
BLACK SWAN, THE

Release Date
1942

Production Studio	Country of Origin	Running Time (Minutes)
TWENTIETH CENTURY FOX	**USA**	**85**

Producer
Robert Bassler

Director
Henry King

Principal Performers
Tyrone Power, Maureen O'Hara, Laird Cregar, Thomas Mitchell, George Sanders, Anthony Quinn, George Zucco, Edward Ashley.

Literary Original and Date of Production
BLACK SWAN, THE   1932

Author and Biographical Dates
Rafael Sabatini   1875-1950

Codings of 16 mm Distribution Agencies	Recommended Viewing
FNC	**16 mm Film, B & W**

SUMMARIES	THEME INDICATORS
	ADVENTURE
Literary Original	**MARINE**
This Caribbean adventure is a model of piratical life and lore. The dialogue and action accurately portray the 1700s while captivating the imagination with details of ships and nautical maneuvering. The buccaneer Henry Morgan changes his ways when appointed governor of Jamaica. He enlists the aid of adventurous friends to sweep the seas of the Caribbean clear of pirates.	**DRAMA**
	ROMANCE
	ETHICS
	HISTORICAL

Film Version: **Recommended**
A vigorous and exciting costume piece, with plenty of fast action, heroics, broad humor, and solid characterization by a competent cast of primary and secondary actors. The original story line is retained in its major essentials, but most of the film script features new material.

Full Film Title
BORN FREE

Release Date
1966

Production Studio
BRITISH LION/COLUMBIA

Country of Origin
Great Britain

Running Time (Minutes)
95

Producer
Sam Jaffe

Director
James Hill

Principal Performers
Virginia McKenna, Bill Travers, Geoffrey Keen, Peter Luckoye.

Literary Original and Date of Production
BORN FREE 1960

Author and Biographical Dates
Joy Adamson 1910-

Codings of 16 mm Distribution Agencies

ALB	ARG	BUC	CCC	CHA	CIN	CWF	FPC	ICS
KER	MAC	MOD	NAT	NEW	ROA	SEL	SWA	TFC
TWY	VCI	WCF	WEL	WHO	WIL			

Recommended Viewing
Recommended Reading
16 mm Film, Color

SUMMARIES

Literary Original
This best-seller is a compilation of three earlier books by the same author, *Born Free, Living Free,* and *Forever Free.* It relates a dramatic, unique human-animal relationship. A lion cub, Elsa, is reared to maturity by a Kenya game warden and his wife. Elsa has difficulty returning to life in the wild and remembers her human friends even after adjusting to the laws of her own nature.

Film Version: **Highly recommended**
The unique camera coverage of wild animals in their natural surroundings, accepting and living with humans, makes this documentary reconstruction of a real-life story a memorable film experience, and a natural audience pleaser in any presentation of ecological issues.

THEME INDICATORS
ADVENTURE
DOCUMENTARY
CULTURAL
ECOLOGY
ETHICS
FAMILY

Full Film Title
CAINE MUTINY, THE

Release Date
1954

Production Studio
COLUMBIA

Country of Origin
USA

Running Time (Minutes)
125

Producer
Stanley Kramer

Director
Edward Dmytryk

Principal Performers
Humphrey Bogart, Jose Ferrer, Van Johnson, Fred MacMurray, Robert Francis, May Wynn, Tom Tully, E. G. Marshall.

Literary Original and Date of Production
CAINE MUTINY, THE   1951

Author and Biographical Dates
Herman Wouk   1915-

Codings of 16 mm Distribution Agencies

ARG	BUC	BUD	CCC	CHA	CIN	CON	CWF	IMA
KPF	MAC	MOD	NAT	ROA	SWA	TFC	TWY	VCI
WCF	WEL	WHO

Recommended Viewing
Recommended Reading
16 mm Film, Color

SUMMARIES

THEME INDICATORS
ADVENTURE
MARINE
DRAMA
ETHICS
HISTORICAL
WAR

Literary Original
The sustained narrative power of this best-seller begins on the Caine, a World War II mine sweeper. Citing his cowardly and inept methods, disgruntled officers confront Captain Queeg and relieve him of his command. They subsequently face the consequences of their actions before a naval court and learn as much of themselves as of their captain.

Film Version: **Recommended**
The original best-selling novel (which was also successfully adapted for the stage) is here somewhat condensed to highlight the main episodes of action at sea, with an emphasis on the interplay of psychological tensions in the climactic trial scenes. Notable for intelligent and sensitive performances by the main actors.

Full Film Title
CALL OF THE WILD

Release Date
1935

Production Studio	Country of Origin	Running Time (Minutes)
UNITED ARTISTS	**USA**	**78**

Producer
Darryl F. Zanuck

Director
William A. Wellman

Principal Performers
Clark Gable, Loretta Young, Jack Oakie, Reginald Owen, Frank Conroy.

Literary Original and Date of Production
CALL OF THE WILD, THE   1903

Author and Biographical Dates
Jack London   1876-1916

Codings of 16 mm Distribution Agencies
FNC

Recommended Viewing
Recommended Reading
16 mm Film, B & W

SUMMARIES

THEME INDICATORS
ADVENTURE
DRAMA
ROMANCE
ECOLOGY
HISTORICAL

Literary Original
A dog, Buck, is stolen from his home and forcibly converted to service as a sled dog in the Klondike. Treated harshly by man and beast alike, he becomes ruthless in his own defense. Finally with John Thornton as his master, Buck finds a companion to serve and love. When Thornton is murdered, Buck flees to the wilderness and becomes the leader of a pack of wolves.

Film Version
Apart from the title and the setting, little has been retained of the source material in this adaptation of a novel into a standard Hollywood star vehicle. However, some impression may still come across of the hardships and dangers of pioneer life in the far north.

Full Film Title
CALL OF THE WILD, THE

Release Date
1972

Production Studio
METRO-GOLDWYN-MAYER/EMI

Country of Origin
USA

Running Time (Minutes)
105

Producer
Harry Alan Towers

Director
Ken Annakin

Principal Performers
Charlton Heston, Michele Mercier, Raimund Harmstorf, George Eastman.

Literary Original and Date of Production
CALL OF THE WILD, THE   1903

Author and Biographical Dates
Jack London   1876-1916

Codings of 16 mm Distribution Agencies
MAC

Recommended Reading
16 mm Film, Color

SUMMARIES

THEME INDICATORS
ADVENTURE
DRAMA
ECOLOGY
HISTORICAL

Literary Original
A dog named Buck is stolen from his home and forcibly converted to service as a sled dog in the Klondike. Treated harshly by man and beast alike, he becomes ruthless in his own defense. Finally with John Thornton as his master, Buck finds a companion to serve and love. When Thornton is murdered, Buck flees to the wilderness and becomes the leader of a pack of wolves.

Film Version
This more recent version follows the original story more closely but still fails to be convincing as a presentation of the author's intention to promote interest and understanding of the interrelationship of man and beast in the wilderness.

Full Film Title
CANTERVILLE GHOST, THE

Release Date
1943

Production Studio
METRO-GOLDWYN-MAYER

Country of Origin
USA

Running Time (Minutes)
95

Producer
Arthur Field

Director
Jules Dassin

Principal Performers
Charles Laughton, Robert Young, Margaret O'Brien, Peter Lawford, William Gargan, Rags Ragland, Una O'Connor, Mike Mazurki.

Literary Original and Date of Production
CANTERVILLE GHOST, THE 1887

Author and Biographical Dates
Oscar Wilde   1856-1900

Codings of 16 mm Distribution Agencies
FNC

Recommended Viewing
Recommended Reading
16 mm Film, B & W

SUMMARIES

THEME INDICATORS
ADVENTURE
FANTASY
MILITARY
COMEDY
CHILDREN
CULTURAL

Literary Original
In the 1880s, an American family buys and occupies an old English mansion, and their unromantic and matter-of-fact ways produce problems for the resident ghost. The daughter, Victoria Otis, succeeds in bringing peace to the unhappy phantom and marries his descendant, the Duke of Canterville.

Film Version
Much of the lightness and imagination of the original story has disappeared in the artificial addition of a twentieth-century setting to the original story. However, the performances by Charles Laughton and Margaret O'Brien provide some relief by lightening a heavy-handed treatment.

Full Film Title
CAPTAIN BLOOD

Release Date
1935

Production Studio
WARNER

Country of Origin
USA

Running Time (Minutes)
119

Director
Michael Curtiz

Principal Performers
Errol Flynn, Olivia de Havilland, Basil Rathbone, Lionel Atwill, Guy Kibbee, Ross Alexander, Henry Stephenson, Forrester Harvey, Donald Meek.

Literary Original and Date of Production
CAPTAIN BLOOD   1922

Author and Biographical Dates
Rafael Sabatini   1875-1950

Codings of 16 mm Distribution Agencies
UAS

Recommended Viewing
Recommended Reading
16 mm Film, B & W

SUMMARIES

Literary Original
Young Peter Blood is falsely accused of treason and exiled to the Caribbean. In this seventeenth-century setting, the Englishman leads an uprising of slaves, captures a Spanish ship, and becomes a gentleman corsair. Though a rebel, he never commits or approves of dishonorable deeds. As reward for his virtue, he gains a colonial governorship and the hand of Miss Arabella Bishop. The text is a model of Sabatini's penchant for historical accuracy.

Film Version: **Recommended**

Successful as a period adventure film, this unsubtle version of the original novel leans more heavily on rapid and exciting action than on strong production values and established Errol Flynn as the exponent of the swashbuckling costume extravaganza.

THEME INDICATORS
ADVENTURE
MARINE
DRAMA
ROMANCE
ETHICS
HISTORICAL

Full Film Title
CAPTAIN HORATIO HORNBLOWER, R.N.

Release Date
1951

Production Studio
WARNERS

Country of Origin
USA

Running Time (Minutes)
117

Producer
Raoul Walsh

Director
Raoul Walsh

Principal Performers
Gregory Peck, Virginia Mayo, Robert Beatty, James Robertson Justice, Denis O'Dea, Terence Morgan, Richard Hearne, James Kenney, Stanley Baker.

Literary Original and Date of Production
CAPTAIN HORATIO HORNBLOWER   1939

Author and Biographical Dates
Cecil Scott Forester   1899-1966

Codings of 16 mm Distribution Agencies
CHA   ICS   MAC   MOD
NAT   ROA   WCF   WHO

Recommended Viewing
Recommended Reading
16 mm Film, Color

SUMMARIES

THEME INDICATORS
ADVENTURE
MARINE
DRAMA
ROMANCE
HISTORICAL
WAR

Literary Original
During the 1790s, the gallant Captain Hornblower, under orders from England, commands the Lydia, a thirty-six gun frigate. He is to assist a rebellion against Spain and sink her vessel, Natividad. After doing battle with his nation's enemies, he at long last returns home to fame, fortune, and romance. Battle scenes are colorfully described in this retrospective of the British navy.

Film Version
Episodes from the original, extended series of novels have been telescoped into a single narrative script, which conveys little of the period flavor so carefully researched and portrayed by the author. The result is a two-dimensional representation of some highlights of a sea saga, without distinction in production or acting performances.

Full Film Title
CAPTAINS COURAGEOUS

Release Date
1937

Production Studio
METRO-GOLDWYN-MAYER

Country of Origin
USA

Running Time (Minutes)
116

Producer
Louis D. Lighton

Director
Victor Fleming

Principal Performers
Spencer Tracy, Freddy Bartholomew, Lionel Barrymore, Mickey Rooney, Melvyn Douglas, Charley Grapewin, Christian Rub, John Carradine.

Literary Original and Date of Production
CAPTAINS COURAGEOUS: A STORY OF THE GRAND BANKS 1897

Author and Biographical Dates
Rudyard Kipling   1865-1936

Codings of 16 mm Distribution Agencies
FNC

Recommended Viewing
Recommended Reading
16 mm Film, B & W

SUMMARIES

THEME INDICATORS
- ADVENTURE
- MARINE
- DRAMA
- CHILDREN
- CULTURAL
- ECOLOGY
- ETHICS
- FAMILY
- RACIAL

Literary Original
In the 1890s, Harvey Cheyne, the spoiled son of a rich family, falls overboard from a cruise ship. He is rescued by fishermen on a schooner. Tossed from his accustomed luxury to a world where only strength and cunning are respected, Harvey struggles to persevere. The rugged sea life transforms his snobbish youth to self-reliant maturity. His personal development is admired at a reunion with his parents.

Film Version: **Very highly recommended**
Strong performances by a well-selected cast convey most of the spirit and atmosphere of the original work in a production that still has a strong appeal for family audiences in spite of its age and rather old-fashioned style.

Full Film Title
CHARLOTTE'S WEB

Release Date
1973

Production Studio
PARAMOUNT

Country of Origin
USA

Running Time (Minutes)
94

Director
Charles A. Nichols/Iwao Takamoto

Principal Performers
Animation

Literary Original and Date of Production
CHARLOTTE'S WEB 1952

Author and Biographical Dates
Elwyn Brooks White 1899-

Codings of 16 mm Distribution Agencies
PAR

Recommended Viewing
Recommended Reading
16 mm Film, Color

SUMMARIES

THEME INDICATORS
ANIMATION
FANTASY
COMEDY
ECOLOGY
ETHICS

Literary Original
Young Fern lives on a country farm. She rescues Wilbur, a runty pig, from the slaughterhouse and supervises his development. In his barn home, Wilbur is befriended by the philosophic spider, Charlotte, who supports his dwindling morale. The story provides an objective view of life and death.

Film Version: **Highly recommended**
The animation film version brings the story vividly alive in a successful presentation of the gentle whimsy, philosophical depth, and attention to local color of the original.

Full Film Title
CHIMES AT MIDNIGHT

Release Date
1966

Production Studio
INTERNATIONAL FILMS ESPANOLA/ALPINE

Country of Origin
Spain

Running Time (Minutes)
119

Producer
Alessandro Tasca

Director
Orson Welles

Principal Performers
Orson Welles, Keith Baxter, John Gielgud, Margaret Rutherford, Jeanne Moreau, Norman Rodway, Alan Webb, Marina Vlady.

Literary Original and Date of Production
KING HENRY THE FOURTH/KING HENRY THE FIFTH (plays) 1598-1600

Author and Biographical Dates
William Shakespeare 1564-1616

Codings of 16 mm Distribution Agencies
JAN

Recommended Viewing
Recommended Reading
16 mm Film, B & W

SUMMARIES

THEME INDICATORS
ADVENTURE
MILITARY
DRAMA
ETHICS
HISTORICAL
WAR

Literary Original
Extracts are presented of the plays *King Henry The Fourth* and *King Henry The Fifth* by William Shakespeare. Sir John Falstaff finds favor with the young prince but loses his influence when the prince is called to the stern duties of kingship.

Film Version: **Recommended**
In a typically personal interpretation, Orson Welles (who also scripted and directed the production) gives a sustained study of the dramatic episodes that illustrate the character of Sir John Falstaff. The presentation is uneven but always original with occasional brilliancies and excellent support performances by a cast of seasoned players.

Full Film Title
CHITTY CHITTY BANG BANG

Release Date
1968

Production Studio
UNITED ARTISTS

Country of Origin
USA

Running Time (Minutes)
142

Producer
Albert R. Broccoli

Director
Richard Taylor

Principal Performers
Dick Van Dyke, Sally Ann Howes, Lionel Jeffries, Gert Frobe, Anna Quayle, Benny Hill, James Robertson Justice, Robert Helpmann.

Literary Original and Date of Production
CHITTY CHITTY BANG BANG, THE MAGICAL CAR   1964

Author and Biographical Dates
Ian Fleming   1908-1964

Codings of 16 mm Distribution Agencies
CWF   ROA   UAS   WCF   WHO

Recommended Viewing
Recommended Reading
16 mm Film, Color

SUMMARIES

THEME INDICATORS
ADVENTURE
FANTASY
COMEDY
DRAMA
CHILDREN
FAMILY

Literary Original
In this fantasy for pre- to early teens, Commander Caractacus Potts saves a racing car from the junkyard. To his surprise, the car possesses magical powers. It flies and demonstrates an uncanny talent for saving the Potts family from troublesome situations.

Film Version
The original story has been lengthened as an entertainment vehicle with the addition of songs, additional episodes, and trick photography. In the result, the story line has become rather disjointed, but young audiences will probably react uncritically to the situational comedy sequences rather than the variable quality of the production.

Full Film Title
CHRISTMAS CAROL, A

Release Date
1938

Production Studio
METRO-GOLDWYN-MAYER

Country of Origin
USA

Running Time (Minutes)
68

Producer
Joseph L. Mankiewcz

Director
Edwin L. Marin

Principal Performers
Reginald Owen, Terry Kilburn, Ann Rutherford, Gene Lockhart, Leo J. Carroll, Lynne Carver.

Literary Original and Date of Production
CHRISTMAS CAROL, A   1843

Author and Biographical Dates
Charles Dickens   1812-1870

Codings of 16 mm Distribution Agencies
FNC

Recommended Viewing
Recommended Reading
16 mm Film, B & W

SUMMARIES

Literary Original
Scrooge is a rich miser who is visited on Christmas Eve by the ghost of his dead partner and the spirits of Christmas Past, Present, and To-come. The visions they bring him of the punishment of avarice so impress him that he rises on Christmas Day a changed man, full of charity and goodwill to all.

THEME INDICATORS
FANTASY
COMEDY
DRAMA
ETHICS
FAMILY
HISTORICAL
RELIGIOUS

Film Version: **Recommended**
A thoroughgoing traditional version of the original, which recaptures the atmosphere and flavor of the annual winter season classic from Victorian England, with competent interpretations of the stock characters and careful attention to period detail.

Full Film Title
CHRISTMAS CAROL, A

Release Date
1951

Production Studio
RENOWN/UNITED ARTISTS

Country of Origin
Great Britain

Running Time (Minutes)
86

Producer
Brian Desmond-Hurst

Director
Brian Desmond-Hurst

Principal Performers
Alastair Sim, Mervyn Johns, Hermione Baddeley, Jack Warner, Kathleen Harrison, Michael Hordern, George Cole, Glyn Dearman.

Literary Original and Date of Production
CHRISTMAS CAROL, A   1843

Author and Biographical Dates
Charles Dickens   1812-1870

Codings of 16 mm Distribution Agencies
MAC   VCI

Recommended Viewing
Recommended Reading
16 mm Film, B & W

SUMMARIES

Literary Original
Scrooge is a rich miser who is visited on Christmas Eve by the ghost of his dead partner and the spirits of Christmas Past, Present, and To-come. The visions they bring him of the punishment of avarice so impress him that he rises on Christmas Day a changed man, full of charity and goodwill to all.

THEME INDICATORS
- **FANTASY**
- **COMEDY**
- **DRAMA**
- **CULTURAL**
- **ETHICS**
- **FAMILY**
- **HISTORICAL**
- **RELIGIOUS**

Film Version: **Highly recommended**
A sombre characterization of Scrooge, special effects that reflect the anguish of a troubled soul, and adherence to the original text distinguish this adaptation, which was produced in England.

Full Film Title
CINDERELLA

Release Date
1950

Production Studio	Country of Origin	Running Time (Minutes)
DISNEY	**USA**	**75**

Producer
Walt Disney

Director
Ben Sharpsteen

Principal Performers
Animation

Literary Original and Date of Production
CINDERELLA

Author and Biographical Dates
Charles Perrault   1628-1703 (and numerous later translators and imitators)

Recommended Viewing
Recommended Reading
35 mm Film, Color

SUMMARIES

THEME INDICATORS
ANIMATION
FANTASY
MUSICAL
COMEDY
DRAMA
CHILDREN
ETHICS
FAMILY
FEMINISM

Literary Original
The legendary little sister Cinderella is relegated to housework while her elder sisters attend a ball. A fairy godmother intercedes, and Cinderella attends the ball where a handsome prince falls in love with her. During her hasty departure, Cinderella loses a glass slipper, which the prince uses in his subsequent search for his lady.

Film Version: **Very highly recommended**
This cartoon version displays the Disney magic for creating delightfully artistic features. A host of animal friends have been added to amuse Cinderella and the audience. The splendid coloration, music, and animation are certain to entertain, but Bruno Bettelheim's discussion of Cinderella in *The Uses of Enchantment* should be read by adults in connection with seeing this film.

Full Film Title
CONNECTICUT YANKEE, A

Release Date
1931

Production Studio
TWENTIETH CENTURY FOX

Country of Origin
USA

Running Time (Minutes)
96

Director
David Butler

Principal Performers
Will Rogers, Maureen O'Sullivan, Myrna Loy, Frank Albertson, William Farnum, Mitchell Harris, Brandon Hurst, William V. Mong.

Literary Original and Date of Production
CONNECTICUT YANKEE IN KING ARTHUR'S COURT, A   1889

Author and Biographical Dates
Mark Twain (Samuel Langhorne Clemens)   1835-1910

Recommended Viewing
Recommended Reading
35 mm Film, B & W

SUMMARIES

THEME INDICATORS
ADVENTURE
FANTASY
COMEDY
CULTURAL
HISTORICAL

Literary Original
An industrialist from New England is struck on the head and awakes in the England of 528 AD. He astonishes King Arthur's men with his knowledge and powers and replaces Merlin as court magician. During his absence, his many innovations, including trains and telegraph, are destroyed by church decree. Finally, under a spell from Merlin, the Yankee is returned to the nineteenth century.

Film Version: **Recommended**
A famous homespun character of American stage and cinema carries the action in this adaptation, which captures more of the satiric spirit of the original than its incident.

Full Film Title
COUNT OF MONTE CRISTO, THE

Release Date
1934

Production Studio
UNITED ARTISTS

Country of Origin
USA

Running Time (Minutes)
127

Producer
Edward Small

Director
Rowland V. Lee

Principal Performers
Robert Donat, Elissa Landi, Louis Calhern, Sidney Blackmer, Raymond Walburn, O. P. Heggie, William Farnum, Georgia Caine.

Literary Original and Date of Production
COUNT OF MONTE-CRISTO, THE   1844

Author and Biographical Dates
Alexandre Dumas   1802-1870

Codings of 16 mm Distribution Agencies
**ALB   BUD   KPF   MOG   SEL   TWF   WHO
WIL   WRS**

Recommended Viewing
Recommended Reading
16 mm Film, B & W

SUMMARIES

Literary Original
In nineteenth-century France, Edmond Dantès is unjustly charged with political crimes by his enemies. They condemn him to perpetual imprisonment. In a dramatic episode, Dantès escapes to the island of Monte Cristo, where he discovers a treasure. With this new wealth, he contrives to settle accounts with his accusers.

THEME INDICATORS
**ADVENTURE
CRIME
DRAMA
ETHICS
HISTORICAL**

Film Version: **Highly recommended**
This film version is a prestige production with a faithful retelling of the original story, supported in its effects by fine acting, well-written script, and accurate detail of period and location.

Full Film Title
CYRANO DE BERGERAC

Release Date
1950

Production Studio
UNITED ARTISTS

Country of Origin
USA

Running Time (Minutes)
112

Producer
Stanley Kramer

Director
Michael Gordon

Principal Performers
Jose Ferrer, Mala Powers, William Prince, Morris Carnovsky, Ralph Clanton, Virginia Farmer, Edgar Barrier, Elena Verdugo.

Literary Original and Date of Production
CYRANO DE BERGERAC (play)   1897

Author and Biographical Dates
Edmond Rostand (trans. Brian C. Hooker)   1868-1918

Codings of 16 mm Distribution Agencies
IVY

Recommended Viewing
Recommended Reading
16 mm Film, B & W

SUMMARIES

Literary Original
Poet, swordsman, and philosopher, the long-nosed Cyrano is in love with the beautiful Roxane. She, however, loves Christian who, though inarticulate, wishes to grace her with love letters. Cyrano offers to write the letters, which eventually win the heart of Roxane for Christian. Cyrano keeps the secret even after Christian dies in battle. Roxane learns the truth years later on the day Cyrano is killed.

THEME INDICATORS
ADVENTURE
MILITARY
COMEDY
DRAMA
ROMANCE
BIOGRAPHICAL
ETHICS
FEMINISM
HISTORICAL
WAR

Film Version: **Recommended**
The film loses something of the high romantic quality of the original French verse play and retains something of the static slow pace of the stage action. Despite this, it succeeds in communicating the essence of the famous central character, and the atmosphere of the troubled period in which he lived and wrote.

Full Film Title
DADDY LONG LEGS

Release Date
1955

Production Studio
TWENTIETH CENTURY FOX

Country of Origin
USA

Running Time (Minutes)
126

Producer
Samuel G. Engel

Director
Jean Negulesco

Principal Performers
Fred Astaire, Leslie Caron, Terry Moore, Thelma Ritter, Fred Clark, Charlotte Austin, Larry Keating, Kathryn Givney.

Literary Original and Date of Production
DADDY LONG LEGS   1912

Author and Biographical Dates
Jean Webster   1876-1916

Codings of 16 mm Distribution Agencies
FNC

Recommended Reading
16 mm Film, Color

SUMMARIES

Literary Original
Through the support of an anonymous benefactor, Judy Abbott, a seventeen-year-old orphan, is enabled to leave the John Grier Home for a college education. She falls in love with an older man, Jervis Pendleton, who before their marriage reveals the secret of his identity as her sponsor and patron.

THEME INDICATORS
MUSICAL
COMEDY
ROMANCE
CHILDREN
FAMILY
FEMINISM

Film Version
An extended adaptation of the story line, exploited as the basis for a song-and-dance comedy allowing displays of performing talents by the gifted and famous featured stars.

Full Film Title
DARBY O'GILL AND THE LITTLE PEOPLE

Release Date
1959

Production Studio
DISNEY

Country of Origin
USA

Running Time (Minutes)
93

Producer
Walt Disney

Director
Robert Stevenson

Principal Performers
Albert Sharpe, Janet Munro, Sean Connery, Jimmy O'Dea, Kieron Moore, Estelle Winwood, Walter Fitzgerald, Denis O'Dea, J. G. Devlin, Jack McGowran.

Literary Original and Date of Production
DARBY O'GILL AND THE GOOD PEOPLE (stories)   1903

Author and Biographical Dates
Herminie Templeton Kavanagh

Codings of 16 mm Distribution Agencies
CCC   DIS   FNC   MAC   MOD   NEW   ROA
SWA   TWY

Recommended Viewing

16 mm Film, Color

SUMMARIES

Literary Original
Darby O'Gill is a wily old Irish workman who, in a series of stories, engages in an ongoing battle of wits with leprechauns and fairies in an attempt to use their magic powers to his own advantage. Although he cannot triumph over their supernatural abilities, he is cunning enough to draw some benefits for himself and his family from his encounters with the little folk.

THEME INDICATORS
- **ANIMATION**
- **FANTASY**
- **COMEDY**
- **ROMANCE**
- **FAMILY**
- **FEMINISM**

Film Version: **Recommended**
The innocent fairytale fantasy of the original stories has been adequately interpreted and enhanced by the Disney studios' film magic in special effects and the addition of musical and dance sequences.

Full Film Title
DAVID COPPERFIELD

Release Date
1935

Production Studio
METRO-GOLDWYN-MAYER

Country of Origin
USA

Running Time (Minutes)
133

Producer
David O. Selznick

Director
George Cukor

Principal Performers
W.C. Fields, Freddie Bartholomew, Lionel Barrymore, Edna May Oliver, Frank Lawton, Maureen O'Sullivan, Basil Rathbone, Lewis Stone.

Literary Original and Date of Production
DAVID COPPERFIELD 1850

Author and Biographical Dates
Charles Dickens 1812-1870

Codings of 16 mm Distribution Agencies
FNC

Recommended Viewing
Recommended Reading
16 mm Film, B & W

SUMMARIES

THEME INDICATORS
DRAMA
ROMANCE
CHILDREN
CULTURAL
ETHICS
FAMILY
FEMINISM
HISTORICAL

Literary Original
Orphaned at an early age and unhappy in his period in boarding school, David Copperfield lives in poverty and misery during an apprenticeship in nineteenth-century London. He runs away and is kindly received by a country aunt and a number of friends. He grows up to marry and become a successful writer. On the death of his first wife, he remarries happily. (The host of vividly drawn secondary characters includes the optimistic Mr. Micawber and the scheming Uriah Heep.)

Film Version: **Very highly recommended**
Although the production inevitably condenses and compresses the action and range of characters in a lengthy original, it still brilliantly succeeds in preserving and conveying the essence of Dickens's work. The acting is studded with excellent and definitive performances, and the overall effect is of a near-perfect translation from literature into cinema.

Full Film Title
DAVID COPPERFIELD

Release Date
1969

Production Studio
TWENTIETH CENTURY FOX

Country of Origin
USA

Running Time (Minutes)
118

Producer
Frederich H. Brogger

Director
Delbert Mann

Principal Performers
Richard Attenborough, Lawrence Olivier, Michael Redgrave, Ralph Richardson, Edith Evans, Emlyn Williams, James Donald, Anna Massey, Pamela Franklin.

Literary Original and Date of Production
DAVID COPPERFIELD   1850

Author and Biographical Dates
Charles Dickens   1812-1870

Recommended Viewing
Recommended Reading
35 mm Film, Color

SUMMARIES

THEME INDICATORS
DRAMA
CHILDREN
ETHICS
FAMILY
FEMINISM
HISTORICAL

Literary Original
Orphaned at an early age and unhappy in his period in boarding school, David Copperfield lives in poverty and misery during an apprenticeship in nineteenth-century London. He runs away and is kindly received by a country aunt and a number of friends. He grows up to marry and become a successful writer. On the death of his first wife, he remarries happily. (The host of vividly drawn secondary characters includes the optimistic Mr. Micawber and the scheming Uriah Heep.)

Film Version
Adapted for television presentation, this version skims over the main narrative episodes without exploration of character or development of atmosphere.

Full Film Title
DOCTOR DOLITTLE

Release Date
1967

Production Studio
TWENTIETH CENTURY FOX

Country of Origin
USA

Running Time (Minutes)
152

Producer
Arthur P. Jacobs

Director
Richard Fleischer

Principal Performers
Rex Harrison, Anthony Newley, Samantha Eggar, Richard Attenborough, Peter Bull, Muriel Landers, William Dix, Geoffrey Holder, Portia Nelson.

Literary Original and Date of Production
DOCTOR DOLITTLE... (series)   1920-1953

Author and Biographical Dates
Hugh Lofting   1886-1947

Codings of 16 mm Distribution Agencies
FNC

Recommended Viewing
Recommended Reading
16 mm Film, Color

SUMMARIES

THEME INDICATORS
ADVENTURE
FANTASY
MARINE
MUSICAL
ECOLOGY

Literary Original
Doctor Dolittle is the wonder of the nineteenth-century scientific community. In an English village, he masters the languages of 500 animal species. Due to his unconventional behavior, he is committed to an asylum from which he escapes. With help from seals, whales, and human sympathizers, he searches for the Great Pink Sea Snail.

Film Version
The Hugh Lofting novels have been run together to provide a script that gives opportunities for musical numbers and visual re-creations of the strange imaginary creatures sought out by the eccentric doctor. In the process, much of the fantasy is lost.

Full Film Title
DOCTOR JEKYLL AND MR. HYDE

Release Date
1932

Production Studio
PARAMOUNT

Country of Origin
USA

Running Time (Minutes)
90

Producer
Rouben Mamoulian

Director
Rouben Mamoulian

Principal Performers
Fredric March, Miriam Hopkins, Rose Hobart, Holmes Herbert, Halliwell Hobbes, Edgar Norton.

Literary Original and Date of Production
STRANGE CASE OF DR. JEKYLL AND MR. HYDE, THE   1886

Author and Biographical Dates
Robert Louis Stevenson   1850-1894

Codings of 16 mm Distribution Agencies
FNC

Recommended Viewing
Recommended Reading
16 mm Film, B & W

SUMMARIES

THEME INDICATORS
ADVENTURE
CRIME
FANTASY
MONSTER
DRAMA
TRAGEDY
ETHICS
HISTORICAL

Literary Original
In nineteenth-century London, the philanthropic Dr. Jekyll is preoccupied with separating the good and evil sides of human nature. He concocts a potion that alters his character and unleashes the qualities of the monstrous Mr. Hyde. Though there is an antidote, he commits a murder while under the potion's influence. Moving ever deeper into the world of evil, he finally commits suicide.

Film Version: **Very highly recommended**
A successful film version of the classic novel, which in its time broke new ground by its innovations in makeup, photography, and special effects, and it still remains effective for its evocation of atmosphere, the quality of its acting performances, and its power to convey the spirit of horror and personal tragedy of the original.

Full Film Title
DOCTOR JEKYLL AND MR. HYDE

Release Date
1941

Production Studio
METRO-GOLDWYN-MAYER

Country of Origin
USA

Running Time (Minutes)
122

Producer
Victor Fleming

Director
Victor Fleming

Principal Performers
Spencer Tracy, Ingrid Bergman, Lana Turner, Ian Hunter, C. Aubrey Smith, Donald Crisp, Sara Allgood.

Literary Original and Date of Production
STRANGE CASE OF DR. AND MR. HYDE, THE 1886

Author and Biographical Dates
Robert Louis Stevenson   1850-1894

Codings of 16 mm Distribution Agencies
FNC

Recommended Viewing
Recommended Reading
16 mm Film, B & W

SUMMARIES

THEME INDICATORS
- **CRIME**
- **FANTASY**
- **MONSTER**
- **DRAMA**
- **TRAGEDY**
- **ETHICS**
- **HISTORICAL**

Literary Original
In nineteenth-century London, the philanthropic Dr. Jekyll is preoccupied with separating the good and evil sides of human nature. He concocts a potion that alters his character and unleashes the qualities of the monstrous Mr. Hyde. Though there is an antidote, he commits a murder while under the potion's influence. Moving ever deeper into the world of evil, he finally commits suicide.

Film Version: **Recommended**

This version represents an honest but flawed interpretation of the story, with surprising weaknesses in casting and acting performances. Dream sequences have been added without doing anything constructive to explain the action or develop dramatic tension. The general effect is of an elaborate and careful attempt at modernization of technique, which does not quite succeed.

Full Film Title
DR. SYN

Release Date
1937

Production Studio
GAUMONT

Country of Origin
Great Britain

Running Time (Minutes)
80

Director
Roy William Neill

Principal Performers
George Arliss, Margaret Lockwood, John Loder, Roy Emerton, Graham Moffatt, Frederick Burtwell.

Literary Original and Date of Production
DR. SYN   1938

Author and Biographical Dates
Arthur Russell Thorndike   1885-1972

Codings of 16 mm Distribution Agencies
BUD   CFM

Recommended Viewing
Recommended Reading
16 mm Film, B & W

SUMMARIES

THEME INDICATORS
ADVENTURE
MILITARY
DRAMA
CULTURAL
ETHICS
HISTORICAL

Literary Original
In the 1780s during the reign of George III, the king's men come to the British town of Dymchurch to crush a ring of smugglers. Involved in the illegal trade operation are the town's vicar, schoolmaster, and village sexton.

Film Version: **Recommended**
This is a lively rendition, authenticated by a skillful reproduction of the mood and atmosphere of devil-may-care piratic life.

Full Film Title
DOCTOR SYN ALIAS THE SCARECROW

Release Date
1964

Production Studio
DISNEY

Country of Origin
USA

Running Time (Minutes)
98

Producer
William Anderson

Director
James Neilson

Principal Performers
Patrick McGoohan, Sean Scully, Kay Walsh, Tony Britton, George Cole.

Literary Original and Date of Production
DR. SYN   1915

Author and Biographical Dates
Arthur Russell Thorndike   1885-1972

Codings of 16 mm Distribution Agencies
AIM   BUC   CCC   COU   CWF   DIS
FNC   MOD   NEW   ROA   SWA   TWY

Recommended Viewing
Recommended Reading
16 mm Film, Color

SUMMARIES

Literary Original
In the 1780s during the reign of George III, the king's men come to the British town of Dymchurch to crush a ring of smugglers. Involved in the illegal trade operation are the town's vicar, schoolmaster, and village sexton.

THEME INDICATORS
ADVENTURE
MILITARY
DRAMA
CULTURAL
ETHICS
HISTORICAL
WAR

Film Version
This undistinguished version of the original was produced for television. The text has been altered to create a well-intended, if not benevolent, corsair of the seas.

Full Film Title
DRUMS ALONG THE MOHAWK

Release Date
1939

Production Studio
TWENTIETH CENTURY FOX

Country of Origin
USA

Running Time (Minutes)
103

Producer
Raymond Griffith

Director
John Ford

Principal Performers
Claudette Colbert, Henry Fonda, Edna May Oliver, Eddie Collins, John Carradine, Doris Bowdon, Jessie Ralph, Arthur Shields.

Literary Original and Date of Production
DRUMS ALONG THE MOHAWK   1936

Author and Biographical Dates
Walter D. Edmonds   1903-

Codings of 16 mm Distribution Agencies
FNC

Recommended Viewing
Recommended Reading
16 mm Film, Color

SUMMARIES

Literary Original
During the Revolutionary War era, Gil Martin and his wife Lana are among farmers who attempt to settle in the Mohawk Valley of upper New York. The local militia repeatedly battle the British soldiers billeted in Canada and reinforced by Iroquois warriors. A model of courage, Lana at one point rescues her two children from marauding Indians. Eventually the British forces are routed and scattered in the wilderness.

THEME INDICATORS
ADVENTURE
MILITARY
DRAMA
CULTURAL
ECOLOGY
ETHICS
HISTORICAL
RACIAL
WAR

Film Version: **Highly recommended**
A very viewable example of the strong directorial style of John Ford, maintaining the essentials of the original story, and using every opportunity to develop film conventions in action, dialogue, and the interplay of personalities.

Full Film Title
DUMBO

Release Date
1972

Production Studio	Country of Origin	Running Time (Minutes)
DISNEY	**USA**	**110**

Producer
Disney Studios

Director
Ben Sharpsteen

Principal Performers
Animation

Literary Original and Date of Production
DUMBO

Author and Biographical Dates
Helen Aberson and Harold Pearl

Codings of 16 mm Distribution Agencies
AIM FNC NAT ROA SWA

Recommended Viewing

16 mm Film, Color

SUMMARIES

THEME INDICATORS
ANIMATION
FANTASY
COMEDY
CHILDREN
FAMILY

Literary Original
Dumbo is a baby elephant, born to a mother who is a circus performer. He has unusually large ears and because of this handicap is mistreated and relegated to a clown act. However, when it is discovered that he can use his ears to fly, he becomes a star and the pride of his loving mother.

Film Version: **Very highly recommended**
A delightful and charming animation film, expanding on the original story in musical numbers and the limitless effects of cartoon photography.

Full Film Title
ELEPHANT BOY

Release Date
1937

Production Studio
UNITED ARTISTS

Country of Origin
USA

Running Time (Minutes)
80

Producer
Alexander Korda

Director
Robert Flaherty/Zoltan Korda

Principal Performers
Sabu, Walter Hudd, Allan Jeayes, W. E. Holloway, Bruce Gordon, D. J. Williams.

Literary Original and Date of Production
TOOMAI OF THE ELEPHANTS 1893

Author and Biographical Dates
Rudyard Kipling 1865-1936

Codings of 16 mm Distribution Agencies
BUD   ICS   ROA

Recommended Viewing
Recommended Reading
16 mm Film, B & W

SUMMARIES

THEME INDICATORS
ADVENTURE
DRAMA
CHILDREN
CULTURAL
ECOLOGY
RACIAL

Literary Original
In nineteenth-century British India, a young boy is taunted for his knowledge of the ways of elephants. He is retained by the government to lead an expedition into their unexplored territories.

Film Version: **Recommended**
The simple story line is followed as far as necessary, to allow near documentary coverage of elephants and other animals in their natural environment. At this level, the adaptation is successful and full of visual appeal for children.

Full Film Title
ELUSIVE PIMPERNEL, THE

Release Date
1950

Production Studio
BRITISH LION FILMS

Country of Origin
Great Britain

Running Time (Minutes)
109

Producer
Samuel Goldwyn/Alexander Korda

Director
Michael Powell/Emeric Pressburger

Principal Performers
David Niven, Margaret Leighton, Jack Hawkins, Cyril Cusack, Robert Coote, David Hutcheson.

Literary Original and Date of Production
SCARLET PIMPERNEL, THE   1905

Author and Biographical Dates
Baroness Emma Magdalena Orczy   1865-1947

Recommended Viewing
Recommended Reading
35 mm Film, Color

SUMMARIES

THEME INDICATORS
- **ADVENTURE**
- **DRAMA**
- **CULTURAL**
- **ETHICS**
- **HISTORICAL**

Literary Original
Sir Percy Blakeney poses as a decadent fop while being the courageous mastermind behind the organization that snatches victims of the French Revolution from imprisonment and death by the guillotine. In a series of daring encounters, he defeats his archenemy the fanatic revolutionary Citizen Chauvelin.

Film Version: **Recommended**
This expensive and elaborately mounted remake of *The Scarlet Pimpernel* **fails to outclass the 1934 original in the quality of its acting or the communication of the excitement of the original story.**

Full Film Title
EMIL AND THE DETECTIVES

Release Date
1964

Production Studio
DISNEY

Country of Origin
USA

Running Time (Minutes)
99

Producer
Peter V. Herald

Director
Peter Tewksbury

Principal Performers
Walter Slezak, Bryan Russell, Roger Mobley, Heinz Schubert, Peter Ehrlich, Cindy Cassell, Elsa Wagner, Wolfgang Volz.

Literary Original and Date of Production
EMIL AND THE DETECTIVES 1929 (trans. Eileen Hall, 1931)

Author and Biographical Dates
Erich Kastner 1899-1974

Recommended Viewing
Recommended Reading
35 mm Film, Color

SUMMARIES

THEME INDICATORS
ADVENTURE
CRIME
DRAMA
CHILDREN
ETHICS

Literary Original
In the Berlin of 1929, a schoolboy, Emil, is en route to visit his grandmother. When asleep, he is robbed by his compartment companion. Determined to regain his money, he follows the thief and, enlisting the aid of others, captures the perpetrator.

Film Version: **Recommended**
A filmed account of the tale of crime and detection in an urban setting, amiably produced on location in Germany by the Disney studios.

Full Film Title
FIRST MEN IN THE MOON, THE

Release Date
1964

Production Studio
COLUMBIA PRODUCTIONS

Country of Origin
USA

Running Time (Minutes)
103

Producer
Charles H. Schneer/Ray Harryhausen

Director
Nathan Juran

Principal Performers
Edward Judd, Lionel Jeffries, Martha Hyer, Erik Chitty, Betty McDowall, Miles Malleson, Laurence Herder, Peter Finch.

Literary Original and Date of Production
FIRST MEN IN THE MOON, THE   1901

Author and Biographical Dates
Herbert George Wells   1866-1946

Codings of 16 mm Distribution Agencies
ARG   BUC   CCC   CWF   MAC   MOD
NAT   ROA   SWA   TFC   TWY   VCI   WCF

Recommended Viewing
Recommended Reading
16 mm Film, Color

SUMMARIES

THEME INDICATORS
ADVENTURE
FANTASY
SCIENCE FICTION
DRAMA
HISTORICAL

Literary Original
Bedford and Cavor, two Englishmen of the late nineteenth century, develop a gravity-resisting combination of metals from which they build a sphere and take off into space. They land on the moon, to find plant life and antlike Selenites, which live below the surface. They capture the astronauts, but Bedford succeeds in escaping and returning to Earth to tell the story and include radio reports from the captive Cavor.

Film Version: **Recommended**
As the fictional flights of fancy of H.G. Wells in the 1900s have been outstripped by the real achievements of the space age, this treatment of his novel has been slanted towards a comic period adventure calculated to entertain young modern audiences. The result is enjoyable fun, with a rather slow narrative pace, without any of the serious intentions of the original.

Full Film Title
FIVE WEEKS IN A BALLOON

Release Date
1962

Production Studio	Country of Origin	Running Time (Minutes)
TWENTIETH CENTURY FOX	**USA**	**101**

Producer
Irwin Allen

Director
Irwin Allen

Principal Performers
Red Buttons, Fabian, Barbara Eden, Cedric Hardwicke, Peter Lorre, Richard Haydn, Barbara Luna, Billy Gilbert, Herbert Marshall, Reginald Owen.

Literary Original and Date of Production
FIVE WEEKS IN A BALLOON   1863

Author and Biographical Dates
Jules Verne   1828-1905

Codings of 16 mm Distribution Agencies	Recommended Viewing
FNC	
	16 mm Film, Color

SUMMARIES

Literary Original

A dauntless British explorer, Dr. Samuel Fergusson, makes a daring experiment by sailing the Victoria balloon from Zanzibar on the trade winds across unknown East Africa in 1862. He takes his crew on this novel voyage of discovery safely through the dangers presented by jungle animals, strange monsters, and all the reputed perils of darkest Africa of the period.

THEME INDICATORS
ADVENTURE
DRAMA
ECOLOGY
HISTORICAL
RACIAL

Film Version

The intention in this film adaptation was to inject humor into the original adventure story, but the capable cast of actors do not entirely succeed in carrying out the planned change of emphasis, and the net result is an unsatisfactory production that has only distant echoes of the original work.

Full Film Title
FORTUNES OF CAPTAIN BLOOD, THE

Release Date
1950

Production Studio
COLUMBIA

Country of Origin
USA

Running Time (Minutes)
91

Producer
Harry Joe Brown

Director
Gordon Douglas

Principal Performers
Louis Hayward, Patricia Medina, George Macready, Lowell Gilmore, Alfonso Bedoya, Dona Drake, Wilton Graff, Curt Bois, Lumsden Hure.

Literary Original and Date of Production
CAPTAIN BLOOD   1922

Author and Biographical Dates
Rafael Sabatini   1875-1950

Codings of 16 mm Distribution Agencies
NEW   ROA

Recommended Viewing
Recommended Reading
16 mm Film, B & W

SUMMARIES

THEME INDICATORS
ADVENTURE
MARINE
DRAMA
ROMANCE
HISTORICAL

Literary Original
Young Peter Blood is falsely accused of treason and exiled to the Caribbean. In this seventeenth century setting, the Englishman leads an uprising of slaves, captures a Spanish ship, and becomes a gentleman corsair. Though a rebel, he never commits or approves of dishonorable deeds. As reward for his virtue, he gains a colonial governorship and the hand of Miss Arabella Bishop. The text is a model of Sabatini's penchant for historical accuracy.

Film Version
The altered plot line allows the creation of another sea-saga film, which generally fails to generate the excitement, romance, or historical accuracy of Sabatini's adventurous original.

Full Film Title
FOUR FEATHERS, THE

Release Date
1939

Production Studio
UNITED ARTISTS

Country of Origin
USA

Running Time (Minutes)
130

Producer
Alexander Korda/Irving Asher

Director
Zolton Korda

Principal Performers
John Clements, Ralph Richardson, C. Aubrey Smith, Allan Jeayes, Jack Allen, Donald Gray, Frederick Culley, Amid Taftazani, Henry Oscar, John Laurie.

Literary Original and Date of Production
FOUR FEATHERS, THE 1902

Author and Biographical Dates
Alfred Edward Woodley Mason   1865-1948

Codings of 16 mm Distribution Agencies
CHA   ICS   MOG

Recommended Viewing
Recommended Reading
16 mm Film, Color

SUMMARIES

Literary Original
A young officer of the British army in the late nineteenth century is given four white feathers, symbolic of an accusation of cowardice. He proves his courage and redeems his honor by rescuing a group of fellow officers held captive in the Sudan.

THEME INDICATORS
ADVENTURE
MILITARY
DRAMA
CULTURAL
ETHICS
HISTORICAL
RACIAL
WAR

Film Version: **Highly recommended**
An example of a successful transfer from literary to film format of an adventure story, with first-class production values, impeccable acting performances, and a general impression of careful and painstaking handling of the original material.

Full Film Title
FRANKENSTEIN

Release Date
1931

Production Studio
UNIVERSAL

Country of Origin
USA

Running Time (Minutes)
71

Producer
Carl Laemmle, Jr.

Director
James Whale

Principal Performers
Boris Karloff, Colin Clive, Mae Clarke, John Boles, Frederick Kerr, Dwight Frye.

Literary Original and Date of Production
FRANKENSTEIN OR THE MODERN PROMETHEUS 1818

Author and Biographical Dates
Mary Godwin Shelley 1791-1851

Recommended Viewing
Recommended Reading
35 mm Film, B & W

SUMMARIES

THEME INDICATORS
MONSTER
SCIENCE FICTION
DRAMA
ETHICS

Literary Original
In a setting of gothic mystery and suspense, a scientist pieces together a semi-human being, which he animates by harnessing the lightning. His presumptuous meddling with the forces of nature ends in disaster when his monstrous creation proves to be uncontrollable.

Film Version: **Highly recommended**
Based on little more than the central theme of the original novel, this production has become a cinema classic and the prototype of a genre of horror movies, few of which have ever matched it in power and intensity. The moral message of the dangers of presumptuous experimenting with the forces of nature still comes through strongly, although the setting is not entirely suitable for the sensitive or impressionable viewer.

Full Film Title
FROM THE EARTH TO THE MOON

Release Date
1958

Production Studio
WARNER BROTHERS

Country of Origin
USA

Running Time (Minutes)
100

Producer
Benedict Bogeaus

Director
Byron Haskin

Principal Performers
Joseph Cotten, George Sanders, Henry Daniell, Carl Esmond, Melville Cooper, Don Dubbins, Debra Paget, Patric Knowles.

Literary Original and Date of Production
FROM THE EARTH TO THE MOON   1865

Author and Biographical Dates
Jules Verne   1828-1905

Codings of 16 mm Distribution Agencies
BUD   MAC   VCI   WHO

Recommended Viewing

16 mm Film, Color

SUMMARIES

Literary Original
A group of Civil War veterans design a gigantic gun to fire a manned projectile from Florida over the 250,000-mile trajectory to the moon. A French enthusiast, Michel Ardan, volunteers to mastermind the project and lead the three-man crew, but the unknown factors involved in his calculations produce a tragic finale. (The situation was resolved in a sequel *Round The Moon*.)

Film Version
An unsatisfactory adaptation of the early science-fiction classic, maintaining the nineteenth-century background but inadequately scripted and unconvincingly presented.

THEME INDICATORS
ADVENTURE
FANTASY
SCIENCE FICTION
DRAMA

Full Film Title
GOODBYE MR. CHIPS

Release Date
1939

Production Studio
METRO-GOLDWYN-MAYER

Country of Origin
USA

Running Time (Minutes)
113

Producer
Victor Saville

Director
Sam Wood

Principal Performers
Robert Donat, Greer Garson, Terry Kilburn, John Mills, Paul Von Heinreid, Judith Furse, Lyn Harding, Milton Rosmer, Frederick Leister.

Literary Original and Date of Production
GOODBYE, MR. CHIPS   1933

Author and Biographical Dates
James Hilton   1900-1954

Codings of 16 mm Distribution Agencies
FNC

Recommended Viewing
Recommended Reading
16 mm Film, B & W

SUMMARIES

THEME INDICATORS
COMEDY
DRAMA
CHILDREN
CULTURAL
ETHICS
FAMILY
FEMINISM
HISTORICAL

Literary Original
This best-seller deals sentimentally with the life of an English schoolmaster. The gentle Mr. Chipping was known as Mr. Chips to generations of children in Brookfield. In fond memories, he recalls his life there and the hundreds of boys whom he considered his children. The school is grief-stricken at the eventual death of the amiable old man.

Film Version: **Recommended**
This interpretation of the original novel sticks closely to the sentiment and charm implicit in the material and expands on the opportunities for humor and evocation of period detail. The style may have become slightly dated, but the star performances remain fresh and impressive.

Full Film Title
GOOD EARTH, THE

Release Date
1937

Production Studio
METRO-GOLDWYN-MAYER

Country of Origin
USA

Running Time (Minutes)
138

Producer
Albert Levin

Director
Sidney Franklin

Principal Performers
Paul Muni, Louise Rainer, Walter Connolly.

Literary Original and Date of Production
GOOD EARTH, THE 1931

Author and Biographical Dates
Pearl S. Buck   1892-1973

Codings of 16 mm Distribution Agencies
FNC

Recommended Viewing
Recommended Reading
16 mm Film, B & W

SUMMARIES

Literary Original
In this powerful epic of Chinese peasant life, Wang Lung, a young farmer, marries the faithful O-lan. They have sons together, the earth's crops are abundant, and the family prospers. Eventually, poor crops force them to beg for food. Determined, Wang Lung returns to his land, remarries, and toils to recapture his prosperity.

THEME INDICATORS
ADVENTURE
CULTURAL
ECOLOGY
ETHICS
FAMILY
FEMINISM
HISTORICAL
RACIAL
WAR

Film Version: **Recommended**
Widely acclaimed in its day as a genuine glimpse into the barely known China of the early twentieth century, this earnest treatment of the source material will probably appear outdated and stilted to modern and better informed viewers. However, the film is impressive for the quality of acting displayed by its stars and is an interesting historical example of the movie techniques of the major productions of the 1930s.

Full Film Title
GREATEST STORY EVER TOLD, THE

Release Date
1965

Production Studio	Country of Origin	Running Time (Minutes)
UNITED ARTISTS	**USA**	**.141**

Producer
George Stevens

Director
George Stevens

Principal Performers
Max Von Sydow, Dorothy McGuire, Robert Loggia, Charlton Heston, Michael Anderson, Robert Blake, John Considine, Jamie Farr.

Literary Original and Date of Production
GREATEST STORY EVER TOLD, THE   1949

Author and Biographical Dates
Fulton Oursler   1893-1952

Codings of 16 mm Distribution Agencies	**Recommended Viewing**
MAC UAS	
	16 mm Film, Color
SUMMARIES	THEME INDICATORS
	DRAMA
Literary Original	**BIOGRAPHICAL**
This is a compilation of the stories of Jesus' life	**ETHICS**
from the foretelling of his birth to the ascension.	**HISTORICAL**
	RELIGIOUS

Film Version: **Recommended**
This treatment of the public life and ministry of Christ, almost predictably, falls short of its ambitious intentions but remains a sincere and well-meant, reverent handling of the narrative, with Max von Sydow sustaining most of the interest in a four-hour spectacular.

Full Film Title
GREAT EXPECTATIONS

Release Date
1946

Production Studio
CINEGUILD INCORPORATED

Country of Origin
Great Britain

Running Time (Minutes)
118

Producer
Anthony Havelock-Allan

Director
David Lean

Principal Performers
John Mills, Valerie Hobson, Jean Simmons, Alec Guinness, Bernard Miles, Anthony Wager, Grace Denbigh-Russell, Hay Petrie, Frieda Jackson.

Literary Original and Date of Production
GREAT EXPECTATIONS   1861

Author and Biographical Dates
Charles Dickens   1812-1870

Codings of 16 mm Distribution Agencies
**BUD   CAL   CON   IMA   KPF   LCA   MAC
MOD   ROA   TWY   WCF   WEL   WHO**

Recommended Viewing
Recommended Reading
16 mm Film, B & W

SUMMARIES

THEME INDICATORS
**DRAMA
CHILDREN
CULTURAL
ETHICS
FAMILY
HISTORICAL**

Literary Original
In nineteenth-century England, the orphan Philip Pirrir is reared by his sister and her husband. An unknown benefactor provides for his education, and Pip, as he is called, travels to London. As his dreams of grandeur fade, he returns home to the realities of hard work and family life.

Film Version: **Very highly recommended**
The famous original has been only slightly reduced and modified in content to make a deservedly prestigious presentation reflecting taste, skillful treatment, and elegance of finish in all aspects of production, with particularly noteworthy performances in key and support roles.

Full Film Title
GREYFRIARS BOBBY

Release Date
1961

Production Studio
DISNEY

Country of Origin
USA

Running Time (Minutes)
91

Producer
Walt Disney

Director
Don Chaffey

Principal Performers
Donald Crisp, Laurence Naismith, Alex Mackenzie, Kay Walsh, Duncan Macrae, Andrew Cruickshank, Rosalie Crutchley, Moultrie Kelsall, Joyce Carey.

Literary Original and Date of Production
GREYFRIARS BOBBY 1912

Author and Biographical Dates
Eleanor Atkinson 1863-1942

Codings of 16 mm Distribution Agencies
**AIM BUC CCC COU DIS FNC FPC
MAC MOD NEW ROA SWA TFC TWY**

Recommended Viewing
Recommended Reading
16 mm Film, Color

SUMMARIES

THEME INDICATORS
COMEDY
DRAMA
CHILDREN
CULTURAL
ECOLOGY
HISTORICAL

Literary Original
Bobby, a little Scotch terrier, preferred the graveside of his beloved master to the other homes available to him. Admiring townspeople fed and sheltered him there. A wealthy woman heard of his loyalty and had a bronze replica of him erected in the churchyard after his death.

Film Version: **Recommended**
A completely satisfactory film version of an appealing original, executed with all the skill, care, and accurate research typical of the best Disney studio live-action unit productions.

Full Film Title
GULLIVER'S TRAVELS

Release Date
1939

Production Studio
PARAMOUNT

Country of Origin
USA

Running Time (Minutes)
85

Producer
Max Fleischer

Director
Dave Fleischer

Principal Performers
Animation

Literary Original and Date of Production
GULLIVER'S TRAVELS 1726

Author and Biographical Dates
Jonathan Swift   1667-1745

Codings of 16 mm Distribution Agencies

AIM	ARG	BUD	CCC	CFM	CHA	CWF	EMG	FPC
ICS	IMA	IVY	KPF	LEW	MAC	MOG	NAT	NEW
ROA	TFC	TWF	TWY	VCI	WEL	WHO		

Recommended Viewing
Recommended Reading
16 mm Film, Color

SUMMARIES

THEME INDICATORS
ADVENTURE
ANIMATION
FANTASY
DRAMA
CULTURAL
ECOLOGY

Literary Original
In this fantasy, Swift fires caustic social criticism at England in particular and humanity in general. In the imaginary realms of Lilliput and Brobdingnag, Lemuel Gulliver finds that the scale of things, miniature or gigantic, does little to alter human folly. He begins to hate mankind and upon his return to England is repulsed by the sight of his wife and family. Horses remain his only friends.

Film Version
This cartoon for young audiences retains little of the intent of the literary original. The satire has been converted to humorous fantasy, which provides pleasant, lighthearted fun.

Full Film Title
GUNGA DIN

Release Date
1939

Production Studio
RKO RADIO

Country of Origin
USA

Running Time (Minutes)
117

Producer
George Stevens

Director
George Stevens

Principal Performers
Cary Grant, Douglas Fairbanks, Jr., Victor McLaglen, Sam Jaffe, Eduardo Ciannelli, Joan Fontaine, Montagu Love, Robert Coote.

Literary Original and Date of Production
GUNGA DIN 1890

Author and Biographical Dates
Rudyard Kipling 1865-1936

Codings of 16 mm Distribution Agencies
FNC   RKO

Recommended Viewing
Recommended Reading
16 mm Film, B & W

SUMMARIES

Literary Original
Gunga Din was a water carrier for a British Indian regiment. During a fierce battle and with disregard for his own safety, he passed among the slain soldiers still lying in the field, offering drink and comfort to the injured. He embodied the courage and humility so revered by Kipling.

THEME INDICATORS
ADVENTURE
MILITARY
DRAMA
CULTURAL
HISTORICAL
RACIAL
WAR

Film Version: **Recommended**
The original poem serves merely as a peg on which to hang a confection created by expert script writers who provide all the ingredients for a comedy-action adventure never intended to be taken as anything but rousing entertainment.

Full Film Title
HAMLET

Release Date
1948

Production Studio
RANK/TWO CITIES

Country of Origin
Great Britain

Running Time (Minutes)
142

Producer
Laurence Olivier

Director
Laurence Olivier

Principal Performers
Laurence Olivier, Eileen Herlie, Jean Simmons, Felix Aylmer, Norman Wooland, Terence Morgan, Stanley Holloway, Peter Cushing.

Literary Original and Date of Production
HAMLET (Play) 1603

Author and Biographical Dates
William Shakespeare   1564-1616

Codings of 16 mm Distribution Agencies
**CAL   CON   IMA   KPF   LCA   MAC
ROA   TWY**

Recommended Viewing
Recommended Reading
16 mm Film, B & W

SUMMARIES

THEME INDICATORS
**DRAMA
TRAGEDY
ETHICS
HISTORICAL**

Literary Original
Hamlet, Prince of Denmark, determines to avenge the murder of his father by his uncle Claudius, who has married the widowed queen. Torn by irresolution and feigning madness, he drives his beloved Ophelia to her death, kills her father Polonius by mistake, and is himself killed by the treachery of Claudius in a climactic duel scene, which also sees the death of the king, the queen, and Ophelia's brother, Laertes.

Film Version: **Highly recommended**
A commanding interpretation by a master tragedian equally distinguished on the stage and the screen, with the original text trimmed down to concentrate attention on the central dilemma of the doubt-torn prince.

Full Film Title
HAMLET

Release Date
1969

Production Studio	Country of Origin	Running Time (Minutes)
WOODFALL	**Great Britain**	**114**

Producer
Leslie Linder/Martin Ransohoff

Director
Tony Richardson

Principal Performers
Nicol Williamson, Marianne Faithfull, Gordon Jackson, Anthony Hopkins, Mark Dignam, Roger Livesey, Judy Parfitt.

Literary Original and Date of Production
HAMLET (play) 1603

Author and Biographical Dates
William Shakespeare 1564-1616

Codings of 16 mm Distribution Agencies
AIM BUD KPF LCA MAC MMM
MOD ROA SWA WHO

Recommended Viewing
Recommended Reading
16 mm Film, Color

SUMMARIES

THEME INDICATORS
DRAMA
TRAGEDY
ETHICS
HISTORICAL

Literary Original
Hamlet, Prince of Denmark, determines to avenge the murder of his father by his uncle Claudius, who has married the widowed queen. Torn by irresolution and feigning madness, he drives his beloved Ophelia to her death, kills her father Polonius by mistake, and is himself killed by the treachery of Claudius in a climactic duel scene, which also sees the death of the king, the queen, and Ophelia's brother, Laertes.

Film Version: **Recommended**
An interesting and acceptable alternative to the classic style of the Olivier version, showing the central character more as a man of action caught up in events beyond his power to control and with greater emphasis on side plots.

Full Film Title
HEIDI

Release Date
1937

Production Studio **TWO CITIES FILMS**	Country of Origin **USA**	Running Time (Minutes) **88**

Director
Allan Dwan

Principal Performers
Shirley Temple, Jean Hersholt, Arthur Treacher, Helen Westley, Pauline Moore, Mary Nash, Thomas Beck, Sidney Blackmer, Sig Rumann.

Literary Original and Date of Production
HEIDI   1880

Author and Biographical Dates
Johanna Hauser Spyri   1827-1901

Codings of 16 mm Distribution Agencies **FNC**	Recommended Viewing Recommended Reading 16 mm Film, B & W
SUMMARIES	THEME INDICATORS **COMEDY** **DRAMA**
Literary Original **A lonely, homeless child goes to stay with her grandfather high in the Alps. She makes friends with the goatherd, Peter, and learns to love the peace and simplicity of her surroundings.**	**CHILDREN** **CULTURAL** **FAMILY** **FEMINISM** **HISTORICAL**

Film Version: **Recommended**
The story line has been preserved in outline, and recast to offer opportunities for a display of the unique and winsome charm of the public's favorite child star of the 1930s.

Full Film Title
HEIDI

Release Date
1954

Production Studio
UNITED ARTISTS

Country of Origin
USA

Running Time (Minutes)
97

Director
Luigi Comincini

Principal Performers
Elsbeth Sigmund, Heinrich Gretler.

Literary Original and Date of Production
HEIDI   1880

Author and Biographical Dates
Johanna Hauser Spyri   1827-1901

Codings of 16 mm Distribution Agencies
BUC   BUD   CCC   ICS   MAC

Recommended Viewing
Recommended Reading
16 mm Film, B & W

SUMMARIES

THEME INDICATORS
  COMEDY
  DRAMA
  CHILDREN
  CULTURAL
  FAMILY
  FEMINISM
  HISTORICAL

Literary Original
A lonely, homeless child goes to stay with her grandfather high in the Alps. She makes friends with the goatherd, Peter, and learns to love the peace and simplicity of her surroundings.

Film Version: **Recommended**
Authentic scenery and laudable performances eloquently re-create the innocence and grandeur of Spyri's classic story. English dialogue has been dubbed into the film.

Full Film Title
HENRY V

Release Date
1944

Production Studio
RANK/TWO CITIES

Country of Origin
Great Britain

Running Time (Minutes)
137

Producer
Laurence Olivier

Director
Laurence Olivier

Principal Performers
Laurence Olivier, Robert Newton, Leslie Banks, Esmond Knight, Renee Asherson, George Robey, Leo Genn, Ernest Thesiger, Ralph Truman.

Literary Original and Date of Production
KING HENRY THE FIFTH (Play) 1600

Author and Biographical Dates
William Shakespeare 1564-1616

Codings of 16 mm Distribution Agencies
BUD CAL CON CWF IMA KPF LCA
MAC MOD ROA TWY WCF WHO

Recommended Viewing
Recommended Reading
16 mm Film, Color

SUMMARIES

THEME INDICATORS
ADVENTURE
MILITARY
DRAMA
ROMANCE
HISTORICAL
WAR

Literary Original
The young Prince Hal renounces his low companions and irresponsible way of life when called to assume the responsibilities of kingship. He vigorously asserts his claim to territories in France, performs heroically as military commander at the victory of Agincourt, and woos and wins the daughter of the defeated French king.

Film Version: **Very highly recommended**
In an innovative experimental approach, the film treatment moves from the stage of Shakespeare's Globe Theater outward to the wider horizons allowed by cinema techniques. The central character is strongly and intelligently presented, the supporting cast is distinguished, and the entire very satisfying presentation is visually enriched by careful reinforcement of authentic period detail.

Full Film Title
HIGH WIND IN JAMAICA, A

Release Date
1965

Production Studio	Country of Origin	Running Time (Minutes)
TWENTIETH CENTURY FOX	**USA**	**104**

Producer
John Croydon

Director
Alexander Mackendrick

Principal Performers
Anthony Quinn, James Coburn, Dennis Price, Lila Kedrova, Gert Frobe, Kenneth J. Warren, Nigel Davenport, Isabel Dean, Viviane Ventura.

Literary Original and Date of Production
HIGH WIND IN JAMAICA, A   1929

Author and Biographical Dates
Richard Hughes   1900-

Codings of 16 mm Distribution Agencies
FNC

Recommended Viewing
Recommended Reading
16 mm Film, Color

SUMMARIES

Literary Original
This novel was first published as *The Innocent Voyage*. **The Thornton home in the West Indies is destroyed by a hurricane. The children are sent to England. En route they are captured by pirates and begin a voyage of nightmarish quality. The children and the crew never understand each other or the fantastic events that occur.**

THEME INDICATORS
ADVENTURE
CRIME
MARINE
DRAMA
CHILDREN
CULTURAL
ETHICS
FAMILY
HISTORICAL

Film Version: **Recommended**
The psychological interplay of the child and adult characters is strongly stressed in the film version, which opens up the action in sequences of good local color and reworks the ending in an attempt at increased dramatic effect.

Full Film Title
HOUND OF THE BASKERVILLES, THE

Release Date
1939

Production Studio
TCF

Country of Origin
USA

Running Time (Minutes)
80

Producer
Gene Markey

Director
Sidney Lanfield

Principal Performers
Basil Rathbone, Nigel Bruce, Richard Greene, Wendy Barrie, Lionel Atwill, Morton Lowry, John Carradine, Ralph Forbes.

Literary Original and Date of Production
HOUND OF THE BASKERVILLES, THE   1897

Author and Biographical Dates
Sir Arthur Conan Doyle   1859-1930

Codings of 16 mm Distribution Agencies
BUD   FNC   IMA   KPF   LCA   MAC   ROA   TWY

Recommended Viewing
Recommended Reading
16 mm Film, B & W

SUMMARIES

THEME INDICATORS
ADVENTURE
CRIME
DRAMA
ETHICS

Literary Original
Sherlock Holmes and Dr. Watson investigate the murder of Sir Charles Baskerville whose family lies under a legendary curse of haunting by a spectral hound. Blood-curdling howls by night on the lonely moors suggest that the ancestral curse may be coming true, but a second murder leads to the exposure of a cunning human culprit.

Film Version: **Recommended**
The script of the film departs widely from the original story but preserves atmosphere and authenticity in a classic film representation of the famous detective and his staunch companion and admirer, Dr. Watson.

Full Film Title
HOUND OF THE BASKERVILLES, THE

Release Date
1959

Production Studio
UNITED ARTISTS

Country of Origin
USA

Running Time (Minutes)
87

Producer
Anthony Hinds

Director
Terence Fisher

Principal Performers
Peter Cushing, Andre Morell, Christopher Lee, Marla Landi, David Oxley, Ewen Solon, Francis De Wolff.

Literary Original and Date of Production
HOUND OF THE BASKERVILLES, THE   1897

Author and Biographical Dates
Sir Arthur Conan Doyle   1859-1930

Codings of 16 mm Distribution Agencies
MAC   UAS

Recommended Viewing
Recommended Reading
16 mm Film, Color

SUMMARIES

Literary Original
Sherlock Holmes and Dr. Watson investigate the murder of Sir Charles Baskerville, whose family lies under a legendary curse of haunting by a spectral hound. Blood-curdling howls by night on the lonely moors suggest that the ancestral curse may be coming true, but a second murder leads to the exposure of a cunning human culprit.

THEME INDICATORS
ADVENTURE
CRIME
DRAMA
ETHICS

Film Version
A British remake in color, of poor technical finish, and with exaggerated overtones of horror and violence far removed from the Victorian atmosphere of the original material.

Full Film Title
HUCKLEBERRY FINN

Release Date
1974

Production Studio
UNITED ARTISTS

Country of Origin
USA

Running Time (Minutes)
118

Producer
Robert Greehut

Director
J. Lee-Thomson

Principal Performers
Jeff East, Paul Winfield, David Wayne, Harvey Korman, Arthur O'Connell, Gary Merrill, Natalie Trundy.

Literary Original and Date of Production
ADVENTURES OF HUCKLEBERRY FINN, THE   1885

Author and Biographical Dates
Mark Twain (Samuel Clemens)   1835-1910

Codings of 16 mm Distribution Agencies
CWF   ROA   UAS   WCF   WHO

Recommended Reading
16 mm Film, Color

SUMMARIES

Literary Original
Huckleberry Finn and Tom Sawyer run away and sail down the Mississippi on a raft. They fall in with a pair of confidence tricksters and have a series of adventures before shaking off their amusing but undesirable companions and making their way back to their families.

THEME INDICATORS
ADVENTURE
MUSICAL
COMEDY
DRAMA
CHILDREN
CULTURAL
ECOLOGY
FAMILY
HISTORICAL
RACIAL

Film Version
A large-scale version of the classic story with the addition of musical and singing interludes.

Full Film Title
HUNCHBACK OF NOTRE DAME, THE

Release Date
1939

Production Studio
RKO Radio

Country of Origin
USA

Running Time (Minutes)
117

Producer
Pandro S. Berman

Director
William Dieterle

Principal Performers
Charles Laughton, Maureen O'Hara, Sir Cedric Hardwicke, Edmond O'Brien, Alan Marshall, Walter Hampden, Harry Davenport.

Literary Original and Date of Production
Hunchback of Notre Dame, The 1831

Author and Biographical Dates
Victor Hugo   1802-1885

Codings of 16 mm Distribution Agencies
FNC   JAN   RKO

Recommended Viewing
Recommended Reading
16 mm Film, B & W

SUMMARIES

THEME INDICATORS
Adventure
Drama
Romance
Tragedy
Cultural
Ethics
Feminism
Historical

Literary Original
Quasimodo is the deformed bell ringer in the cathedral of Paris in the fifteenth century. He is befriended by the alluring Esmeralda, who has been denounced as a witch and sentenced to death by the hypocritical Claude Frollo. Quasimodo protects her for a time in the cathedral belfry, but ulitmately she is executed. Quasimodo then throws Frollo from the heights of Notre Dame.

Film Version: **Very highly recommended**
A classic film, based on an intelligent adaptation of the original novel, with excellent acting performances, a large and well-handled supporting cast, and masterly contributions from the entire technical-specialist team.

Full Film Title
ICHABOD AND MR. TOAD

Release Date
1949

Production Studio
DISNEY

Country of Origin
USA

Running Time (Minutes)
68

Producer
Ben Sharpsteen

Director
Jack Kinney

Principal Performers
Narrators: Basil Rathbone, Bing Crosby.

Literary Original and Date of Production
LEGEND OF SLEEPY HOLLOW, THE   1820
    and
WIND IN THE WILLOWS, THE   1908

Author and Biographical Dates
Washington Irving   1783-1859
    and
Kenneth Grahame   1859-1932

Codings of 16 mm Distribution Agencies
AIM   BUC   CCC   COU   CWF   FNC   FPC
MAC   MOD   NEW   ROA   SWA   TFC   TWY

Recommended Viewing
Recommended Reading
16 mm Film, Color

SUMMARIES

THEME INDICATORS

Literary Original
In the village of Sleepy Hollow, Ichabod Crane, a superstitious schoolmaster, courts Katrina Van Tassel. Brom Bones, Crane's rival for Katrina, exploits Crane's meak demeanor. Masquerading as a headless horseman, he runs the schoolmaster out of town.
The irrepressible, irresponsible Mr. Toad had a love affair with the new-fangled automobile. His friends Mole and Water Rat set out to save him. Meanwhile, Toad Hall is seized by ruthless weasels. The three companions return and recapture Toad's home.

ANIMATION
FANTASY
COMEDY
ROMANCE

Film Version: **Recommended**
An unusual combination in animation film form of two widely differing literary originals. The story of Ichabod is illustrated with some exaggeration of the creepy overtones sketched in by Washington Irving. Kenneth Grahame's Mr. Toad is pictured at his most pompous and eccentric. Overall, the film provides good visual support with faithful interpretation of action.

Full Film Title
INCREDIBLE JOURNEY, THE

Release Date
1963

Production Studio
DISNEY

Country of Origin
USA

Running Time (Minutes)
80

Producer
James Algar

Director
Fletcher Markle

Principal Performers
Emile Genest, John Drainie, Tommy Tweed, and Muffey, Syn Cat, and Rink.

Literary Original and Date of Production
INCREDIBLE JOURNEY, THE   1961

Author and Biographical Dates
Sheila Burnford   1918-

Codings of 16 mm Distribution Agencies
CCC   DIS   FNC   MAC   NEW   ROA   TWY

Recommended Viewing

16 mm Film, Color

SUMMARIES

THEME INDICATORS
ADVENTURE
DRAMA
ECOLOGY

Literary Original
A Labrador retriever and his two companions, a Siamese cat and an old bull terrier, survive the perils of a 250-mile trek through the Canadian wilderness. They pool their strength, cunning and natural abilities to battle starvation, preditory animals, and the humans who would detain them. A variant of the survival theme in "Bremen Town Musicians" collected by the Brothers Grimm.

Film Version: **Highly recommended**
A tour de force from the Disney live-action studios, which conjures incredible performances from the domestic animals who are the featured players, to make a film certain to succeed with viewing audiences of all ages.

Full Film Title
IN SEARCH OF THE CASTAWAYS

Release Date
1962

Production Studio
DISNEY

Country of Origin
USA

Running Time (Minutes)
100

Producer
Walt Disney

Director
Peter Bolton

Principal Performers
Hayley Mills, Maurice Chevalier, George Sanders, Wilfred Hyde-White, Michael Anderson, Antonio Cifariello, Keith Hamshere, Wilfred Brambell.

Literary Original and Date of Production
CAPTAIN GRANT'S CHILDREN 1868

Author and Biographical Dates
Jules Verne 1828-1905

Recommended Viewing
Recommended Reading
35 mm Film, Color

SUMMARIES

Literary Original
Lord Glenarvan is a Scottish nobleman who comes across a manuscript message in a bottle cast into the sea, giving incomplete indications of the location of a castaway family. To rescue them, he sails halfway around the world, successfully confronting flood, fire, earthquake, and human enemies.

THEME INDICATORS
ADVENTURE
CRIME
MARINE
DRAMA
CHILDREN
CULTURAL
ECOLOGY
FAMILY
HISTORICAL

Film Version: **Highly recommended**
The original search theme has been greatly expanded and elaborated in this rewriting to provide fantasy and adventure in an entertaining and amusing blend of styles calculated to grip the attention of juvenile viewers.

Full Film Title
INVISIBLE MAN, THE

Release Date
1933

Production Studio
UNIVERSAL

Country of Origin
USA

Running Time (Minutes)
71

Producer
Carl Laemmle, Jr.

Director
James Whale

Principal Performers
Claude Rains, Gloria Stuart, Una O'Connor, William Harrigan, E.E. Clive, Dudley Digges.

Literary Original and Date of Production
INVISIBLE MAN, THE   1897

Author and Biographical Dates
Herbert George Wells   1866-1946

Recommended Viewing
Recommended Reading
35 mm Film, B & W

SUMMARIES

THEME INDICATORS
CRIME
SCIENCE FICTION
DRAMA
ETHICS
FAMILY

Literary Original
A scientific amateur in the late nineteenth century discovers how to make himself invisible and terrifies his neighborhood by a criminal career of theft and acts of violence. He is tracked down, trapped, and killed after he threatens to embark on a course of wholesale murder.

Film Version: **Very highly recommended**
Trick photography and all the resources of the special effects department are exploited to the limit to bring off a completely successful visualization of the original story. Even the original message of the importance of remaining within natural human limitations is conveyed effectively.

Full Film Title
IVANHOE

Release Date
1951

Production Studio
METRO-GOLDWYN-MAYER

Country of Origin
USA

Running Time (Minutes)
106

Producer
Pandro S. Berman

Director
Richard Thorpe

Principal Performers
Robert Taylor, Elizabeth Taylor, Joan Fontaine, George Sanders, Emlyn Williams, Guy Rolfe, Robert Douglas, Finlay Currie, Felix Aylmer, Basil Sydney.

Literary Original and Date of Production
IVANHOE   1820

Author and Biographical Dates
Sir Walter Scott   1771-1832

Codings of 16 mm Distribution Agencies
FNC

Recommended Viewing
Recommended Reading
16 mm Film, Color

SUMMARIES

Literary Original

This epitome of the chivalric novel is set in the England of 1194 A.D. The titular hero, Wilfred, Knight of Ivanhoe, loves his father's ward, Rowena. His father Cedric would have her marry Athelstane to restore Saxon supremacy. In this Saxon-Norman power struggle, Richard the Lion Heart, as the Black Knight, and Robin Hood, as Locksley, are prominent characters. King Richard secretly returns to reclaim his throne, and Lady Rowena is wedded to Ivanhoe.

THEME INDICATORS
ADVENTURE
MILITARY
DRAMA
ROMANCE
ETHICS
HISTORICAL

Film Version

A lavish and richly decorated spectacular, which retains only the bare outlines of the Sir Walter Scott novel as the connecting thread for a series of visually splendid scenes of courtly life and the code of medieval chivalry.

Full Film Title
JONATHAN LIVINGSTON SEAGULL

Release Date
1974

Production Studio
PARAMOUNT

Country of Origin
USA

Running Time (Minutes)
114

Producer
Hall Bartlett

Director
Hall Bartlett

Literary Original and Date of Production
JONATHAN LIVINGSTON SEAGULL   1970

Author and Biographical Dates
Richard Bach   1936-

Codings of 16 mm Distribution Agencies
PAR

Recommended Viewing
Recommended Reading
16 mm Film, Color

SUMMARIES

THEME INDICATORS
ADVENTURE
MUSICAL
DRAMA
ECOLOGY
ETHICS

Literary Original
In a parable with strong philosophical and metaphysical overtones, a young sea gull departs from the flock to find his own freedom and seek the perfection of flight. He returns in the end to his fellows in order to impart to them his experiences and encourage them towards the higher wisdom.

Film Version: **Recommended**
Rewritten for the screen by the original author and backed with a strong musical score in the popular style, this production is likely to succeed with audiences who can appreciate, and identify with, the mysticism and symbolism of the theme. Notable for outstanding photography of bird flight.

Full Film Title
JOURNEY TO THE CENTER OF THE EARTH

Release Date
1959

Production Studio	Country of Origin	Running Time (Minutes)
TWENTIETH CENTURY FOX	**USA**	**132**

Producer
Charles Brackett

Director
Henry Levin

Principal Performers
James Mason, Arlene Dahl, Pat Boone, Diane Baker, Peter Ronson, Thayer David, Bob Adler, Alan Napier, Frederick Halliday.

Literary Original and Date of Production
JOURNEY TO THE CENTER OF THE EARTH, A 1864

Author and Biographical Dates
Jules Verne   1828-1905

Codings of 16 mm Distribution Agencies
FNC

Recommended Viewing
Recommended Reading
16 mm Film, Color

SUMMARIES

THEME INDICATORS
ADVENTURE
FANTASY
MONSTER
DRAMA
ROMANCE
ECOLOGY

Literary Original
Axel is a young mineralogist who tells how he wins his sweetheart by accompanying his uncle on a subterranean voyage, which starts in an extinct volcano in Iceland and ends at Stromboli in Sicily. On the way, the party has to negotiate the dangers of the inner seas, with prehistoric creatures and antediluvian monsters.

Film Version: **Highly recommended**
The fantasy and adventure of Verne's original have been skillfully enhanced by well-employed special effects and spectacular colorization to produce captivating illusions that are certain to fascinate all audiences.

Full Film Title
JULIUS CAESAR

Release Date
1953

Production Studio
MGM

Country of Origin
USA

Running Time (Minutes)
121

Producer
John Houseman

Director
Joseph L. Mankiewicz

Principal Performers
John Gielgud, James Mason, Marlon Brando, Greer Garson, Deborah Kerr, Louis Calhern, Edmond O'Brien, George Macready.

Literary Original and Date of Production
JULIUS CAESAR (Play)   1623

Author and Biographical Dates
William Shakespeare   1564-1616

Codings of 16 mm Distribution Agencies
FNC

Recommended Viewing
Recommended Reading
16 mm Film, B & W

SUMMARIES

THEME INDICATORS
- **MILITARY**
- **DRAMA**
- **TRAGEDY**
- **BIOGRAPHY**
- **ETHICS**
- **HISTORICAL**

Literary Original
At the peak of his glory and power as soldier and statesman, Julius Caesar is assassinated by a group of envious conspirators who pose as patriots. (As readers know, motivations for their actions are complex.) Antony exposes the baseness of their real motives and rouses the people of Rome against them. The murderers are forced to flee and go down to military defeat at the battle of Philippi.

Film Version: **Recommended**
A straightforward presentation of the action, which makes the content of the drama more accessible by the portrayal of the main characters as perceptibly modernized participants in the power games of politics and statesmanship.

Full Film Title
JULIUS CAESAR

Release Date
1969

Production Studio
COMMONWEALTH UNITED

Country of Origin
Great Britain

Running Time (Minutes)
116

Producer
Peter Snell

Director
Stuart Burge

Principal Performers
Richard Johnson, Jason Robards, John Gielgud, Charlton Heston, Robert Vaughn, Richard Chamberlain, Diana Rigg, Christopher Lee.

Literary Original and Date of Production
JULIUS CAESAR (Play) 1623

Author and Biographical Dates
William Shakespeare 1564-1616

Codings of 16 mm Distribution Agencies
AIM BUD IVY KPF MAC
MOD ROA VCI WCF WHO

Recommended Viewing
Recommended Reading
16 mm Film, Color

SUMMARIES

THEME INDICATORS
MILITARY
DRAMA
TRAGEDY
BIOGRAPHICAL
ETHICS
HISTORICAL

Literary Original
At the peak of his glory and power as soldier and statesman, Julius Caesar is assassinated by a group of envious conspirators who pose as patriots. (As readers know, motivations for their actions are complex.) Antony exposes the baseness of their real motives and rouses the people of Rome against them. The murderers are forced to flee and go down to military defeat at the battle of Philippi.

Film Version
An oversimple rendering of the story, generally considered to be inferior in acting and production to the MGM 1953 version.

Full Film Title
JUNGLE BOOK, THE

Release Date
1942

Production Studio	Country of Origin	Running Time (Minutes)
UNIVERSAL	**USA**	**115**

Director
Zoltan Korda

Principal Performers
Sabu, Joseph Calleia, John Qualen, Frank Puglia, Rosemary De Camp.

Literary Original and Date of Production
JUNGLE BOOK, THE   1894

Author and Biographical Dates
Rudyard Kipling   1865-1936

Codings of 16 mm Distribution Agencies
BUC   BUD   WHO

Recommended Viewing
Recommended Reading
16 mm Film, Color

SUMMARIES

Literary Original
Left unattended, the infant Mowgli wanders into the jungle. He is reared by wolves and attains prominent status in their pack. Together they battle the dreaded tiger Shere Khan. Questioning his origin, Mowgli seeks out his biological parents in a nearby village and is torn between his two families.

THEME INDICATORS
ADVENTURE
FANTASY
DRAMA
CHILDREN
CULTURAL
ECOLOGY
FAMILY
RACIAL

Film Version
Bearing little relation to the original, this unimpressive effort focuses on the more violent aspects of the jungle, with disregard for the character development of Mowgli.

Full Film Title
KIDNAPPED

Release Date
1971

Production Studio
AMERICAN INTERNATIONAL

Country of Origin
USA

Running Time (Minutes)
100

Director
Delbert Mann

Principal Performers
Michael Caine, Trevor Howard, Jack Hawkins, Donald Pleasence.

Literary Original and Date of Production
KIDNAPPED 1886

Author and Biographical Dates
Robert Louis Stevenson 1850-1894

Codings of 16 mm Distribution Agencies
ARG   BUD   SWA   VCI   WHO

Recommended Viewing
Recommended Reading
16 mm Film, B & W

SUMMARIES

THEME INDICATORS
ADVENTURE
CRIME
MARINE
DRAMA
CHILDREN
ETHICS
FAMILY
HISTORICAL

Literary Original
In the mid-1700s in Scotland, Mr. Balfour died leaving only a letter for his son, David. Following its instructions, David sought his uncle Ebenezer who, upon David's arrival, plotted his abduction to protect an ill-gotten inheritance. Captive on a ship, David met Alan Breck, a wanted criminal. Their friendship, forged of mutual respect, taught David the virtues of loyalty. The pair escaped, plotted, and acquired David's rightful inheritance from Ebenezer.

Film Version: **Recommended**
The Stevenson story and its sequel *Catriana* **have been run together in this well acted but rather slow color remake.**

Full Film Title
KIM

Release Date
1949

Production Studio
METRO-GOLDWYN-MAYER

Country of Origin
USA

Running Time (Minutes)
113

Producer
Leon Gordon

Director
Victor Saville

Principal Performers
Errol Flynn, Dean Stockwell, Paul Lukas, Robert Douglas, Thomas Gomez, Cecil Kellaway, Arnold Moss, Reginald Owen, Laurette Luez.

Literary Original and Date of Production
KIM   1901

Author and Biographical Dates
Rudyard Kipling   1865-1936

Codings of 16 mm Distribution Agencies
FNC

Recommended Viewing
Recommended Reading
16 mm Film, B & W

SUMMARIES

Literary Original
In the 1880s, Kimball O'Hara is the orphaned son of a British soldier in imperial India. The street-wise youth travels with a holy man and learns the ways of the country and its people. When his true identity becomes known, Kim is sent to school against his wishes. While still a boy, he assists the English Secret Service with his knowledge of India.

THEME INDICATORS
ADVENTURE
MILITARY
DRAMA
CHILDREN
CULTURAL
ETHICS
FAMILY
HISTORY
WAR

Film Version
A film version that retains and conveys little of the spirit, atmosphere, or period detail of the original and that remains little more than light entertainment as an adventure story.

Full Film Title
KING KONG

Release Date
1933

Production Studio
RKO Radio

Country of Origin
USA

Running Time (Minutes)
111

Producer
David O. Selznick

Director
Merian C. Cooper/Ernest B. Schoedsack

Principal Performers
Bruce Cabot, Fay Wray, Robert Armstrong, Frank Reicher, Sam Hardy, Noble Johnson, James Flavin, Steve Clemento.

Literary Original and Date of Production
King Kong (story) 1931

Author and Biographical Dates
Edgar Wallace 1875-1932

Codings of 16 mm Distribution Agencies
FNC JAN RKO

Recommended Viewing

16 mm Film, B & W

SUMMARIES

Literary Original
An expedition finds a giant ape on a remote island. It is captured and brought as a sideshow attraction to New York, where it escapes and wreaks havoc before being overcome.

THEME INDICATORS
Adventure
Fantasy
Monster
Drama
Cultural
Ecology
Ethics

Film Version: **Highly recommended**
The original story has become the starting point for a completely cinematic invention, featuring trick effects of all kinds, and the originator of the monster-movie genre. A classic of cinema, still gripping and effective after half a century.

Full Film Title
KING LEAR

Release Date
1970

Production Studio
COLUMBIA

Country of Origin
Great Britain

Running Time (Minutes)
137

Producer
Michael Birkett

Director
Peter Brook

Principal Performers
Paul Scofield, Irene Worth, Alan Webb, Tom Fleming, Susan Engel, Cyril Cusack, Patrick Magee, Jack McGowran.

Literary Original and Date of Production
KING LEAR (Play) 1608

Author and Biographical Dates
William Shakespeare 1564-1616

Codings of 16 mm Distribution Agencies
MAC

Recommended Viewing
Recommended Reading
16 mm Film, B & W

SUMMARIES

THEME INDICATORS
TRAGEDY
CULTURAL
ETHICS
FAMILY
HISTORICAL

Literary Original
In his old age, King Lear divides his kingdom of Britain among his three daughters according to their statements of love for him. The elder daughters, Regan and Goneril, hypocritically express great devotion but go back on their promise to support the aged king. The youngest, Cordelia, is disinherited for her honest and sincere declaration of affection and dies in an attempt to aid her father in his distress. The kingdom is torn by strife. Lear becomes mad and dies, and Regan and Goneril perish miserably.

Film Version: **Recommended**
The lighting, photography, and location settings combine to emphasize the despair and tragedy of the play in an overpoweringly sombre presentation. The acting is competent, and the narrative sequence complete.

Full Film Title
KING OF THE GRIZZLIES

Release Date
1969

Production Studio
DISNEY

Country of Origin
USA

Running Time (Minutes)
93

Producer
Winston Hibler

Director
Ron Kelly

Principal Performers
John Yesno, Chris Wiggins, Hugh Webster, Jack Van Evera, Big Ted.

Literary Original and Date of Production
BIOGRAPHY OF A GRIZZLY, THE   1900

Author and Biographical Dates
Ernest Thompson Seton   1860-1946

Codings of 16 mm Distribution Agencies
AIM   BUC   CCC   CWF   MAC
MOD   NAT   ROA   SWA   TFC

Recommended Viewing

16 mm Film, Color

SUMMARIES

Literary Original
Wahb the bear cub is forced to face alone the dangers of life in the western wilderness — traps, hunters, other animals. He lives out his life as monarch of his territory, to become a legend of the Rockies.

THEME INDICATORS
ADVENTURE
DRAMA
CHILDREN
CULTURAL
ECOLOGY
ETHICS
HISTORICAL

Film Version: **Recommended**
An additional framework featuring human characters has been built around the original simple narrative to give a dramatic interplay between Moki the Indian and Wahb the four-toed bear. The development of this relationship allows for excellent exterior location photography and a portrayal of the life of a grizzly that does credit to the intention and spirit of the source material, if not to its literal re-creation.

Full Film Title
KING RICHARD AND THE CRUSADERS

Release Date
1954

Production Studio
WARNER BROTHERS

Country of Origin
USA

Running Time (Minutes)
114

Producer
Henry Blanke

Director
David Butler

Principal Performers
Rex Harrison, Virginia Mayo, George Sanders, Laurence Harvey, Robert Douglas.

Literary Original and Date of Production
TALISMAN, THE 1825

Author and Biographical Dates
Sir Walter Scott 1771-1832

Recommended Reading
35 mm Film, Color

SUMMARIES

THEME INDICATORS
ADVENTURE
MILITARY
DRAMA
ROMANCE
CULTURAL
ETHICS
FEMINISM
HISTORICAL
WAR

Literary Original
During the Third Crusade, the discouraged and unruly allies of King Richard, bedridden with illness, wish to return to England. Sir Kenneth undertakes a controversial mission and returns with a learned man from the enemy camp of Prince Saladin. With his talisman, the man cures Richard, who then regains control of his forces. King Richard and Prince Saladin meet and depart friends, each admiring the skill and valor of the other.

Film Version
The setting and some episodes of the original novel have been retained, but the film is a travesty, with a routine catalogue of action episodes in costume and no attempt at verisimilitude, sense of period, or faithfulness to the source material.

Full Film Title
KING SOLOMON'S MINES

Release Date
1950

Production Studio
METRO-GOLDWYN-MAYER

Country of Origin
USA

Running Time (Minutes)
102

Producer
Sam Zimbalist

Director
Compton Bennett/Andrew Marton

Principal Performers
Deborah Kerr, Stewart Granger, Richard Carlson.

Literary Original and Date of Production
KING SOLOMON'S MINES   1885

Author and Biographical Dates
H. Rider Haggard   1856-1925

Codings of 16 mm Distribution Agencies
FNC

Recommended Viewing
Recommended Reading
16 mm Film, Color

SUMMARIES

Literary Original
Henry Curtis and Captain John Good enlist the aid of explorer Allan Quatermain in the search for Curtis's brother, not heard from since he departed in quest of the legendary fortunes of King Solomon. In darkest Africa, they survive exposure and bloodthirsty tribesmen before discovering the jewel mines. With a pocketful of diamonds, they escape a death trap and, while returning to civilization, unexpectedly encounter the lost brother.

THEME INDICATORS
ADVENTURE
DRAMA
ROMANCE
CULTURAL
ECOLOGY
ETHICS
HISTORICAL

Film Version
A color remake that sacrifices all but the outline of the original narrative in the interests of photographing the scenery and spectacle of tropical Africa.

Full Film Title
KNIGHTS OF THE ROUND TABLE, THE

Release Date
1954

Production Studio
METRO-GOLDWYN-MAYER

Country of Origin
USA

Running Time (Minutes)
115

Producer
Pandro S. Berman

Director
Richard Thorpe

Principal Performers
Robert Taylor, Ava Gardner, Mel Ferrer, Anne Crawford, Stanley Baker, Felix Aylmer, Maureen Swanson, Gabriel Woolf, Robert Urquhart.

Literary Original and Date of Production
MORTE D' ARTHUR   1469

Author and Biographical Dates
Sir Thomas Malory   1400-1471

Codings of 16 mm Distribution Agencies
FNC

Recommended Viewing
Recommended Reading
16 mm Film, Color

SUMMARIES

THEME INDICATORS
ADVENTURE
MILITARY
DRAMA
CULTURAL
ETHICS
HISTORICAL
WAR

Literary Original
This monumental chronicle is the standard source of many Arthurian legends and espouses knightly chivalry. After the death of his father, King Uther, Arthur proves his right of succession by removing a sword imbedded in a rock. The Lady of the Lake later presented him with Excalibur, his famous sword and symbol of power. King Arthur and his round table of one hundred knights protected and enlarged his realm. On his deathbed, Arthur ordered that Excalibur be thrown back into the lake, where it was caught by a hand and disappeared into the depths.

Film Version
This is a Hollywood costume spectacular filmed mainly in England and Ireland. The scenery is admirable, but repeated departures from the original text produce a string of insufficiently related incidents.

Full Film Title
KON-TIKI

Release Date
1951

Production Studio
RKO RADIO PICTURES

Country of Origin
USA

Running Time (Minutes)
72

Literary Original and Date of Production
KON-TIKE EXPEDITION, THE (trans. F.H. Lyon) 1950

Author and Biographical Dates
Thor Heyerdahl 1914-

Codings of 16 mm Distribution Agencies
BUD   KPF   WCF

Recommended Viewing
Recommended Reading
16 mm Film, B & W

SUMMARIES

THEME INDICATORS
ADVENTURE
MARINE
DOCUMENTARY
CULTURAL
ECOLOGY

Literary Original
An ethnologist, Thor Heyerdahl believed that Polynesia may have been colonized by raft-sailing peoples from Peru. To support his theory, he attempted the Pacific crossing himself. This is a documentary of the trials and triumphs of that sea voyage.

Film Version: **Highly recommended**
Narrated by Thor Heyerdahl, this unique film records the routine and unexpected occurrences of a true-life sea adventure.

Full Film Title
LADY AND THE TRAMP, THE

Release Date
1955

Production Studio
DISNEY

Country of Origin
USA

Running Time (Minutes)
75

Director
Erdman Penner

Principal Performers
Hamilton Luske, Clyde Geronimi, Wilfred Jackson.

Literary Original and Date of Production
LADY AND THE TRAMP, THE   1953

Author and Biographical Dates
Ward Greene   1892-1956

Recommended Viewing

35 mm Film, Color

SUMMARIES

THEME INDICATORS
ANIMATION
ROMANCE
ECOLOGY

Literary Original
Lady, a female spaniel, finds true love and domestic bliss with Tramp, a feisty but irresistible mongrel from the wrong side of the tracks. They prevail against such hazards as evil-minded cats, dog-catchers, and unsympathetic humans.

Film Version: **Recommended**
The simple and well-written original narrative takes on new life and sharper definition in animation film form, retaining all the charm and appeal of its animal characters, who display qualities that would be admirable in their human counterparts.

Full Film Title
LASSIE COME HOME

Release Date
1943

Production Studio
Metro-Goldwyn-Mayer

Country of Origin
USA

Running Time (Minutes)
88

Producer
Samuel Marx

Director
Fred M. Wilcox

Principal Performers
Roddie McDowall, Elizabeth Taylor, Donald Crisp, Edmund Gwenn, Dame May Whittie, Elsa Lanchester, J. Patrick O'Malley, Ben Webster.

Literary Original and Date of Production
Lassie Come Home

Author and Biographical Dates
Eric Knight   1897-1943

Codings of 16 mm Distribution Agencies
FNC

Recommended Viewing

16 mm Film, Color

SUMMARIES

THEME INDICATORS
Adventure
Drama
Children
Cultural
Ecology
Family

Literary Original
A Yorkshire boy owns a prize collie named Lassie. Submitting to economic pressures, the family sells her to a wealthy man who takes her hundreds of miles away to Scotland. Remaining loyal to the boy in England, Lassie escapes from the kennels in Scotland. She endures incredible hardships and returns to her first home.

Film Version: **Recommended**
This film prompted a long series of sequels and imitations but remains the unchallenged best example of the genre. Warmhearted, sentimental, and traditional in its values, it represents an effective visualization of the original story.

Full Film Title
LAST DAYS OF POMPEII, THE

Release Date
1935

Production Studio
RKO Radio

Country of Origin
USA

Running Time (Minutes)
101

Producer
Merian C. Cooper

Director
Ernest B. Schoedsack

Principal Performers
Preston Foster, Basil Rathbone, Alan Hale, Dorothy Cooper.

Literary Original and Date of Production
Last Days of Pompeii, The 1834

Author and Biographical Dates
Sir Edward Bulwer-Lytton 1803-1873

Codings of 16 mm Distribution Agencies
FCE FNC

Recommended Viewing

16 mm Film, B & W

SUMMARIES

THEME INDICATORS
- **Adventure**
- **Drama**
- **Cultural**
- **Ecology**
- **Historical**

Literary Original
A mild earthquake shakes Pompeii on the day Nydia, a blind girl, secretly falls in love with Glaucus, who intends to marry Ione. A day later, the unconcerned citizenry cheer at the deaths of gladiators in the arena. Darkening the sky, the fatal eruption begins. Nydia is accustomed to darkness and leads Glaucus and Ione to the safety of a ship on which the three escape. Heartbroken, Nydia casts herself into the sea.

Film Version: **Recommended**
The Victorian stiffness of the original has not been entirely eliminated from this filmed adaptation, and the acting and production styles now appear rather dated, but the final sequences still convey the feel of the melodramatic literary source material.

Full Film Title
LAST OF THE MOHICANS

Release Date
1936

Production Studio	Country of Origin	Running Time (Minutes)
UNITED ARTISTS	USA	91

Producer
Edward Small

Director
George B. Seitz

Principal Performers
Randolph Scott, Binnie Barnes, Bruce Cabot, Henry Wilcoxon, Heather Angel, Hugh Buckler.

Literary Original and Date of Production
LAST OF THE MOHICANS, THE   1826

Author and Biographical Dates
James Fenimore Cooper   1789-1851

Codings of 16 mm Distribution Agencies	Recommended Viewing
ALB BUD FCE KPF ROA	Recommended Reading
SEL TWY WCF WEL WIL	16 mm Film, B & W

SUMMARIES

Literary Original

In northern New York during the French and Indian Wars of the 1750s, the woodsman Natty Bumppo, known as Hawkeye, agrees to guide Alice and Cora Munro to their British Commander father at Fort William Henry. Though aided by Mohegan friends Chingachgook and his son Uncas, the girls are captured by Magua, a warring Huron, beginning a series of attacks, captures, and rescues. Cora and Uncas die, while the others return to the safety of English territories. Hawkeye and Chingachgook return to the forest.

THEME INDICATORS
ADVENTURE
MILITARY
DRAMA
ROMANCE
CULTURAL
ECOLOGY
ETHICS
FAMILY
HISTORICAL
RACIAL
WAR

Film Version
Rewritten as an action adventure in imitation of the western genre, this version maintains the story outline of the original classic but pays little respect to its historical detail.

Full Film Title
LAST OF THE REDMEN

Release Date
1949

Production Studio
COLUMBIA

Country of Origin
USA

Running Time (Minutes)
77

Producer
Sam Katzman

Director
George Sherman

Principal Performers
Jon Hall, Michael O'Shea, Evelyn Ankers, Julie Bishop, Buster Crabbe.

Literary Original and Date of Production
LAST OF THE MOHICANS, THE   1820

Author and Biographical Dates
James Fenimore Cooper   1789-1851

Recommended Reading
35 mm Film, Color

SUMMARIES

Literary Original

In northern New York during the French and Indian Wars of the 1750s, the woodsman Natty Bumppo, known as Hawkeye, agrees to guide Alice and Cora Munro to their British Commander father at Fort William Henry. Though aided by Mohegan friends Chingachgook and his son Uncas, the girls are captured by Magua, a warring Huron, beginning a series of attacks, captures, and rescues. Cora and Uncas die, while the others return to the safety of English territories. Hawkeye and Chingachgook return to the forest.

THEME INDICATORS
- ADVENTURE
- MILITARY
- DRAMA
- ROMANCE
- CULTURAL
- ECOLOGY
- ETHICS
- FAMILY
- HISTORICAL
- RACIAL
- WAR

Film Version

The Cooper original has been altered considerably to provide the basis for another colonialist-Indian conflict film.

Full Film Title
LEGEND OF LOBO, THE

Release Date
1962

Production Studio
DISNEY

Country of Origin
USA

Running Time (Minutes)
67

Producer
James Algar/Jack Couffer

Director
James Algar

Literary Original and Date of Production
WILD ANIMALS I HAVE KNOWN   1899   (reissued 1959)

Author and Biographical Dates
Ernest Thompson Seton   1860-1946

Codings of 16 mm Distribution Agencies

| AIM | BUC | CCC | COU | CWF | DIS | FNC |
| FPC | MAC | MOD | NEW | ROA | SWA | TFC | TWY |

Recommended Viewing

16 mm Film, Color

SUMMARIES

Literary Original
In New Mexico, the leader of a pack of grey wolves defies his animal and human enemies with diabolic cunning. After losing his mate, Bianca, he is trapped by ranchers, and pines to death in captivity.

THEME INDICATORS
ADVENTURE
DRAMA
ECOLOGY

Film Version: **Recommended**
Infinite patience in open-air photography and the coverage of background detail of life in the wilderness combine to give documentary realism and vividness to the insightful original.

Full Film Title
LIGHT AT THE EDGE OF THE WORLD, THE

Release Date
1972

Production Studio
METRO-GOLDWYN-MAYER/ NATIONAL GENERAL

Country of Origin
USA

Running Time (Minutes)
121

Producer
Kirk Douglas/Ilya Salkind

Director
Kevin Billington

Principal Performers
Kirk Douglas, Yul Brynner, Samantha Eggar, Fernando Rey, Jean-Claude Drouot, Renato Salvatori.

Literary Original and Date of Production
LIGHTHOUSE AT THE END OF THE WORLD, THE (trans. Cranstoun Metcalfe) **1924**

Author and Biographical Dates
Jules Verne   1828-1905

Codings of 16 mm Distribution Agencies
SWA

Recommended Viewing
Recommended Reading
16 mm Film, Color

SUMMARIES

THEME INDICATORS
ADVENTURE
CRIME
MARINE
DRAMA
ECOLOGY
HISTORICAL

Literary Original
The project of building a beacon for shipping on dangerous and isolated Cape Horn is put into effect in the late nineteenth century. Single-handedly, the keeper has to beat off attacks by pirates intent on misusing the lighthouse to lure vessels to their doom and plunder the wrecks.

Film Version
This ponderous, disaster-prone adaptation aims at sensationalism and fails to evoke the intrigue of the Verne novel.

Full Film Title
LIGHT IN THE FOREST, THE

Release Date
1958

Production Studio
DISNEY

Country of Origin
USA

Running Time (Minutes)
93

Producer
Walt Disney

Director
Herschel Daugherty

Principal Performers
James MacArthur, Carol Lynley, Fess Parker, Wendell Corey, Joanne Dru, Jessica Tandy, Joseph Calleia, John McIntire.

Literary Original and Date of Production
LIGHT IN THE FOREST, THE   1953

Author and Biographical Dates
Conrad Richter   1890-1968

Codings of 16 mm Distribution Agencies
**AIM   BUC   CCC   COU   CWF   DIS   FNC   FPC
MAC   MOD   NAT   NEW   ROA   SWA   TFC   TWY**

Recommended Viewing
Recommended Reading
16 mm Film, Color

SUMMARIES

THEME INDICATORS
**ADVENTURE
MILITARY
DRAMA
CHILDREN
CULTURAL
ECOLOGY
ETHICS
FAMILY
HISTORICAL
RACIAL
WAR**

Literary Original
Four-year-old Johnny Butler is captured by Delaware Indians in the mid-1700s. For the next eleven yeas, he matures as part of the tribe. During the Indian Wars of the 1760s, he is rescued by white men and has difficulty adjusting. Finally, he attempts to rejoin his Indian family.

Film Version: **Recommended**
The message of the original is well-captured and preserved in this simple screen adaptation, which follows the story line faithfully and carefully in an effective comment on the clash of cultural values.

Full Film Title
LITTLE LORD FAUNTLEROY

Release Date
1936

Production Studio
UNITED ARTISTS

Country of Origin
USA

Running Time (Minutes)
102

Producer
David O. Selznick

Director
John Cromwell

Principal Performers
Freddie Bartholomew, Dolores Costello.

Literary Original and Date of Production
LITTLE LORD FAUNTLEROY   1886

Author and Biographical Dates
Frances Hodgson Burnett   1849-1924

Codings of 16 mm Distribution Agencies
**AIM   ALB   BUD   CFM   FCE   MAC
MOG   ROA   VCI   WEL   WHO**

Recommended Viewing

16 mm Film, B & W

SUMMARIES

THEME INDICATORS
**DRAMA
CHILDREN
CULTURAL
ETHICS
FAMILY
HISTORY**

Literary Original
Seven-year-old Cedric Errol lives in New York with his mother and English father, who was disinherited for his marriage to an American. On his father's death, the boy is summoned to England, where he wins the hearts of his father's family. Little Lord Fauntleroy is asked to extend a warm invitation to his mother from his British relatives, and the misunderstandings of the past are reconciled.

Film Version: **Recommended**
The period drama is well presented with a respectful, understanding, and humorous preservation of the original story and sound characterization of all the key characters. In the translation, some of the Victorian excesses of the novel have happily been toned down or eliminated.

Full Film Title
LITTLE MEN

Release Date
1940

Production Studio
RKO RADIO PICTURES

Country of Origin
USA

Running Time (Minutes)
84

Producer
Gene Towne

Director
Norman Z. McLeod

Principal Performers
Kay Francis, Jack Oakie.

Literary Original and Date of Production
LITTLE MEN: LIFE AT PLUMFIELD WITH JO'S BOYS   1871

Author and Biographical Dates
Louisa May Alcott   1832-1888

Codings of 16 mm Distribution Agencies
ALB   BUD   IVY   MOG
ROA   TMC   VCI   WHO

Recommended Viewing
Recommended Reading
16 mm Film, B & W

SUMMARIES

THEME INDICATORS
DRAMA
CHILDREN
FAMILY
FEMINISM
HISTORICAL
WAR

Literary Original
In a sequel to *Little Women*, Jo March settles down to married life in New England. She successfully establishes and manages a school for boys and rears her own family.

Film Version
The sentimental, simple story has been revamped considerably to produce a tale of illegal chicanery, which provides entertainment for young audiences.

Full Film Title
LITTLE PRINCE, THE

Release Date
1974

Production Studio
PARAMOUNT

Country of Origin
USA

Running Time (Minutes)
88

Producer
Stanley Donen

Director
Stanley Donen

Principal Performers
Richard Kiley, Bob Fosse, Steven Warner, Gene Wilder, Donna McKechnie, Joss Ackland, Clive Revill, Victor Spinetti, Graham Crowden.

Literary Original and Date of Production
LITTLE PRINCE, THE   1943   (trans. Katherine Woods)

Author and Biographical Dates
Antoine De Saint-Exupéry   1900-1944

Codings of 16 mm Distribution Agencies
PAR

Recommended Viewing
Recommended Reading
16 mm Film, Color

SUMMARIES

THEME INDICATORS
ADVENTURE
FANTASY
COMEDY
DRAMA
CHILDREN
CULTURAL
ECOLOGY
ETHICS

Literary Original
A little prince from asteroid B-612 appears in an African desert where a pilot has made an unscheduled landing. With his astonished earthly audience, the prince discusses conditions and events on other planets and the secret of what is really important in life. After several days, he disappears.

Film Version
The fantasy and imaginative invention of the well-known original have lessened considerably in their effects by the adaptation of the story into musical comedy terms, although certain sequences do recapture something of the whimsical spirit of the original.

= Full Film Title
LITTLE PRINCESS, THE

Release Date
1939

Production Studio
TWENTIETH CENTURY FOX

Country of Origin
USA

Running Time (Minutes)
93

Producer
Gene Markey

Director
Walter Long

Principal Performers
Shirley Temple, Richard Greene, Anita Louise, Ian Hunter, Miles Mander, Cesar Romero, Arthur Treacher.

Literary Original and Date of Production
LITTLE PRINCESS, A   1905

Author and Biographical Dates
Frances Hodgson Burnett   1849-1924

Codings of 16 mm Distribution Agencies
BUD   CFM   EMG   IMA   NEW   ROA   VCI   WEL

Recommended Viewing
Recommended Reading
16 mm Film, Color

SUMMARIES

THEME INDICATORS
COMEDY
DRAMA
CHILDREN
CULTURAL
ETHICS
FAMILY
HISTORICAL

Literary Original
In Victorian London a little rich girl has to adjust to hard living when her father leaves her in a school before going overseas.

Film Version: **Recommended**
The popular original novel has been recast to provide a film script suitable for the talents of the featured child star, but the charm and innocent humor are well conveyed, and the film remains viewable by young audiences.

Full Film Title
LITTLE WOMEN

Release Date
1933

Production Studio
RKO RADIO PICTURES

Country of Origin
USA

Running Time (Minutes)
115

Producer
Kenneth MacGowan

Director
George Cukor

Principal Performers
Katharine Hepburn, Joan Bennett, Paul Lukas, Frances Dee, Jean Parker, Edna May Oliver, Douglas Montgomery, Spring Byington.

Literary Original and Date of Production
LITTLE WOMEN: OR MEG, JO, BETH, AND AMY   1871

Author and Biographical Dates
Louisa May Alcott   1832-1888

Codings of 16 mm Distribution Agencies
FNC

Recommended Viewing
Recommended Reading
16 mm Film, B & W

SUMMARIES

THEME INDICATORS
DRAMA
ROMANCE
CHILDREN
ETHICS
FAMILY
FEMINISM
WAR

Literary Original
In a New England town, Mrs. March and her four daughters face life and love while Mr. March is serving in the Civil War. Meg marries a young tutor. Gentle, frail Beth dies young. Amy is wedded to the high-spirited family friend, Laurie. And Jo, the tomboyish literary member of the family, eventually marries a German professor and starts a school for boys. Structurally, the story follows John Bunyan's *Pilgrim's Progress*.

Film Version: **Very highly recommended**
A screen classic, which also represents a faithful re-creation of the literary work in a splendid visual version.

Full Film Title
LITTLE WOMEN

Release Date
1948

Production Studio
METRO-GOLDWYN-MAYER

Country of Origin
USA

Running Time (Minutes)
121

Producer
Mervyn Leroy

Director
Mervyn Leroy

Principal Performers
June Allyson, Peter Lawford, Margaret O'Brien, Elizabeth Taylor, Janet Leigh, Rossano Brazzi, Mary Astor.

Literary Original and Date of Production
LITTLE WOMEN 1871

Author and Biographical Dates
Louisa May Alcott 1832-1888

Codings of 16 mm Distribution Agencies
FNC

Recommended Viewing
Recommended Reading
16 mm Film, Color

SUMMARIES

THEME INDICATORS
DRAMA
ROMANCE
CHILDREN
ETHICS
FAMILY
FEMINISM
HISTORICAL
WAR

Literary Original
In a New England town, Mrs. March and her four daughters face life and love while Mr. March is serving in the Civil War. Meg marries a young tutor. Gentle, frail Beth dies young. Amy is wedded to the high-spirited family friend Laurie. And Jo, the tomboyish literary member of the family, eventually marries a German professor and starts a school for boys. Structurally, the story follows John Bunyan's *Pilgrim's Progress*.

Film Version: **Recommended**
An acceptable, if oversentimental color remake, without the distinction of the RKO 1933 version.

Full Film Title
LIVING FREE

Release Date
1971

Production Studio
COLUMBIA

Country of Origin
USA

Running Time (Minutes)
92

Director
Jack Couffer

Principal Performers
Susan Hampshire, Nigel Davenport, Geoffrey Keen.

Literary Original and Date of Production
LIVING FREE   1961

Author and Biographical Dates
Joy Adamson   1910-

Codings of 16 mm Distribution Agencies
**BUC   BUD   CCC   CWF   ICS   MOD
ROA   SWA   TWY   WCF   WEL**

Recommended Viewing
Recommended Reading
16 mm Film, Color

SUMMARIES

THEME INDICATORS
**ADVENTURE
DOCUMENTARY
ECOLOGY
FAMILY
RACIAL**

Literary Original
In a continuation of the wildlife story of *Born Free,* **the cubs of Elsa the lioness grow up with their human friends and have to face a return to their way of life in the wild.**

Film Version
A sequel to *Born Free,* **with different performers, lacking the impact of the earlier production but still containing interesting wildlife sequences.**

Full Film Title
LORNA DOONE

Release Date
1934

Production Studio
ATP/ABFD

Country of Origin
Great Britain

Running Time (Minutes)
90

Producer
Basil Dean

Director
Basil Dean

Principal Performers
Margaret Lockwood, John Loder, Victoria Hopper, Roy Emerton, Mary Clare, Edward Rigby, Roger Livesey.

Literary Original and Date of Production
LORNA DOONE 1869

Author and Biographical Dates
Richard Dodridge Blackmore 1825-1900

Codings of 16 mm Distribution Agencies
JAN

Recommended Viewing
Recommended Reading
16 mm Film, B & W

SUMMARIES

THEME INDICATORS
ADVENTURE
DRAMA
ROMANCE
CULTURAL
ETHICS
FEMINISM
HISTORICAL

Literary Original
In seventeenth-century England, the father of schoolboy John Ridd is murdered by the ruthless Doone clan. John, though bent on revenge, falls in love with Lorna, the ward of his father's killer. Their affection withstands years of turmoil, and on their wedding day, Lorna is shot by Carver Doone. In a fierce battle, John kills Carver and hastens to the side of Lorna, who survives her wound.

Film Version: **Recommended**
A straightforward presentation of the story, well photographed and with good acting interpretations in a successful recapturing of a period romance.

Full Film Title
LORNA DOONE

Release Date
1951

Production Studio
COLUMBIA

Country of Origin
USA

Running Time (Minutes)
84

Producer
Edward Small

Director
Phil Karlson

Principal Performers
Barbara Hale, Richard Greene, Anne Howard, William Bishop, Carl Benton Reid, Ron Randell, Sean McClory.

Literary Original and Date of Production
LORNA DOONE   1869

Author and Biographical Dates
Richard Dodridge Blackmore   1825-1900

Codings of 16 mm Distribution Agencies
ICS

Recommended Reading
16 mm Film, Color

SUMMARIES

THEME INDICATORS
ADVENTURE
DRAMA
ROMANCE
CULTURAL
ETHICS
FEMINISM
HISTORICAL

Literary Original
In seventeenth-century England, the father of schoolboy John Ridd is murdered by the ruthless Doone clan. John, though bent on revenge, falls in love with Lorna, the ward of his father's killer. Their affection withstands years of turmoil, and on their wedding day, Lorna is shot by Carver Doone. In a fierce battle, John kills Carver and hastens to the side of Lorna, who survives her wound.

Film Version
An undistinguished color remake, which loses much of the romantic spirit of the original, in an attempt to update the approach and add to the action.

Full Film Title
LOST HORIZON

Release Date
1937

Production Studio
COLUMBIA

Country of Origin
USA

Running Time (Minutes)
118

Producer
Frank Capra

Director
Frank Capra

Principal Performers
Ronald Colman, Jane Wyatt, Edward Everett Horton, John Howard, Thomas Mitchell, Margo, Isabel Jewell, H. B. Warner, Sam Jaffe.

Literary Original and Date of Production
LOST HORIZON   1933

Author and Biographical Dates
James Hilton   1900-1954

Codings of 16 mm Distribution Agencies
ARG   CON   CWF   ICS   KPF   MAC   MOD
NEW   SWA   TWY   WCF   WEL   WHO

Recommended Viewing
Recommended Reading
16 mm Film, B & W

SUMMARIES

THEME INDICATORS
ADVENTURE
FANTASY
DRAMA
ROMANCE
CULTURAL
ECOLOGY
ETHICS
RACIAL
RELIGIOUS

Literary Original
Hugh Conway, hospitalized with amnesia and fatigue, relates a strange story to his friend Rutherford. Kidnapped aboard an airplane, Conway and three companions landed unexpectedly on a Tibetan plateau. Rescuers led them to the lamasery of Shangri-La, a land of serenity and long life. Though he wished to remain, Conway left the valley when his companions begged his assistance. At this point, Conway broke off the narrative, slipped away, and disappeared, possibly in search of Shangri-La.

Film Version: **Very highly recommended**
The utopian and allegorical aspects of the original novel have been rearranged with a new emphasis to blend elements of fantasy and science fiction in a lavish presentation with qualities of acting, special effects, and general production excellence that have given this film classic status.

Full Film Title
LOST WORLD, THE

Release Date
1960

Production Studio
TWENTIETH CENTURY FOX

Country of Origin
USA

Running Time (Minutes)
98

Producer
Irwin Allen

Director
Irwin Allen

Principal Performers
Michael Rennie, Jill St. John, Claude Rains, David Hedison, Fernando Lamas, Richard Haydn, Ray Stricklyn.

Literary Original and Date of Production
LOST WORLD, THE 1912

Author and Biographical Dates
Sir Arthur Conan Doyle   1859-1930

Codings of 16 mm Distribution Agencies
CWF   FNC

Recommended Viewing
Recommended Reading
16 mm Film, Color

SUMMARIES

THEME INDICATORS
- **ADVENTURE**
- **FANTASY**
- **MONSTER**
- **DRAMA**
- **ROMANCE**
- **CULTURAL**
- **ECOLOGY**
- **RACIAL**

Literary Original
An expedition of English scientists and adventurers travels to South America. On a high plateau undisturbed for eons, they discover a world comprised of prehistoric life forms. Among them is a tribe of man-apes, representing the missing links in man's development. Returning to London, the adventurers confront an incredulous audience with irrefutable proof, a young pterodactyl.

Film Version
This film attempt to modernize and sensationalize Sir Arthur Conan Doyle's material does not succeed, and the result is lame and unconvincing.

Full Film Title
MACBETH

Release Date
1948

Production Studio
REPUBLIC

Country of Origin
USA

Running Time (Minutes)
89

Producer
Orson Welles

Director
Orson Welles

Principal Performers
Orson Welles, Jeanette Nolan, Dan O'Herlihy, Roddy McDowall, Edgar Barrier, Robert Coote.

Literary Original and Date of Production
MACBETH (Play)   1623

Author and Biographical Dates
William Shakespeare   1564-1616

Codings of 16 mm Distribution Agencies
BUD   CHA   FCE   IMA   IVY   KPF   MAC   MOD
ROA   SEL   TFC   TWY   WCF   WEL   WHO

Recommended Viewing
Recommended Reading
16 mm Film, B & W

SUMMARIES

Literary Original

Macbeth, Thane of Cawdor, is told by three witches after a victory in battle that he will be king of Scotland and becomes obsessed by the prophecy. Encouraged by his wife in his ambitions, he plots with her to murder the reigning king while he is their guest and continues with a chain of cruel killings. Lady Macbeth goes mad and kills herself, and Macbeth is slain when his enemies besiege him alone in his castle of Dunsinane.

THEME INDICATORS
ADVENTURE
CRIME
MILITARY
DRAMA
TRAGEDY
BIOGRAPHICAL
CULTURAL
ETHICS
FEMINISM
HISTORICAL
WAR

Film Version

This version by Orson Welles condenses the action in a series of dark and claustrophobic settings, to give a very controversial interpretation, debatable in quality and uneven in execution.

Full Film Title
MACBETH

Release Date
1972

Production Studio
COLUMBIA

Country of Origin
Great Britain

Running Time (Minutes)
120

Producer
Andrew Braunsberg

Director
Roman Polanski

Principal Performers
Jon Finch, Francesca Annis, Martin Shaw, Nicholas Selby, John Stride.

Literary Original and Date of Production
MACBETH (Play)   1623

Author and Biographical Dates
William Shakespeare   1564-1616

Codings of 16 mm Distribution Agencies
SWA

Recommended Viewing
Recommended Reading
16 mm Film, Color

SUMMARIES

Literary Original

Macbeth, Thane of Cawdor, is told by three witches after a victory in battle that he will be king of Scotland and becomes obsessed by the prophecy. Encouraged by his wife in his ambitions, he plots with her to murder the reigning king while he is their guest and continues with a chain of cruel killings. Lady Macbeth goes mad and kills herself, and Macbeth is slain when his enemies besiege him alone in his castle of Dunsinane.

THEME INDICATORS
ADVENTURE
CRIME
MILITARY
DRAMA
TRAGEDY
BIOGRAPHICAL
CULTURAL
ETHICS
FEMINISM
HISTORICAL
WAR

Film Version
This version by Roman Polanski selects for emphasis the violence and bloodshed of the play to present an interpretation in which sensationalism is preferred to dramatic insight or the poetry of high tragedy.

Full Film Title
MADAME CURIE

Release Date
1943

Production Studio
METRO-GOLDWYN-MAYER

Country of Origin
USA

Running Time (Minutes)
124

Producer
Sidney Franklin

Director
Mervyn Leroy

Principal Performers
Greer Garson, Walter Pidgeon, Henry Travers, Albert Basserman, Robert Walker, C. Aubrey Smith, Dame May Whitty, Victor Francen.

Literary Original and Date of Production
MADAME CURIE 1938

Author and Biographical Dates
Eve Curie 1904-

Codings of 16 mm Distribution Agencies
FNC

Recommended Viewing
Recommended Reading
16 mm Film, B & W

SUMMARIES

Literary Original
This is the biography of Madame Curie as written by her daughter, Eve Curie. It details her early life, marriage, and scientific endeavors in Paris in the early 1900s. The events surrounding Curie's work as codiscoverer of radium are made clear for the nontechnical reader.

THEME INDICATORS
DOCUMENTARY
ROMANCE
BIOGRAPHICAL
ECOLOGY
FAMILY
FEMINISM
HISTORICAL

Film Version: **Recommended**
The filmed biography tends to glamorize and overdramatize both characters and incidents, but the story recaptures and communicates the courage, persistence, and dedication that remain the central themes in the life of a pioneer researcher.

Full Film Title
MAN FOR ALL SEASONS, A

Release Date
1966

Production Studio	Country of Origin	Running Time (Minutes)
COLUMBIA/HIGHROAD	**USA**	**120**

Producer
Fred Zinnemann

Director
Fred Zinnemann

Principal Performers
Paul Schofield, Wendy Hiller, Leo McKern, Robert Shaw, Orson Welles, Susannah York, Nigel Davenport, John Hurt, Corin Redgrave, Colin Blakely.

Literary Original and Date of Production
MAN FOR ALL SEASONS (Play) 1960

Author and Biographical Dates
Robert Bolt 1924-

Codings of 16 mm Distribution Agencies	Recommended Viewing
SWA	Recommended Reading
	16 mm Film, Color

SUMMARIES | THEME INDICATORS

Literary Original
As chancellor of England, Sir Thomas More cannot in good conscience approve King Henry VIII's actions in divorcing Queen Catherine to marry Anne Boleyn. He goes to the executioner's block for his principles in 1535, sacrificing life, family, fortune, and power.

THEME INDICATORS:
ADVENTURE
DRAMA
TRAGEDY
BIOGRAPHICAL
CULTURAL
ETHICS
FAMILY
FEMINISM
HISTORICAL
RELIGIOUS

Film Version: **Very highly recommended**
The author of the original stage play rewrote the material for the screen, and the production represents an impeccable version of the historic story, with obvious excellence in every aspect of the preparation.

Full Film Title
MAN IN THE IRON MASK, THE

Release Date
1939

Production Studio
United Artists

Country of Origin
USA

Running Time (Minutes)
119

Producer
Edward Small

Director
James Whale

Principal Performers
Louis Hayward, Joan Bennett, Warren William, Alan Hale, Bert Roach, Miles Mander, Joseph Schildkraut, Montagu Love.

Literary Original and Date of Production
Man in the Iron Mask, The   1847

Author and Biographical Dates
Alexandre Dumas   1802-1870

Codings of 16 mm Distribution Agencies
ALB   BUD   KPF   MOG   NAT   NEW   VCI   WRS

Recommended Viewing
Recommended Reading
16 mm Film, B & W

SUMMARIES

THEME INDICATORS
Adventure
Military
Drama
Cultural
Historical

Literary Original
King Louis XIV of France has a mysterious prisoner condemned to perpetual isolation and anonymity in an iron mask. His intrigues are foiled by the courage and dash of the Three Musketeers.

Film Version: **Recommended**
The classic original story has become even more complicated in this screen adaptation, but the pace of the action and the quality of the performances make the film an adequate re-creation of the feel and spirit of Alexandre Dumas's roistering period adventure.

Full Film Title
MARK OF ZORRO, THE

Release Date
1940

Production Studio
TWENTIETH CENTURY FOX

Country of Origin
USA

Running Time (Minutes)
92

Director
Rouben Mamoulian

Principal Performers
Tyrone Power, Linda Darnell, Basil Rathbone, Gale Sondergaard, Eugene Pallette, J. Edward Bromberg, Montagu Love, Janet Beecher.

Literary Original and Date of Production
MARK OF ZORRO, THE (The Curse of Capistrano)   1924

Author and Biographical Dates
Johnston McCulley   1883-1958

Codings of 16 mm Distribution Agencies
FNC

Recommended Viewing
Recommended Reading
16 mm Film, B & W

SUMMARIES

THEME INDICATORS
ADVENTURE
DRAMA
CULTURAL
ETHICS
HISTORICAL

Literary Original
A young Spanish aristocrat masquerades as an idle and worthless fop to conceal his true identity as Zorro, the masked outlaw. As a dashing swordsman and horseman, he champions the cause of commoners against a tyrannical governor.

Film Version: **Highly recommended**
The film script writers have embroidered the already exciting and colorful original with a series of action sequences and dramatic developments that make this production a gripping and thrilling adventure piece certain to succeed with boys of all ages.

Full Film Title
MARY POPPINS

Release Date
1964

Production Studio
DISNEY

Country of Origin
USA

Running Time (Minutes)
140

Producer
Walt Disney/Bill Walsh

Director
Robert Stevenson

Principal Performers
Julie Andrews, Dick Van Dyke, David Tomlinson, Glynis Johns, Ed Wynn, Hermione Baddeley, Karen Dotrice, Matthew Garber, Elsa Lanchester.

Literary Original and Date of Production
MARY POPPINS (and series)   1934-1963

Author and Biographical Dates
Pamela Lyndon Travers   1906-

Recommended Viewing
Recommended Reading
35 mm Film, Color

SUMMARIES

Literary Original
Drifting down into the London of 1910, a "practically perfect" nanny takes the two Banks children into her charge and tidies up their family life in a series of unusual adventures. With a change of the wind, she sails away on her parasol as placidly as she had arrived.

THEME INDICATORS
FANTASY
MUSICAL
COMEDY
ROMANCE
CHILDREN
CULTURAL
FAMILY
FEMINISM

Film Version: **Very highly recommended**
The studio resources of special effects, the addition of a musical score, and the contributions of a highly talented cast of players combine splendidly to bring the fantasy and invention of the original novel from the printed page to the screen. A near classic of children's films.

Full Film Title
MASTER OF BALLANTRAE, THE

Release Date
1953

Production Studio
WARNER

Country of Origin
USA

Running Time (Minutes)
88

Director
William Keighley

Principal Performers
Errol Flynn, Beatrice Campbell, Roger Livesey, Anthony Steel, Yvonne Furneaux, Felix Aylmer, Mervyn Johns.

Literary Original and Date of Production
MASTER OF BALLANTRAE, THE 1889

Author and Biographical Dates
Robert Louis Stevenson 1850-1894

Codings of 16 mm Distribution Agencies
SWA

Recommended Viewing
Recommended Reading
16 mm Film, Color

SUMMARIES

THEME INDICATORS
- **ADVENTURE**
- **MARINE**
- **DRAMA**
- **ETHICS**
- **FAMILY**
- **HISTORICAL**
- **WAR**

Literary Original
In the mid-1700s, two brothers join opposing warring factions to insure the safety of the family estate, regardless of the outcome. In the victorious camp, Henry marries the sweetheart of the absent James. Upon his return, James goads Henry into a duel after which they again part. Henry and his family flee to New York, and James follows. In a tangle of trickery and tragedy, they die together in the American wilderness.

Film Version
This film version repeats the story line of the original novel, but somehow fails to stimulate interest or convey any feeling for the dramatic values of Stevenson's classic.

Full Film Title
MEET ME IN ST. LOUIS

Release Date
1944

Production Studio
METRO-GOLDWYN-MAYER

Country of Origin
USA

Running Time (Minutes)
113

Producer
Arthur Freed

Director
Vincente Minnelli

Principal Performers
Judy Garland, Margaret O'Brien, Lucille Bremer, Joan Carroll, Mary Astor, Tom Drake, Harry Davenport, Marjorie Main, Hugh Marlowe, Chil Wills.

Literary Original and Date of Production
MEET ME IN ST. LOUIS 1942

Author and Biographical Dates
Sally Benson 1900-1972

Codings of 16 mm Distribution Agencies
FNC

Recommended Viewing

16 mm Film, Color

SUMMARIES

Literary Original
These chapters in the lives of the Smith family contain humor and heartache. Occurring in St. Louis in 1903 and 1904, they center around the escapades of Tootie who, at six years of age, is the youngest Smith daughter.

THEME INDICATORS
MUSICAL
COMEDY
ROMANCE
CHILDREN
FAMILY
FEMINISM
HISTORICAL

Film Version: **Highly recommended**
The warmth, atmosphere, and period quality of the original novel have been retained, and the narrative sequence respected in an adaptation that agreeably combines appealing acting performances and a series of well-mounted musical numbers.

Full Film Title
MIDSUMMER NIGHT'S DREAM, A

Release Date
1935

Production Studio
WARNER

Country of Origin
USA

Running Time (Minutes)
117

Producer
Max Reinhardt

Director
Max Reinhardt

Principal Performers
James Cagney, Dick Powell, Jean Muir, Ross Alexander, Olivia de Havilland, Joe E. Brown, Hugh Herbert, Arthur Treacher, Frank McHugh, Mickey Rooney.

Literary Original and Date of Production
MIDSUMMER NIGHT'S DREAM, A   1600

Author and Biographical Dates
William Shakespeare   1564-1616

Codings of 16 mm Distribution Agencies
UAS

Recommended Viewing
Recommended Reading
16 mm Film, B & W

SUMMARIES

THEME INDICATORS
FANTASY
COMEDY
ROMANCE

Literary Original
A complex plot interweaves the stories of pairs of lovers of Athenian nobles and commoners, a quarrel between the king and queen of the fairies, and the attempts of a group of workmen to stage a classical play. When the humans enter an enchanted forest, the fairies bring about happy endings to their problems in a series of mischievous pranks and magic-working spells.

Film Version: **Recommended**
Derived from a successful stage presentation on Broadway, this film version carries the central dramatic action of the original comedy in a typically Hollywood treatment for its period, with lavish sets, decors, costume, and makeup. Unique as a screen version, it is surprisingly effective as support material in making visual many aspects of the play that may be difficult to imagine from a straightforward reading.

Full Film Title
MIRACLE OF THE WHITE STALLIONS, THE

Release Date
1962

Production Studio
DISNEY

Country of Origin
USA

Running Time (Minutes)
118

Producer
Peter V. Herald

Director
Arthur Hiller

Principal Performers
Robert Taylor, Lilli Palmer, Eddie Albert, Curt Jurgens.

Literary Original and Date of Production
WHITE STALLIONS OF VIENNA (trans. Frances Hogarth Gaute)   1963

Author and Biographical Dates
Alois Podhajsky

Codings of 16 mm Distribution Agencies

| AIM | BUC | CCC | COU | CWF | DIS | FNC | FPC |
| MAC | MOD | NAT | NEW | ROA | SWA | TFC | TWY |

Recommended Viewing

16 mm Film, Color

SUMMARIES

Literary Original
The manager of the Spanish Riding School in Vienna escapes with his famous Lippizaner horses from the Nazi occupation in World War II.

THEME INDICATORS
ADVENTURE
DRAMA
ECOLOGY
ETHICS
HISTORICAL
WAR

Film Version: **Recommended**
A straightforward recounting of the true-life original adventure story, with splendid photography of the famous horses and interesting details of their training and performance.

Full Film Title
MOBY DICK

Release Date
1954

Production Studio
WARNER BROTHERS

Country of Origin
USA

Running Time (Minutes)
115

Producer
John Huston

Director
John Huston

Principal Performers
Gregory Peck, Richard Basehart, Leo Genn, Orson Welles, James Robertson Justice, Harry Andrews, Bernard Miles, Noel Purcell, Edric Connor, Mervyn Johns.

Literary Original and Date of Production
MOBY DICK 1851

Author and Biographical Dates
Herman Melville 1819-1891

Codings of 16 mm Distribution Agencies
UAS

Recommended Viewing
Recommended Reading
16 mm Film, Color

SUMMARIES

THEME INDICATORS
ADVENTURE
MARINE
MONSTER
DRAMA
TRAGEDY
ECOLOGY
ETHICS
HISTORICAL

Literary Original
From a nineteenth-century New England whaling port, Captain Ahab drives himself and his men in his obsessional pursuit of the great white whale. Ahab, having lost a leg in a previous encounter, is dehumanized by his vengeance. He and crew are sacrificed, while only the unselfish Ishmael, the narrator, is spared.

Film Version: **Recommended**
A slow-moving recapitulation of the famous story, preserving all the essentials of the action and dénouement, without great distinction in the acting but with much authentic and interesting technical detail.

Full Film Title
MRS. WIGGS OF THE CABBAGE PATCH

Release Date
1934

Production Studio
UNIVERSAL/PARAMOUNT

Country of Origin
USA

Running Time (Minutes)
80

Producer
Douglas MacLean

Director
Norman Taurog

Principal Performers
W.C. Fields, Pauline Lord, Zasu Pitts, Evelyn Venable, Kent Taylor, Charles Middleton, Donald Meek, Edith Fellows.

Literary Original and Date of Production
MRS. WIGGS OF THE CABBAGE PATCH   1901

Author and Biographical Dates
Alice Hegan Rice   1870-1942

Codings of 16 mm Distribution Agencies
UNI

Recommended Viewing

16 mm Film, B & W

SUMMARIES

Literary Original
A widowed mother plans and sacrifices to advance her five children, despite her poverty and the difficulties of the conditions in small-town America in the 1880s.

THEME INDICATORS
**DRAMA
CHILDREN
ETHICS
FAMILY
FEMINISM
HISTORICAL**

Film Version
Made in the Depression years, the spirit of the original has been somewhat distorted in this adaptation, which now has a flat and dated quality.

Full Film Title
MRS. WIGGS OF THE CABBAGE PATCH

Release Date
1942

Production Studio
PARAMOUNT

Country of Origin
USA

Running Time (Minutes)
80

Director
Ralph Murphy

Principal Performers
Fay Bainter, Hugh Herbert, Vera Vague, Barbara Britton, Carl Switzer, Moroni Olsen, Billy Lee.

Codings of 16 mm Distribution Agencies
UNI

Recommended Viewing

16 mm Film, B & W

SUMMARIES

Literary Original
A widowed mother plans and sacrifices to advance her five children, despite her poverty and the difficulties of the conditions in small-town America in the 1880s.

THEME INDICATORS
DRAMA
CHILDREN
ETHICS
FAMILY
FEMINISM
HISTORICAL

Film Version
A remake, which follows closely the 1934 original film version but does not rise any higher than the earlier production in conveying the sympathy and humor of the source material.

Full Film Title
MUDLARK, THE

Release Date
1950

Production Studio	Country of Origin	Running Time (Minutes)
TWENTIETH CENTURY FOX	**USA**	**100**

Producer
Nunally Johnson

Director
Jean Negulesco

Principal Performers
Irene Dunne, Alec Guinness, Andrew Ray, Beatrice Campbell, Finlay Currie, Anthony Steel, Raymond Lovell, Marjorie Fielding, Constance Smith.

Literary Original and Date of Production
MUDLARK, THE   1949

Author and Biographical Dates
Theodore Bonnet   1865-1920

Codings of 16 mm Distribution Agencies
FNC

Recommended Viewing

16 mm Film, B & W

SUMMARIES

Literary Original
A youth from London's lower class desires an audience with Queen Victoria. In achieving his goal, he begins a series of events by which the queen is brought out of her retirement. Most of the life of Benjamin Disraeli is presented in the text.

THEME INDICATORS
DRAMA
BIOGRAPHICAL
CHILDREN
CULTURAL
ETHICS
FAMILY
FEMINISM
HISTORICAL

Film Version: **Recommended**
The original story line is followed with careful attention to its period setting, and any improbabilities in the fictional episodes are compensated for by the convincing realism of performance by the principal actors.

Full Film Title
MY FRIEND FLICKA

Release Date
1943

Production Studio	Country of Origin	Running Time (Minutes)
TWENTIETH CENTURY FOX	**USA**	**90**

Producer
Ralph Dietrich

Director
Harold Schuster

Principal Performers
Preston Foster, Rita Johnson, Roddy McDowall, James Bell, Jeff Corey, Diana Hale, Arthur Loft.

Literary Original and Date of Production
MY FRIEND FLICKA   1943

Author and Biographical Dates
Mary O'Hara (Mary O'Hara Alsop)   1885-

Codings of 16 mm Distribution Agencies
FNC

Recommended Viewing
Recommended Reading
16 mm Film, Color

SUMMARIES

THEME INDICATORS
DRAMA
CHILDREN
ECOLOGY
FAMILY

Literary Original
Ten-year-old Ken lives on a western ranch. His father gives a young filly to him to raise as his own. Flicka has a wild temperament and almost dies trying to escape. She is saved by the care of Ken, whose own life is threatened in the process.

Film Version: **Recommended**
The film script for this production was written by the author from her novel, and the very successful result remains a popular and appealing production suitable for family audiences.

Full Film Title
MY SIDE OF THE MOUNTAIN

Release Date
1969

Production Studio
PARAMOUNT

Country of Origin
USA

Running Time (Minutes)
100

Producer
Robert B. Radnitz

Director
James B. Clark

Principal Performers
Ted Eccles, Theodore Bikel, Tudi Wiggins, Frank Perry, Peggi Loder, Gina Dick, Karen Pearson, Danny McIlravey, Cosette Lee.

Literary Original and Date of Production
MY SIDE OF THE MOUNTAIN   1959

Author and Biographical Dates
Jean Craighead George   1919-

Codings of 16 mm Distribution Agencies
PAR

Recommended Viewing

16 mm Film, Color

SUMMARIES

THEME INDICATORS
- **ADVENTURE**
- **COMEDY**
- **DRAMA**
- **CHILDREN**
- **ECOLOGY**
- **FAMILY**

Literary Original
Thirteen-year-old Sam Gribley is inspired by his readings of Henry Thoreau to run away from home with his pet raccoon Gus, and returns to his family after a year, well-content with his experiment of fending for himself by finding food, clothing, and shelter in the wild.

Film Version: **Highly recommended**
The film is a strong and straightforward version of the story, with exceptionally fine outdoor photography shot on location in the Swiss Alps.

Full Film Title
MYSTERIOUS ISLAND, THE

Release Date
1961

Production Studio	Country of Origin	Running Time (Minutes)
COLUMBIA	**USA**	**100**

Producer
Charles H. Schneer

Director
Cy Endfield

Principal Performers
Michael Craig, Joan Greenwood, Michael Callan, Gary Merrill, Herbert Lom, Beth Logan, Percy Herbert, Dan Jackson, Nigel Green.

Literary Original and Date of Production
MYSTERIOUS ISLAND, THE   1874

Author and Biographical Dates
Jules Verne   1828-1905

Codings of 16 mm Distribution Agencies
ARG BUC CCC CHA CWF FPC KER KPF LEW
MAC MOD NAT NEW ROA SWA TFC TWY VCI
WEL WHO

Recommended Viewing
Recommended Reading
16 mm Film, Color

SUMMARIES

Literary Original
During the American Civil War, a group of northern sympathizers escapes in a balloon from internment in the South. They are blown far out over the Pacific and land on a desert island, where they survive natural dangers and attacks by pirates. The crazed genius Captain Nemo finally comes to their rescue in his submarine.

THEME INDICATORS
ADVENTURE
FANTASY
MONSTER
DRAMA
ECOLOGY
HISTORICAL
WAR

Film Version: **Recommended**
The Jules Verne original has been rewritten to provide a script giving scope for the introduction of well-handled studio re-creations of prehistoric creatures. The production values are high, the acting competent, and the general result is a good adventure film, with strong juvenile appeal.

Full Film Title
NATIONAL VELVET

Release Date
1944

Production Studio
METRO-GOLDWYN-MAYER

Country of Origin
USA

Running Time (Minutes)
123

Producer
Pandro S. Berman

Director
Clarence Brown

Principal Performers
Elizabeth Taylor, Mickey Rooney, Donald Crisp, Arthur Treacher, Anne Revere, Angela Lansbury, Juanita Quigley, Jack Jenkins, Alec Craig.

Literary Original and Date of Production
NATIONAL VELVET   1935

Author and Biographical Dates
Enid Bagnold   1889-

Codings of 16 mm Distribution Agencies
FNC

Recommended Viewing
Recommended Reading
16 mm Film, Color

SUMMARIES

THEME INDICATORS
ADVENTURE
DRAMA
CHILDREN
CULTURAL
ECOLOGY
FAMILY

Literary Original
A troublesome horse that would jump 5-foot fences rather than respond to command is raffled off. A local fourteen-year-old girl, Velvet, wins the horse and is certain of its greatness. With Velvet as jockey, the horse wins the Grand National, an English Classic race, bringing the pair world-wide recognition.

Film Version: **Recommended**
A handsomely produced visualization of the story, which originally achieved great success through the performances of the young leading actors but appears less convincing and interesting today.

Full Film Title
NICHOLAS NICKLEBY

Release Date
1953

Production Studio
EALING STUDIOS

Country of Origin
Great Britain

Running Time (Minutes)
105

Producer
John Croydon

Director
Alberto Cavalcanti

Principal Performers
Sir Cedric Hardwicke, Stanley Holloway, Alfred Drayton, Bernard Miles, Dame Sybil Thorndike.

Literary Original and Date of Production
NICHOLAS NICKLEBY   1839

Author and Biographical Dates
Charles Dickens   1812-1870

Codings of 16 mm Distribution Agencies
BUD   KPF   LCA   ROA

Recommended Viewing
Recommended Reading
16 mm Film, B & W

SUMMARIES

THEME INDICATORS
ADVENTURE
DRAMA
CHILDREN
CULTURAL
ETHICS
FAMILY
HISTORICAL

Literary Original
Nicholas Nickleby is a young Englishman who leaves in disgust after a period as usher in a brutally run boarding school, joins a troupe of actors, and finally becomes a successful merchant. His life story is complicated by the constant but unsuccessful attempts of his grasping uncle Ralph to interfere with his plans and harm his family and friends.

Film Version: **Recommended**
A trimmed-down version of the Dickens original, competently produced and performed, but with a rather lightweight final effect in its portrayal of the ups and downs in the dramatic life of the central character.

Full Film Title
NORTHWEST PASSAGE

Release Date
1940

Production Studio
METRO-GOLDWYN-MAYER

Country of Origin
USA

Running Time (Minutes)
126

Producer
Hunt Stromberg

Director
King Vidor

Principal Performers
Spencer Tracy, Robert Young, Walter Brennan, Ruth Hussey, Nat Pendleton, Louis Hector, Robert Barrat, Lumsden Hare.

Literary Original and Date of Production
NORTHWEST PASSAGE   1937

Author and Biographical Dates
Kenneth Roberts   1885-1957

Codings of 16 mm Distribution Agencies
FNC

Recommended Viewing
Recommended Reading
16 mm Film, Color

SUMMARIES

THEME INDICATORS
ADVENTURE
MILITARY
DRAMA
CULTURAL
ECOLOGY
HISTORICAL
RACIAL
WAR

Literary Original
The narrator of this historical novel is Langdon Towne from Kittery, Maine. He relates the episodes of Major Robert Rogers who led an expedition against Indians and sought an overland route to the Pacific.

Film Version: **Highly recommended**
With only a partial treatment of the original story line, the film version concentrates on the heroic endurance and boldness of the explorers embarking on their quest to provide a convincing and informative account of pioneer life.

Full Film Title
OLD YELLER

Release Date
1958

Production Studio
DISNEY

Country of Origin
USA

Running Time (Minutes)
83

Producer
Walt Disney

Director
Robert Stevenson

Principal Performers
Dorothy McGuire, Fess Parker, Tommy Kirk, Kevin Corcoran, and Spike.

Literary Original and Date of Production
OLD YELLER   1957

Author and Biographical Dates
Fred Gipson   1908-1973

Recommended Viewing

35 mm Film, Color

SUMMARIES

Literary Original
In the 1860s, Travis lives with his family in their log home in Texas. The fourteen-year-old is left in charge of the farm when his father departs on a cattle drive to distant Abilene. A stray dog, Old Yeller, wanders onto the ranch and becomes a pet, defender, and family member.

THEME INDICATORS
- ADVENTURE
- WESTERN
- DRAMA
- CHILDREN
- ECOLOGY
- FAMILY
- HISTORICAL

Film Version: **Recommended**
A standard straightforward rendering of the story, with all the excellence of technique of the Disney studios in their presentation of a simple, direct story line shot with a good feel of outdoor life.

Full Film Title
OLIVER TWIST

Release Date
1948

Production Studio
CINEGUILD INCORPORATED

Country of Origin
Great Britain

Running Time (Minutes)
116

Producer
Anthony Havelock-Allen

Director
David Lean

Principal Performers
Robert Newton, Alec Guinness, Kay Walsh, Francis L. Sullivan, John Howard Davies, Henry Stephenson, Mary Clare, Anthony Newley, Ralph Truman, Diana Dors.

Literary Original and Date of Production
OLIVER TWIST   1839

Author and Biographical Dates
Charles Dickens   1812-1870

Codings of 16 mm Distribution Agencies
JAN

Recommended Viewing
Recommended Reading
16 mm Film, B & W

SUMMARIES

Literary Original
Born in the workhouse, orphan Oliver Twist is unhappy in his apprenticeship and runs off to London, where he is recruited into a gang of juvenile thieves. The criminals who have ensnared him are brought to justice, he learns the secret of his parentage, and escapes from the squalor of his surroundings when he is adopted and educated by a kindly patron.

THEME INDICATORS
ADVENTURE
CRIME
DRAMA
CHILDREN
CULTURAL
ETHICS
FAMILY
HISTORICAL

Film Version: **Very highly recommended**
The story is condensed and compressed in this film narrative, which concentrates on the dramatic turning points and the major characters to provide a strong and persuasive series of character performances to convey all the spirit and incident of the Dickens novel.

=================== Full Film Title
ONE HUNDRED AND ONE DALMATIANS

Release Date
1961

Production Studio	Country of Origin	Running Time (Minutes)
DISNEY	**USA**	**79**

Producer
Ken Peterson

Director
Wolfgang Reithermann

Principal Performers
Animation

Literary Original and Date of Production
ONE HUNDRED AND ONE DALMATIANS   1957

Author and Biographical Dates
Dodie Smith   1896-

Recommended Viewing

35 mm Film, Color

SUMMARIES

Literary Original
Animals and good-hearted humans combine forces to rescue scores of helpless dalmatians from the clutches of the horrible Cruella De Ville, who has designs on the pelts to make an unusual fur coat for herself.

THEME INDICATORS
**ANIMATION
CRIME
FANTASY
COMEDY
DRAMA
ECOLOGY
ETHICS
FAMILY
FEMINISM**

Film Version: **Highly recommended**
The potential for larger-than-life characterization and invention of incident provided by film animation is once again exploited by the Disney production staff to turn an already amusing original into a hilarious and touching suspense comedy, with an acceptable exaggeration of good and bad characters and many well-judged additional twists of the story line.

Full Film Title
OTHELLO

Release Date
1951

Production Studio
MERCURY

Country of Origin
USA/France

Running Time (Minutes)
91

Producer
Orson Welles

Director
Orson Welles

Principal Performers
Orson Welles, Micheal MacLiammoir, Fay Compton, Robert Cook, Suzanne Cloutier, Michael Laurence, Hilton Edwards, Doris Dowling.

Literary Original and Date of Production
OTHELLO (Play)   1622

Author and Biographical Dates
William Shakespeare   1564-1616

Codings of 16 mm Distribution Agencies
CON

Recommended Viewing
Recommended Reading
16 mm Film, B & W

SUMMARIES

THEME INDICATORS
CRIME
MILITARY
DRAMA
TRAGEDY
ETHICS
FAMILY
FEMINISM
HISTORICAL
RACIAL

Literary Original
Othello is an African Moor who rises to command the armies of Venice and marries the daughter of a senator. His evil lieutenant, Iago, maliciously poisons his mind by lying insinuations against the fidelity of the beautiful Desdemona, his wife. In jealous rage, Othello smothers her and takes his own life in despair.

Film Version: **Recommended**
A low-budget, reduced version of the plot line, with scanty production values and a highly personal but interesting portrayal of the title role by Orson Welles, who was also responsible for script and direction.

Full Film Title
OTHELLO

Release Date
1965

Production Studio
BHE

Country of Origin
Great Britain

Running Time (Minutes)
166

Producer
Richard Goodwin

Director
Stuart Burge

Principal Performers
Laurence Olivier, Frank Finlay, Joyce Redman, Maggie Smith, Derek Jacobi, Robert Lang, Anthony Nicholls.

Literary Original and Date of Production
OTHELLO (Play)   1622

Author and Biographical Dates
William Shakespeare   1564-1616

Codings of 16 mm Distribution Agencies
SWA

Recommended Viewing
Recommended Reading
16 mm Film, Color

SUMMARIES

Literary Original
Othello is an African Moor who rises to command the armies of Venice and marries the daughter of a senator. His evil lieutenant, Iago, maliciously poisons his mind by lying insinuations against the fidelity of the beautiful Desdemona, his wife. In jealous rage, Othello smothers her and takes his own life in despair.

THEME INDICATORS
CRIME
MILITARY
DRAMA
TRAGEDY
ETHICS
FAMILY
FEMINISM
HISTORICAL
RACIAL

Film Version: **Recommended**
The filmed version of a notable stage presentation by the National Theater in England, centered on an excellent performance by Lord Olivier in an unusual interpretation of the personality of the Moor.

Full Film Title
PETER PAN

Release Date
1953

Production Studio
RKO Radio

Country of Origin
USA

Running Time (Minutes)
77

Producer
Disney Studios

Director
Hamilton Luske, Clyde Geronimi, Wilfred Jackson.

Principal Performers
Animation

Literary Original and Date of Production
Peter Pan (Play) 1904

Author and Biographical Dates
Sir James Matthew Barrie 1860-1937

Codings of 16 mm Distribution Agencies
DIS SWA

Recommended Viewing
Recommended Reading
16 mm Film, Color

SUMMARIES

Literary Original
Peter Pan is a boy who never wants to grow up. With the fairy Tinker Bell, he visits the children of the Darling family, and takes them on a trip to Never-Never-Land. They have adventures with pirates led by the menacing Captain Hook, who nearly succeeds in poisoning Peter. All return safely to the Darling home, but Peter refuses to stay.

THEME INDICATORS
Adventure
Animation
Crime
Fantasy
Marine
Comedy
Drama
Children
Cultural
Ethics
Family

Film Version: **Highly recommended**
This animation cartoon treatment of the original play script adds to the potential for fantasy effects, without reducing the credibility of the Barrie characters.

Full Film Title
PICKWICK PAPERS, THE

Release Date
1952

Production Studio
RENOWN PICTURE CORPORATION

Country of Origin
Great Britain

Running Time (Minutes)
115

Director
Noel Langley

Principal Performers
James Donald, Hermione Gingold, James Hayter, Nigel Patrick, Kathleen Harrison, Joyce Grenfell, Donald Wolfit, George Robey.

Literary Original and Date of Production
PICKWICK PAPERS, THE 1837

Author and Biographical Dates
Charles Dickens 1812-1870

Codings of 16 mm Distribution Agencies
BUD   KPF   VCI   WHO

Recommended Viewing
Recommended Reading
16 mm Film, B & W

THEME INDICATORS
COMEDY
CULTURAL
HISTORICAL

SUMMARIES

Literary Original
Mr. Pickwick is the jovial figure on whom center the activities of a group of picturesque and eccentric friends. The records of the coterie feature such innocent amusements as trips to the country, social evenings, and dinner parties. The series climaxes in a breach of promise suit brought by Mr. Pickwick's designing landlady. As a result, he serves a term of imprisonment and on his release settles down quietly to edit the papers of the club.

Film Version: **Recommended**
Episodes from the well-beloved Dickens classic have been selected for treatment in a loosely structured sequence of humorous scenes featuring the major characters of the Pickwick Club, with a highlight of the breach of promise case brought by Mrs. Bardell.

Full Film Title
PINOCCHIO

Release Date
1940

Production Studio
DISNEY

Country of Origin
USA

Running Time (Minutes)
88

Producer
Walt Disney

Director
Ben Sharpsteen/Hamilton Luske

Principal Performers
Animation

Literary Original and Date of Production
ADVENTURES OF PINCCHIO 1883 (trans. M.A. Murray, 1892)

Author and Biographical Dates
Carlo Collodi (Carlo Lorenzini) 1826-1890

Recommended Viewing
35 mm Film, Color

SUMMARIES

THEME INDICATORS
**ADVENTURE
ANIMATION
CRIME
FANTASY
MARINE
MONSTER
MUSICAL
COMEDY
DRAMA
CHILDREN
CULTURAL
FAMILY**

Literary Original
Gepetto, the old puppet maker, makes a marvellous wooden doll that behaves like a mischievous boy. The puppet runs away, has a series of encounters with fairies, animals, and strange beings, is swallowed by a dog fish, and finds himself at home again. He turns into a real boy and settles down to being good. This story and *The Divine Comedy* **are probably the best known Italian classics.**

Film Version: **Very highly recommended**
The techniques of film animation, with the added resources of sound track and music result in a magic visualization of the classic Italian story. All the incidents are presented in an amalgam of delightful color, captivating cartoon characterizations, and action that make the presentation pure fun.

Full Film Title
PLANET OF THE APES

Release Date
1968

Production Studio
TWENTIETH CENTURY FOX

Country of Origin
USA

Running Time (Minutes)
112

Producer
Arthur P. Jacobs

Director
Franklin J. Schaffner

Principal Performers
Charlton Heston, Roddy McDowall, Kim Hunter, Maurice Evans, James Whitmore, James Daly, Linda Harrison, Robert Gunner, Lou Wagner, Woodrow Parfrey.

Literary Original and Date of Production
PLANET OF THE APES   1963

Author and Biographical Dates
Pierre Boulle   1912-

Codings of 16 mm Distribution Agencies
FNC

Recommended Viewing
Recommended Reading
16 mm Film, Color

SUMMARIES

Literary Original
Two French airmen make an unscheduled landing on the planet Soror and observe the structured society of the civilized Simian inhabitants. The men are captured and treated like other Sororian humans. One is sold to a zoo, the other is used as a laboratory animal.

THEME INDICATORS
- ADVENTURE
- FANTASY
- MONSTER
- SCIENCE FICTION
- DRAMA
- CULTURAL
- ECOLOGY
- ETHICS
- RACIAL

Film Version: **Highly recommended**
This film version explores the central theme of the original novel with all the resources of studio tricks and effects to present a thought-provoking and high-grade science-fiction essay, with convincing and memorable effect.

Full Film Title
POLLYANNA

Release Date
1960

Production Studio
DISNEY

Country of Origin
USA

Running Time (Minutes)
134

Producer
George Golitzen

Director
David Swift

Principal Performers
Hayley Mills, Jane Wyman, Richard Egan, Karl Malden, Adolphe Menjou, Agnes Moorehead.

Literary Original and Date of Production
POLLYANNA 1912

Author and Biographical Dates
Eleanor Hodgman Porter 1868-1920

Codings of 16 mm Distribution Agencies

| AIM | BUC | CCC | COU | CWF | DIS | FNC |
| MAC | MOD | NAT | NEW | ROA | SWA | TFC | TWY |

Recommended Viewing
Recommended Reading
16 mm Film, Color

SUMMARIES

THEME INDICATORS
COMEDY
DRAMA
CHILDREN
CULTURAL
ETHICS
FAMILY
FEMINISM
HISTORICAL

Literary Original

A poor twelve-year-old orphan girl in 1912 faces up to the problems of life by looking on the bright side of things, changes the way of life of a crusty bachelor, a hypochondriac, a fire-and-brimstone preacher, and her wealthy aunt, and wins over the townspeople to her side in playing her "glad game."

Film Version: **Recommended**
This lengthy and overserious film adaptation of an old classic falls short of establishing the central character as a cheerful and optimistic model for imitation.

Full Film Title
PRIDE AND PREJUDICE

Release Date
1940

Production Studio
METRO-GOLDWYN-MAYER

Country of Origin
USA

Running Time (Minutes)
118

Director
Robert Z. Leonard

Principal Performers
Greer Garson, Laurence Olivier, Edmund Gwenn, Ann Rutherford, Mary Boland, Melville Cooper, Edna May Oliver, Maureen O'Sullivan, Marsha Hunt.

Literary Original and Date of Production
PRIDE AND PREJUDICE   1813

Author and Biographical Dates
Jane Austen   1775-1817

Codings of 16 mm Distribution Agencies
FNC

Recommended Viewing
Recommended Reading
16 mm Film, B & W

SUMMARIES

THEME INDICATORS
  COMEDY
  DRAMA
  ROMANCE
  CULTURAL
  ETHICS
  FAMILY
  FEMINISM
  HISTORICAL

Literary Original
Mrs. Bennet's goal is to find husbands for her five daughters, an endeavor that receives no support from Mr. Bennet. Daughter Elizabeth becomes prejudiced against Darcy, a suitor, because of his arrogance born of his awareness of Mrs. Bennet's intentions. However, he falls in love with Elizabeth and presents a rather reserved proposal of marriage, which Elizabeth refuses. They are wedded when they overcome their individual pride and prejudice.

Film Version: **Highly recommended**
Intelligent writing, good casting and acting, and careful production combine to make this a very acceptable film version of the Helen Jerome stage play based on Jane Austen's famous novel.

Full Film Title
PRISONER OF ZENDA, THE

Release Date
1937

Production Studio
UNITED ARTISTS

Country of Origin
USA

Running Time (Minutes)
101

Producer
David O. Selznick

Director
John Cromwell

Principal Performers
Ronald Colman, Douglas Fairbanks, Jr., Madeleine Carroll, David Niven, Raymond Massey, Mary Astor, C. Aubrey Smith, Montagu Love.

Literary Original and Date of Production
PRISONER OF ZENDA, THE 1894

Author and Biographical Dates
Anthony Hope 1863-1933

Codings of 16 mm Distribution Agencies
FNC

Recommended Viewing
Recommended Reading
16 mm Film, B & W

SUMMARIES

THEME INDICATORS
ADVENTURE
CRIME
DRAMA
CULTURAL
ETHICS
HISTORICAL

Literary Original
In nineteenth-century Ruritania, it is hoped that the uncanny resemblance of Englishman Rudolf Rassendyll to King Rudolf will be of assistance to the king's men. Threatened by conspirators, King Rudolf is detained while Rassendyll impersonates him in public. The ruse is uncovered, however, and the king is kidnapped and subsequently wounded in an escape. Rassendyll, meanwhile, has fallen in love with the loyal Flavia, who is betrothed to the king.

Film Version: **Very highly recommended**
A classic of the costume adventure genre, this film represents a very close reproduction of the story line, characterization, and romantic setting of the original novel. The acting, dialogue, camera work, and overall finish are all equally satisfying and sure to have their effect on viewers of all ages.

Full Film Title
PRISONER OF ZENDA, THE

Release Date
1952

Production Studio
METRO-GOLDWYN-MAYER

Country of Origin
USA

Running Time (Minutes)
100

Producer
Pandro S. Berman

Director
Richard Thorpe

Principal Performers
Stewart Granger, Deborah Kerr, James Mason, Louis Calhern, Robert Douglas, Jane Greer, Lewis Stone.

Literary Original and Date of Production
PRISONER OF ZENDA, THE   1894

Author and Biographical Dates
Anthony Hope   1863-1933

Codings of 16 mm Distribution Agencies
FNC

Recommended Viewing
Recommended Reading
16 mm Film, Color

SUMMARIES

THEME INDICATORS
ADVENTURE
CRIME
DRAMA
CULTURAL
ETHICS
HISTORICAL

Literary Original
In nineteenth-century Ruritania, it is hoped that the uncanny resemblance of Englishman Rudolf Rassendyll to King Rudolf will be of assisance to the king's men. Threatened by conspirators, King Rudolf is detained while Rassendyll impersonates him in public. The ruse is uncovered, however, and the king is kidnapped and subsequently wounded in an escape. Rassendyll, meanwhile, has fallen in love with the loyal Flavia, who is betrothed to the King.

Film Version: **Recommended**
An expensive, highly colored remake, which in all respects falls short of the standards set by the 1937 production.

Full Film Title
QUENTIN DURWARD

Release Date
1955

Production Studio
METRO-GOLDWYN-MAYER

Country of Origin
USA

Running Time (Minutes)
101

Producer
Pandro S. Berman

Director
Richard Thorpe

Principal Performers
Robert Taylor, Kay Kendall, Robert Morley, George Cole, Alec Clunes, Duncan Lamont, Laya Raki, Marius Goring.

Literary Original and Date of Production
QUENTIN DURWARD 1823

Author and Biographical Dates
Sir Walter Scott 1771-1832

Codings of 16 mm Distribution Agencies
FNC

Recommended Viewing

16 mm Film, Color

SUMMARIES

Literary Original
In 1468, a young Scottish adventurer is entrusted by the French King Louis with the mission of escorting a beautiful countess through dangerous territory. Durward protects her from attack by villainous enemies and after many adventures wins her hand by defeating the murderous William de la Marck, Wild Boar of the Ardennes.

THEME INDICATORS
ADVENTURE
CRIME
DRAMA
ROMANCE
CULTURAL
ETHICS
FAMILY
FEMINISM
HISTORICAL

Film Version
The original story has been followed in only the sketchiest outline in this historical costume adventure, which is acceptable enough as action-filled entertainment without showing any outstanding qualities.

Full Film Title
QUO VADIS?

Release Date
1949

Production Studio
METRO-GOLDWYN-MAYER

Country of Origin
USA

Running Time (Minutes)
171

Producer
Sam Zimbalist

Director
Mervyn LeRoy

Principal Performers
Robert Taylor, Deborah Kerr, Peter Ustinov, Leo Genn, Patricia Laffan, Finlay Currie, Abraham Sofaer, Marina Berti, Felix Aylmer.

Literary Original and Date of Production
QUO VADIS? 1896

Author and Biographical Dates
Henry Sienkewicz 1846-1916

Codings of 16 mm Distribution Agencies
FNC

Recommended Viewing

16 mm Film, Color

SUMMARIES

THEME INDICATORS
ADVENTURE
MILITARY
DRAMA
TRAGEDY
CULTURAL
ETHICS
FEMINISM
HISTORICAL
RELIGIOUS

Literary Original
Set in the Rome of the emperor Nero, the novel, originally written in Polish, narrates the love story of Ligia, a beautiful Christian girl, and Vicinius, who is converted by her influence from his pagan outlook. Condemned to a horrible death in the arena, Ligia is rescued from martyrdom by the bravery and strength of her faithful servant Ursus, to be united with Vicinius.

Film Version: **Recommended**
This lengthy film expands on the visual possibilities of a studio re-creation of the spectacles of ancient Rome to an extent that slows down the development of the plot and the portrayal of characters, but the original narrative is well reproduced, and the well-researched historical detail adds to an understanding of the period.

Full Film Title
RAILWAY CHILDREN, THE

Release Date
1970

Production Studio
UNIVERSAL

Country of Origin
USA

Running Time (Minutes)
108

Producer
Robert Lynn

Director
Lionel Jeffries

Principal Performers
Jenny Agutter, Dinah Sheridan, Bernard Cribbins, William Mervyn, Iain Cuthbertson, Sally Thomsett, Peter Bromilow, Ann Lancaster.

Literary Original and Date of Production
RAILWAY CHILDREN, THE   1906

Author and Biographical Dates
Edith Nesbit   1858-1924

Codings of 16 mm Distribution Agencies
MOD   UNI

Recommended Viewing
Recommended Reading
16 mm Film, Color

SUMMARIES

THEME INDICATORS
- **ADVENTURE**
- **COMEDY**
- **DRAMA**
- **CHILDREN**
- **CULTURAL**
- **ETHICS**
- **FAMILY**
- **FEMINISM**
- **HISTORICAL**

Literary Original
When their father is unjustly sent to prison, a family moves north from London, in 1904, to a house beside a railway in Yorkshire. They find new friends to support them in their bid to clear the family name.

Film Version: **Very highly recommended**
A successful film adaptation, respectful of the original story, with a wealth of well-managed period atmosphere, competent performances, and a generally happy and refreshing feeling in its development.

Full Film Title
REBECCA OF SUNNYBROOK FARM

Release Date
1938

Production Studio
TWENTIETH CENTURY FOX

Country of Origin
USA

Running Time (Minutes)
80

Producer
Darryl F. Zanuck

Director
Allan Dwan

Principal Performers
Shirley Temple, Randolph Scott, Jack Haley, Gloria Stuart, Phyllis Brooks, Helen Westley, Slim Summerville, Bill Robinson, Alan Dinehart.

Literary Original and Date of Production
REBECCA OF SUNNYBROOK FARM 1903

Author and Biographical Dates
Kate Douglas Wiggin 1856-1923

Codings of 16 mm Distribution Agencies
FNC

Recommended Viewing

16 mm Film, B & W

SUMMARIES

Literary Original
Rebecca Randall has such a cheerful and lovable disposition that she wins the hearts of all the neighborhood when she goes to live on a farm with her Aunt Miranda. On the death of her aunt, she inherits the property and continues to live there among her friends.

THEME INDICATORS
MUSICAL
COMEDY
DRAMA
CHILDREN
CULTURAL
FAMILY
FEMINISM
HISTORICAL

Film Version
The title of the original story has been retained, but the entire plot line recast and modernized in a conventional Hollywood script, which results in a disappointingly routine musical with limited entertainment values.

Full Film Title
RED BADGE OF COURAGE, THE

Release Date
1951

Production Studio	Country of Origin	Running Time (Minutes)
METRO-GOLDWYN-MAYER	**USA**	**69**

Producer
Gottfried Reinhardt

Director
John Huston

Principal Performers
Audie Murphy, Bill Mauldin, Douglas Dick, Royal Dano, John Dierkes, Arthur Hunnicutt, Robert Easton Burke, Smith Ballew, Glenn Strange.

Literary Original and Date of Production
RED BADGE OF COURAGE, THE   1895

Author and Biographical Dates
Stephen Crane   1871-1900

Codings of 16 mm Distribution Agencies
FNC

Recommended Viewing
Recommended Reading
16 mm Film, B & W

SUMMARIES

Literary Original
A farm boy who volunteers for the Union Army during the Civil War, Henry Fleming flees from the enemy in a moment of panic during the battle of Chancellorsville. He overcomes his shame and remorse to return to his comrades-in-arms and share their hardships and dangers. War is not glamorized.

THEME INDICATORS
ADVENTURE
MILITARY
DRAMA
ETHICS
HISTORICAL
WAR

Film Version: **Highly recommended**
Director John Huston's prestigious presentation captures vividly the spirit of the original novel, with a balance of emphasis between the impressions of the young hero and the scenes of war in which he is engulfed. The cast of characters is well selected and well handled, and the background of action conveys an authentic atmosphere of the Civil War period.

Full Film Title
RICHARD III

Release Date
1956

Production Studio
LONDON FILMS

Country of Origin
Great Britain

Running Time (Minutes)
161

Producer
Laurence Olivier

Director
Laurence Olivier

Principal Performers
Laurence Olivier, Claire Bloom, Ralph Richardson, Cedric Hardwicke, Stanley Baker, Alice Clunes, John Gielgud, Pamela Brown, Michael Gough.

Literary Original and Date of Production
KING RICHARD THE THIRD (Play)   1597

Author and Biographical Dates
William Shakespeare   1564-1616

Codings of 16 mm Distribution Agencies
JAN

Recommended Viewing
Recommended Reading
16 mm Film, Color

SUMMARIES

THEME INDICATORS
  ADVENTURE
  CRIME
  MILITARY
  DRAMA
  TRAGEDY
  BIOGRAPHICAL
  CULTURAL
  ETHICS
  FEMINISM
  HISTORICAL
  WAR

Literary Original
The hunchbacked and malevolent Richard of Gloucester ruthlessly clears his way to the throne of England in a course of treacherous and blood-stained intrigues involving the destruction of all who oppose his ambitions of power. His excesses bring about an armed rebellion, and he is defeated and slain in the battle of Bosworth Field.

Film Version: **Very highly recommended**
The dramatic Shakespearean plot has been reshaped and even extended as an in-depth study of a devious and intriguing schemer intent on power. The acting is first class, and the production deliberately follows for the most part traditional stage conventions, rather than the wider range of effects possible in the cinema, to give an overall effect of closeup familiarity and comprehension of the central tragic character.

Full Film Title
RING OF BRIGHT WATER

Release Date
1968

Production Studio
RANK FILM DISTRIBUTION

Country of Origin
Great Britain

Running Time (Minutes)
107

Producer
Joseph Strick

Director
Jack Couffer

Principal Performers
Bill Travers, Virginia McKenna, Peter Jeffrey, Jameson Clark, Heiena Gloag, W. H. D. Joss, Roddy McMillan, Jean Taylor-Smith, Archie Duncan.

Literary Original and Date of Production
RING OF BRIGHT WATER   1960

Author and Biographical Dates
Gavin Maxwell   1914-1969

Codings of 16 mm Distribution Agencies
FNC

Recommended Viewing
Recommended Reading
16 mm Film, Color

SUMMARIES

THEME INDICATORS
DRAMA
CULTURAL
ECOLOGY

Literary Original
The author retires to the pastoral setting of his Scottish Highland retreat and notes the antics of two pet otters, Mijbil and Edal, that provide companionship after the loss of his faithful dog.

Film Version: **Recommended**
The true-life original account of a return to nature has been well reconstructed with a generally successful effect due to the pleasing photography of location exteriors and animal sequences.

Full Film Title
ROBE, THE

Release Date
1953

Production Studio
TWENTIETH CENTURY FOX

Country of Origin
USA

Running Time (Minutes)
135

Producer
Frank Ross

Director
Henry Koster

Principal Performers
Richard Burton, Jean Simmons, Victor Mature, Michael Rennie, Jay Robinson, Dean Jagger, Torin Thatcher, Richard Boone.

Literary Original and Date of Production
ROBE, THE   1942

Author and Biographical Dates
Lloyd Cassel Douglas   1877-1951

Codings of 16 mm Distribution Agencies
FNC

Recommended Viewing

16 mm Film, Color

SUMMARIES

Literary Original
Marcellus is a young Roman officer who comes into possession of the cloak taken from Christ before the crucifixion on Calvary. The relic exercises a strange and all-consuming influence on him, allowing him no peace until he is converted to Christianity.

THEME INDICATORS
**ADVENTURE
MILITARY
DRAMA
CULTURAL
ETHICS
HISTORICAL
RELIGIOUS**

Film Version: **Highly recommended**
The first feature produced in the Cinemascope process, this film version exploits the potential of the technique for spectacular effects, but without sacrificing the essentials of the original story line or obscuring its message. The production is rich and generous, and the overall development guarantees attention and interest by the viewer.

Full Film Title
ROMEO AND JULIET

Release Date
1936

Production Studio
MGM

Country of Origin
USA

Running Time (Minutes)
127

Producer
Irving Thalberg

Director
George Cukor

Principal Performers
Leslie Howard, Norma Shearer, John Barrymore, Basil Rathbone, Edna May Oliver, C. Aubrey Smith, Reginald Denny.

Literary Original and Date of Production
ROMEO AND JULIET (Play)   1597

Author and Biographical Dates
William Shakespeare   1564-1616

Codings of 16 mm Distribution Agencies
FNC

Recommended Viewing
Recommended Reading
16 mm Film, B & W

SUMMARIES

Literary Original

Young Romeo and Juliet belong to the powerful rival families of Montague and Capulet. They fall in love and are married in secret. Romeo is banished after a fatal street brawl, and Juliet is betrothed by her parents to a young nobleman. To escape her predicament she takes a potion and simulates death. Believing her really dead, Romeo takes poison in her tomb, and when Juliet recovers consciousness she, too, kills herself in grief.

THEME INDICATORS
ADVENTURE
DRAMA
ROMANCE
TRAGEDY
CULTURAL
ETHICS
FAMILY
FEMINISM
HISTORICAL

Film Version: **Recommended**

The romance and poetry of Shakespeare's tragedy of star-crossed lovers has been emphasized in this now dated but still interesting treatment. No effort was spared to produce the intended dramatic effects, and the acting interpretations of the central characters remain fine examples of technique.

Full Film Title
ROMEO AND JULIET

Release Date
1968

Production Studio	Country of Origin	Running Time (Minutes)
PARAMOUNT	**Great Britain**	**152**

Producer
Dino De Laurentis

Director
Franco Zeffirelli

Principal Performers
Leonard Whiting, Olivia Hussy, John McEnery, Michael York, Pat Heywood, Milo O'Shea, Paul Hardwick, Natasha Parby.

Literary Original and Date of Production
ROMEO AND JULIET (Play)   1597

Author and Biographical Dates
William Shakespeare   1564-1616

Codings of 16 mm Distribution Agencies
PAR

Recommended Viewing
Recommended Reading
16 mm Film, Color

SUMMARIES

THEME INDICATORS
- ADVENTURE
- DRAMA
- ROMANCE
- TRAGEDY
- CULTURAL
- ETHICS
- FAMILY
- FEMINISM
- HISTORICAL

Literary Original
Young Romeo and Juliet belong to the powerful rival families of Montague and Capulet. They fall in love and are married in secret. Romeo is banished after a fatal street brawl, and Juliet is betrothed by her parents to a young nobleman. To escape her predicament, she takes a potion and simulates death. Believing her really dead, Romeo takes poison in her tomb, and when Juliet recovers consciousness she, too, kills herself in grief.

Film Version: **Recommended**
Youthful leading actors, well-selected location settings, and an opening up of the action have been combined in this most recent remake to preserve the story while appealing to the tastes and attitudes of modern viewers. The general result is successful, and the film has achieved wide popularity as a classic adapted to the contemporary outlook.

Full Film Title
SAVAGE SAM

Release Date
1963

Production Studio
DISNEY

Country of Origin
USA

Running Time (Minutes)
103

Producer
Bill Anderson

Director
Norman Tokar

Principal Performers
Brian Keith, Tommy Kirk, Kevin Corcoran, Dewey Martin, Jeff York, Royal Dano, Marta Kristen, Rafael Campos, Slim Pickens, Pat Hogan.

Literary Original and Date of Production
SAVAGE SAM 1962

Author and Biographical Dates
Fred Gipson 1908-1973

Codings of 16 mm Distribution Agencies
AIM BUC CCC COU CWF DIS FNC
MAC MOD NAT NEW ROA SWA TFC TWY

Recommended Viewing

16 mm Film, Color

SUMMARIES

Literary Original
In this sequel to *Old Yeller*, **the hound Savage Sam leads rescuers on the trail of fifteen-year-old Travis, his younger brother Arliss, and their adolescent neighbor, all of whom have been captured by Indians.**

THEME INDICATORS
ADVENTURE
MILITARY
WESTERN
DRAMA
CHILDREN
CULTURAL
ECOLOGY
FAMILY
HISTORICAL
RACIAL
WAR

Film Version: **Recommended**
What this Disney adaptation loses in departing from the original text it makes up in suspense and scenery. It is an acceptable boy-and-dog yarn for children.

Full Film Title
SCARAMOUCHE

Release Date
1952

Production Studio
METRO-GOLDWYN-MAYER

Country of Origin
USA

Running Time (Minutes)
115

Producer
Carey Wilson

Director
George Sidney

Principal Performers
Stewart Granger, Eleanor Parker, Mel Ferrer, Janet Leigh, Henry Wilcoxon, Nina Foch, Lewis Stone, Robert Coote, Richard Anderson.

Literary Original and Date of Production
SCARAMOUCHE 1921

Author and Biographical Dates
Rafael Sabatini 1875-1950

Codings of 16 mm Distribution Agencies
FNC

Recommended Viewing

16 mm Film, Color

SUMMARIES

Literary Original
In France at the time of the Revolution, André-Louis Moreau resolves to avenge the murder of his friend by a rich nobleman. Under the guise of an actor in a travelling troupe, he tracks down his quarry but finds that he has a crisis of conscience when he confronts him at last.

THEME INDICATORS
ADVENTURE
CRIME
DRAMA
ROMANCE
CULTURAL
ETHICS
HISTORICAL

Film Version: **Recommended**
A high-grade adventure story, romantic and exciting, emerges from this adaptation of the novel, with a film evocation of the turbulence, violence, and drama of the period of the French Revolution.

Full Film Title
SCARLET PIMPERNEL, THE

Release Date
1935

Production Studio
UNITED ARTISTS

Country of Origin
USA

Running Time (Minutes)
98

Producer
Alexander Korda

Director
Harold Young

Principal Performers
Leslie Howard, Merle Oberon, Raymond Massey, Nigel Bruce, Bramwell Fletcher, Joan Gardner, Walter Rilla.

Literary Original and Date of Production
SCARLET PIMPERNEL, THE 1905

Author and Biographical Dates
Baroness Emma Magdalena Orczy   1865-1947

Codings of 16 mm Distribution Agencies
BUC   BUD   EMG   KPF   VCI   WHO

Recommended Viewing
Recommended Reading
16 mm Film, B & W

SUMMARIES

Literary Original
Sir Percy Blakeney poses as a decadent fop while being the courageous mastermind behind the organization that snatches victims of the French Revolution from imprisonment and death by the guillotine. In a series of daring encounters he defeats his archenemy the fanatic revolutionary Citizen Chauvelin.

THEME INDICATORS
ADVENTURE
DRAMA
CULTURAL
ETHICS
HISTORICAL

Film Version: **Very highly recommended**
Masterful performances and historically accurate backgrounds combine in this first class period adventure that captures the intent of the author.

Full Film Title
SCROOGE

Release Date
1970

Production Studio
WATERBURY

Country of Origin
Great Britain

Running Time (Minutes)
118

Producer
Leslie Bricusse/Robert Solo

Director
Ronald Neame

Principal Performers
Albert Finney, Alec Guinness, Edith Evans, Kenneth More, Michael Medwin, Laurence Naismith, David Collings, Roy Kinnear.

Literary Original and Date of Production
CHRISTMAS CAROL, A   1843

Author and Biographical Dates
Charles Dickens   1812-1870

Codings of 16 mm Distribution Agencies
MOD   SWA   TWY

Recommended Viewing
Recommended Reading
16 mm Film, Color

SUMMARIES

THEME INDICATORS
- FANTASY
- COMEDY
- DRAMA
- CULTURAL
- ETHICS
- FAMILY
- HISTORICAL
- RELIGIOUS

Literary Original
Scrooge is a rich miser who is visited on Christmas Eve by the ghost of his dead partner and the spirits of Christmas Past, Present, and To-come. The visions they bring him of the punishment of avarice so impress him that he rises on Christmas Day a changed man, full of charity and goodwill to all.

Film Version
A musical version of the story, with special effects and trick photography.

Full Film Title
SEA HAWK, THE

Release Date
1940

Production Studio
WARNER BROTHERS

Country of Origin
USA

Running Time (Minutes)
130

Producer
Hal B. Wallis/Henry Blanke

Director
Michael Curtiz

Principal Performers
Errol Flynn, Brenda Marshall, Flora Robson, Henry Daniell, Claude Rains, Donald Crisp, Alan Hale, Una O'Connor, Gilbert Roland.

Literary Original and Date of Production
SEA HAWK, THE   1915

Author and Biographical Dates
Rafael Sabatini   1875-1950

Codings of 16 mm Distribution Agencies
UAS

Recommended Viewing

16 mm Film, B & W

SUMMARIES

Literary Original
Sir Oliver Tressilian is the gentleman commander of one of a number of British ships that confronts and disperses the Spanish Armada. Exemplifying the courageous qualities of a Barbary corsair, he acquires the title of Sakr-el-Bahr — Hawk of the Sea.

THEME INDICATORS
ADVENTURE
MARINE
DRAMA
ROMANCE
CULTURAL
HISTORICAL
WAR

Film Version: **Recommended**
The original novel has been loosely reshaped and expanded into a scenario for scenes of action and adventure featuring the typical displays of swordsmanship, seamanship, and athletic bravado of a Hollywood historical spectacular.

Full Film Title
SEA WOLF, THE

Release Date
1941

Production Studio	Country of Origin	Running Time (Minutes)
WARNERS	**USA**	**100**

Producer
Henry Blanke

Director
Michael Curtiz

Principal Performers
Edward G. Robinson, Ida Lupino, John Garfield, Alexander Knox, Gene Lockhart, Barry Fitzgerald, Stanley Ridges, Francis McDonald.

Literary Original and Date of Production
SEA WOLF, THE   1904

Author and Biographical Dates
Jack London   1876-1916

Codings of 16 mm Distribution Agencies
UAS

Recommended Viewing
Recommended Reading
16 mm Film, B & W

SUMMARIES

THEME INDICATORS
ADVENTURE
MARINE
DRAMA
ETHICS

Literary Original
After a shipwreck in 1904, Humphrey Van Weyden is saved from the Pacific by the crew of the maniacal Captain Wolf. Surviving the vacillations of Wolf's irascible character, Hump falls in love with a rescued girl, Maud Brewster. Ignoring pleas for safe passage home, Wolf takes the pair north, where they escape. A mutiny ensures Wolf's death, and the lovers find safety aboard a United States revenue cutter.

Film Version: **Recommended**
The original story line has been modernized and modified in a film version that remains viewable for the acting of its main performers.

Full Film Title
SECRET GARDEN, THE

Release Date
1949

Production Studio
METRO-GOLDWYN-MAYER

Country of Origin
USA

Running Time (Minutes)
93

Director
Fred M. Wilcox

Principal Performers
Margaret O'Brien, Herbert Marshall, Gladys Cooper, Elsa Lanchester, Dean Stockwell, Brian Roper.

Literary Original and Date of Production
SECRET GARDEN, THE   1911

Author and Biographical Dates
Frances Hodgson Burnett   1849-1924

Codings of 16 mm Distribution Agencies
FNC

Recommended Viewing
Recommended Reading
16 mm Film, B & W

SUMMARIES

Literary Original
Mary Lennox is sent home from India, after an illness, to a Yorkshire cottage and finds a sick boy living there. By giving attention to a long-neglected walled garden, she discovers a magic force that brings back health and happiness to all the tenants of the property.

THEME INDICATORS
ADVENTURE
COMEDY
DRAMA
CHILDREN
CULTURAL
ETHICS
FAMILY
FEMINISM
HISTORICAL

Film Version: **Recommended**
A quiet, careful, and well-produced film version of the novel, appealing and convincing in its overall effect and with a firm underlining to one of the author's messages, the need to seek contentment in familiar surroundings.

Full Film Title
SHANE

Release Date
1953

Production Studio
PARAMOUNT

Country of Origin
USA

Running Time (Minutes)
118

Producer
George Stevens

Director
George Stevens

Principal Performers
Alan Ladd, Jean Arthur, Van Heflin, Jack Palance, Brandon De Wilde.

Literary Original and Date of Production
SHANE   1949

Author and Biographical Dates
Jack Schaefer   1907-

Codings of 16 mm Distribution Agencies
PAR

Recommended Viewing
Recommended Reading
16 mm Film, Color

SUMMARIES

Literary Original
In the 1880s in Wyoming, a drifter rides into the lives of a peaceful homesteading family, buckles on his gun belt to defend their interests against the brutalities of a ruthless cattle baron, and rides on after squaring accounts, leaving the young son of the family to lament the passing of his hero.

THEME INDICATORS
ADVENTURE
CRIME
WESTERN
DRAMA
CHILDREN
ETHICS
FAMILY
HISTORICAL

Film Version: **Very highly recommended**
The strong and dramatic plot line of the novel has been well developed and reinforced to make a classic of the western film genre, which provides excellent family viewing and a strong moral message.

Full Film Title
SHE

Release Date
1965

Production Studio
METRO-GOLDWYN-MAYER

Country of Origin
USA

Running Time (Minutes)
106

Producer
Michael Carreras/Aida Young

Director
Robert Day

Principal Performers
Ursula Andress, Peter Cushing, Bernard Cribbins, John Richardson, Rosenda Monteros, Christopher Lee, Andre Morell, John Maxim.

Literary Original and Date of Production
SHE: A HISTORY OF ADVENTURE 1887

Author and Biographical Dates
H. Rider Haggard   1856-1925

Codings of 16 mm Distribution Agencies
FNC

Recommended Viewing

16 mm Film, Color

SUMMARIES

Literary Original
The mysterious and queenly Ayesha (or "she-who-must-be-obeyed") reveals to a young Englishman that he is the reincarnation of her long-dead love. She then brings him to Kôr, the capital of her secret realm in upper Africa, where she perishes in the Sacred Flame, leaving him to wait another 2,000 years for their next reunion.

THEME INDICATORS
ADVENTURE
FANTASY
DRAMA
ROMANCE
CULTURAL
ECOLOGY
ETHICS
FEMINISM

Film Version
The central sequences set in the fabled city of Kôr have been isolated as the basis for a costume spectacular, which has little relation to the intentions of the author and misses any spark of inspiration or interest.

Full Film Title
SO DEAR TO MY HEART

Release Date
1948

Production Studio
DISNEY

Country of Origin
USA

Running Time (Minutes)
82

Director
Harold Schuster

Principal Performers
Burl Ives, Beulah Bondi, Bobby Driscoll, Harry Carey.

Literary Original and Date of Production
MIDNIGHT AND JEREMIAH   1943

Author and Biographical Dates
Sterling North   1906-1974

Codings of 16 mm Distribution Agencies

| AIM | BUC | CCC | COU | CWF | DIS | FNC |
| MOD | NAT | NEW | ROA | SWA | TFC | TWY |

Recommended Viewing

16 mm Film, Color

SUMMARIES

THEME INDICATORS
DRAMA
CHILDREN
ECOLOGY
ETHICS
FAMILY
HISTORY

Literary Original
In 1910, young Jeremiah lived on an Indiana farm. To the surprise of his contemptuous grandfather, Jeremiah's pet black lamb Midnight won honors at a county fair. During the ensuing jubilation, Midnight ran away, only to return on Christmas Eve to his heartbroken master.

Film Version: **Recommended**
The original story is re-created in a blend of live action and animation film techniques to give a good overall impression of period, action, and character as intended by the author.

= Full Film Title
SONG OF BERNADETTE, THE

Release Date
1944

Production Studio
TWENTIETH CENTURY FOX

Country of Origin
USA

Running Time (Minutes)
156

Producer
William Perlberg

Director
Henry King

Principal Performers
Jennifer Jones, William Eythe, Charles Bickford, Vincent Price, Lee J. Cobb, Gladys Cooper, Anne Revere, Roman Bohnen.

Literary Original and Date of Production
THE SONG OF BERNADETTE 1942

Author and Biographical Dates
Franz Werfel 1890-1945

Recommended Viewing
Recommended Reading
35 mm Film, B & W

SUMMARIES

THEME INDICATORS
DRAMA
FAMILY
RELIGIOUS

Literary Original
A French country girl in the town of Lourdes in the Pyrenees has a vision of the Virgin Mary and has to face the scepticism and doubt of her community. In the end, her conviction and faith prevail, and the scene of the apparition becomes a center of pilgrimage.

Film Version: **Highly recommended**
The film is a reverent and respectful recounting of the story, in which the simplicity and sincerity of the theme dominate the conversion into cinematic terms of the central character and her contemporaries, hostile or supportive.

Full Film Title
SOUND OF MUSIC, THE

Release Date
1965

Production Studio
TWENTIETH CENTURY FOX

Country of Origin
USA

Running Time (Minutes)
174

Producer
Robert Wise/Saul Chaplin

Director
Robert Wise

Principal Performers
Julie Andrews, Christopher Plummer, Eleanor Parker, Richard Haydn, Peggy Wood, Charmian Carr, Heather Menzies, Nicolas Hammond.

Literary Original and Date of Production
STORY OF THE TRAPP FAMILY SINGERS, THE   1949

Author and Biographical Dates
Maria Augusta Trapp   1905-

Codings of 16 mm Distribution Agencies
FNC

Recommended Viewing
Recommended Reading
16 mm Film, Color

SUMMARIES

Literary Original
Maria, a young novice, leaves her convent to become tutor to the seven children of widower Baron Von Trapp. Later she marries him and escapes with her children from the Nazi police during the Salzburg Music Festival of 1938.

THEME INDICATORS
ADVENTURE
MUSICAL
DRAMA
ROMANCE
BIOGRAPHICAL
CHILDREN
CULTURAL
ETHICS
FAMILY
FEMINISM
HISTORICAL
RELIGIOUS

Film Version: **Very highly recommended**
The film treatment preserves the main lines of the biographical original but expands far beyond it into an unusual form of musical, approximating film opera. The songs, settings, and performances are all of high quality, and the whole film is by now a classic of family cinema.

Full Film Title
STORM OVER THE NILE

Release Date
1955

Production Studio
GENERAL FILM DISTRIBUTORS

Country of Origin
Great Britain

Running Time (Minutes)
107

Producer
Zoltan Korda

Director
Zoltan Korda/ Terence Young

Principal Performers
Anthony Steil, Laurence Harvey, James Robertson Justice, Mary Ure, Geoffrey Keen, Ronald Lewis, Ian Carmichael.

Literary Original and Date of Production
FOUR FEATHERS, THE   1902

Author and Biographical Dates
Alfred Edward Woodley Mason   1865-1948

Recommended Viewing
Recommended Reading
35 mm Film, Color

SUMMARIES

Literary Original
A young officer of the British army in the late nineteenth century is given four white feathers, symbolic of an accusation of cowardice. He proves his courage and redeems his honor by rescuing a group of fellow officers held captive in the Sudan.

THEME INDICATORS
ADVENTURE
MILITARY
DRAMA
CULTURAL
ETHICS
HISTORICAL
RACIAL
WAR

Film Version
A remake of *The Four Feathers*, which preserves the original plot but lacks any distinctions or interest in its routine recapitulation of the story.

Full Film Title
SUMMER MAGIC

Release Date
1963

Production Studio
DISNEY

Country of Origin
USA

Running Time (Minutes)
100

Producer
Walt Disney/Ron Miller

Director
James Neilson

Principal Performers
Hayley Mills, Burl Ives, Dorothy McGuire, Deborah Walley, Eddie Hodges, Una Merkel, Jimmy Mathers, Michael J. Pollard, Wendy Turner, Peter Brown, James Stacy.

Literary Original and Date of Production
MOTHER CAREY'S CHICKENS   1911

Author and Biographical Dates
Kate Douglas Wiggin   1856-1923

Codings of 16 mm Distribution Agencies

| AIM | BUC | CCC | COU | CWF | DIS | FNC |
| MAC | MOD | NAT | NEW | ROA | TFC | |

Recommended Viewing

16 mm Film, Color

SUMMARIES

THEME INDICATORS
- COMEDY
- DRAMA
- CHILDREN
- FAMILY
- FEMINISM
- HISTORICAL

Literary Original
The widowed Mrs. Carey, her four children, and their obstinate cousin acquire a deserted house. Together they renovate its bleak interior, while uniting in love and loyalty to defy the frustrations of adversity.

Film Version: **Recommended**
An accurate and successful remake of Kate Douglas Wiggin's *Mother Carey's Chickens*, with a good cast and all the production expertise of the Disney studios.

Full Film Title
SWISS FAMILY ROBINSON, THE

Release Date
1940

Production Studio
RKO RADIO

Country of Origin
USA

Running Time (Minutes)
84

Producer
Gene Towne/Graham Baker

Director
Edward Ludwig

Principal Performers
Thomas Mitchell, Edna Best, Freddie Bartholomew, Tim Holt, Terry Kilburn.

Literary Original and Date of Production
SWISS FAMILY ROBINSON, THE 1813

Author and Biographical Dates
John [Rudolf] Wyss 1781-1830

Codings of 16 mm Distribution Agencies
BUD   FCE   ICS   MOG

Recommended Viewing
Recommended Reading
16 mm Film, B & W

SUMMARIES

THEME INDICATORS
ADVENTURE
MARINE

Literary Original
A Swiss family is shipwrecked, in the nineteenth century, on its way to the New World. Beached on a deserted coastline, the parents and their children make adjustments to their new way of life, which includes treehouses, coexistence with wild animals, and encounters with pirates. This is one of the hundreds of island stories descended from Robinson Crusoe.

COMEDY
DRAMA
CHILDREN
CULTURAL
ECOLOGY
FAMILY
HISTORICAL

Film Version
A reduced version of the original narrative is used in this film version to provide a rather stiff and low-key interpretation, with emphasis on the drama of the central situation. The result is adequate but lacking in highlights in the production or the acting.

Full Film Title
SWISS FAMILY ROBINSON

Release Date
1960

Production Studio
DISNEY

Country of Origin
USA

Running Time (Minutes)
128

Producer
Bill Anderson

Director
Ken Annakin

Principal Performers
John Mills, Dorothy McGuire, James MacArthur, Janet Munro, Sessue Hayakawa, Tommy Kirk, Kevin Corcoran, Cecil Parker, Andy Ho, Milton Reid, Larry Taylor.

Literary Original and Date of Production
SWISS FAMILY ROBINSON, THE   1813

Author and Biographical Dates
Johann Wyss   1781-1830

Codings of 16 mm Distribution Agencies
DIS   FNC   MOD

Recommended Viewing
Recommended Reading
16 mm Film, Color

SUMMARIES

THEME INDICATORS
ADVENTURE
MARINE
COMEDY
DRAMA
CHILDREN
CULTURAL
ECOLOGY
FAMILY
HISTORICAL

Literary Original
A Swiss family is shipwrecked, in the nineteenth century, on its way to the New World. Beached on a deserted coastline, the parents and their children make adjustments to their new way of life, which includes treehouses, coexistence with wild animals, and encounters with pirates. This is one of the hundreds of island stories descended from Robinson Crusoe.

Film Version: **Recommended**
A colorful and lively remake, with the story line amplified and varied to give openings for additional comedy and adventure sequences, in an enjoyable entertainment offering of simple fun in a family setting.

Full Film Title
SWORD IN THE STONE, THE

Release Date
1963

Production Studio
DISNEY

Country of Origin
USA

Running Time (Minutes)
75

Producer
Ken Peterson

Director
Wolfgang Reithermann

Principal Performers
Animation

Literary Original and Date of Production
SWORD IN THE STONE, THE 1938

Author and Biographical Dates
Terence Hanbury White   1906-1964

Recommended Viewing
Recommended Reading
35 mm Film, Color

SUMMARIES

THEME INDICATORS
ADVENTURE
ANIMATION
FANTASY
COMEDY
DRAMA
CHILDREN
CULTURAL
ECOLOGY
ETHICS

Literary Original
Merlin the wizard trains the young Arthur by his love and magic to realize that knowledge is power. Ultimately, the boy proves his right to the kingship of England by drawing the symbolic sword from the stone in which it is fixed.

Film Version: **Highly recommended**
This feature-length animation film recounts all of the main action of the novel, but loses something of the whimsy and imaginative inventiveness of the original in its treatment of tradition, folklore and magic.

Full Film Title
TALE OF TWO CITIES, A

Release Date
1935

Production Studio
METRO-GOLDWYN-MAYER

Country of Origin
USA

Running Time (Minutes)
128

Director
Jack Conway

Principal Performers
Ronald Colman, Elizabeth Allan.

Literary Original and Date of Production
TALE OF TWO CITIES, A   1859

Author and Biographical Dates
Charles Dickens   1812-1870

Codings of 16 mm Distribution Agencies
FNC

Recommended Viewing
Recommended Reading
16 mm Film, B & W

SUMMARIES

Literary Original
Sidney Carton is a dissolute English lawyer who is the identical double of a French nobleman, Charles Darney, whose wife, Lucie, Carton also loves. When the Frenchman is caught up in the turmoil of the Revolution of 1789 and condemned to be guillotined, Carton smuggles him out of prison and takes his place on the scaffold.

THEME INDICATORS
ADVENTURE
DRAMA
TRAGEDY
CULTURAL
ETHICS
HISTORICAL

Film Version: **Highly recommended**
An abridged account of the Dickens story, backed by strong and effective evocation of the historical background, giving a generally satisfying impression of the tone and spirit of the original.

Full Film Title
TALE OF TWO CITIES, A

Release Date
1957

Production Studio
RANK FILM DISTRIBUTION

Country of Origin
Great Britain

Running Time (Minutes)
117

Producer
Betty Fox

Director
Ralph Thomas

Principal Performers
Dirk Bogarde, Dorothy Tutin, Cecil Parker, Stephen Murray, Athene Seyler, Paul Guers, Alfie Bass, Rosalie Crutchley.

Literary Original and Date of Production
TALE OF TWO CITIES, A 1859

Author and Biographical Dates
Charles Dickens   1812-1870

Codings of 16 mm Distribution Agencies
BUD   KPF   LCA   MAC
MOD   ROA   TWY   WHO

Recommended Viewing
Recommended Reading
16 mm Film, B & W

SUMMARIES

THEME INDICATORS
ADVENTURE
DRAMA
TRAGEDY
CULTURAL
ETHICS
HISTORICAL

Literary Original

Sidney Carton is a dissolute English lawyer who is the identical double of a French nobleman, Charles Darney, whose wife, Lucie, Carton also loves. When the Frenchman is caught up in the turmoil of the Revolution of 1789 and condemned to be guillotined, Carton smuggles him out of prison and takes his place on the scaffold.

Film Version: **Recommended**
An adequate remake illustrating the main episodes of the novel, with a rather deliberate development of the story line but good background detail and competent acting.

Full Film Title
TAMING OF THE SHREW, THE

Release Date
1967

Production Studio
COLUMBIA

Country of Origin
USA

Running Time (Minutes)
122

Producer
Richard McWhorter

Director
Franco Zeffirelli

Principal Performers
Richard Burton, Elizabeth Taylor, Michael York, Michael Hordern, Cyril Cusack, Alfred Lynch, Natasha Pyne, Alan Webb, Victor Spinetti.

Literary Original and Date of Production
THE TAMING OF THE SHREW   1623

Author and Biographical Dates
William Shakespeare   1564-1616

Codings of 16 mm Distribution Agencies
| AIM | CCC | CTC | CTH | CWF | IMA | MAC |
| MOD | SEL | SWA | TWY | WCF | WEL | WHO |

Recommended Viewing
Recommended Reading
16 mm Film, Color

SUMMARIES

THEME INDICATORS
COMEDY
CULTURAL
ETHICS
FAMILY
FEMINISM
HISTORICAL

Literary Original
Petruchio demonstrates the success of fighting fire with fire in his wooing of the wayward Katherina, whose violence and bad temper have repelled other suitors. By heavy-handed tactics in courtship and married life, he overbears her shrewishness, until she submits to being an obedient and gentle wife.

Film Version: **Recommended**
The comedy elements of the Shakespeare play have been emphasized in this film version, which takes every opportunity to develop broadly humorous sequences of rapid action and boisterous incident. The overall effect is of a slightly off-center interpretation, suitable for modern audiences but not overrespectful of the original material.

Full Film Title
TARZAN THE APE MAN

Release Date
1932

Production Studio
METRO-GOLDWYN-MAYER

Country of Origin
USA

Running Time (Minutes)
99

Director
W. S. Van-Dyke

Principal Performers
Johnny Weissmuller, Maureen O'Sullivan, C. Aubrey Smith, Doris Lloyd, Forrester Harvey, Ivory Williams.

Literary Original and Date of Production
TARZAN OF THE APES   1912

Author and Biographical Dates
Edgar Rice Burroughs   1875-1950

Codings of 16 mm Distribution Agencies
FNC

Recommended Viewing
Recommended Reading
16 mm Film, B & W

SUMMARIES

Literary Original
Shipwrecked on a deserted coast of Africa, the parents of the infant Lord Greystone are killed by apes, which take the boy and leave a dead juvenile ape in his place. Tarzan matures in his jungle home by combining the cunning of man and instincts of his ape family. When he encounters a party of white hunters, including the beautiful Jane, he is forced to choose between civilization and life in the wild.

THEME INDICATORS
ADVENTURE
COMEDY
DRAMA
ROMANCE
ECOLOGY
FAMILY

Film Version: **Recommended**
The essentials of the original story line are followed in this film version, which glamorized the jungle settings and exploited the contact of man and jungle beast for sensational effect but which nevertheless succeeded in establishing a new subgenre of adventure film that has produced a host of inferior imitations.

Full Film Title
THAT DARN CAT

Release Date
1965

Production Studio
DISNEY

Country of Origin
USA

Running Time (Minutes)
116

Producer
Bill Walsh/Ron Miller

Director
Robert Stevenson

Principal Performers
Hayley Mills, Dean Jones, Dorothy Provine, Roddy McDowall, Elsa Lanchester, Neville Brand, William Demarest, Frank Gorshin, Richard Eastham.

Literary Original and Date of Production
UNDERCOVER CAT   1963

Author and Biographical Dates
Gordon Gordon and Mildred Gordon   1912-

Codings of 16 mm Distribution Agencies
AIM   CCC   CWF   DIS   FNC   FPC   MAC
MOD   NAT   NEW   ROA   SWA   TFC   TWY

Recommended Viewing

16 mm Film, Color

SUMMARIES

THEME INDICATORS
ADVENTURE
CRIME
COMEDY
DRAMA
ECOLOGY
ETHICS
FAMILY

Literary Original
D.C. is a resourceful Siamese cat who carries an appeal for help from a bank teller taken hostage during a robbery and leads F.B.I. agents and rescuers a merry dance during the mission to locate and extricate the prisoner.

Film Version: **Recommended**
As rewritten for the screen by the original authors, the story takes on new dimensions through the performance of the feline lead, who adds to the fun by setting the pace for the support cast of human actors.

Full Film Title
THIRD MAN ON THE MOUNTAIN

Release Date
1959

Production Studio
DISNEY

Country of Origin
USA

Running Time (Minutes)
105

Producer
William H. Anderson

Director
Ken Annakin

Principal Performers
Michael Rennie, James MacArthur, Janet Munro, James Donald, Herbert Lom, Laurence Naismith.

Literary Original and Date of Production
BANNER IN THE SKY   1954

Author and Biographical Dates
James Ramsey Ullman   1907-1971

Codings of 16 mm Distribution Agencies
AIM   BUC   CCC   COU   FNC   MAC   MOD
NAT   NEW   ROA   SWA   TWF   TWY

Recommended Viewing
Recommended Reading
16 mm Film, Color

SUMMARIES

Literary Original

In an attempt to conquer an Alpine mountain, teenaged Rudy learns that courage and conviction are the inseparable partners of physical prowess in the struggle for success.

THEME INDICATORS
ADVENTURE
DRAMA
CHILDREN
CULTURAL
ECOLOGY
ETHICS
FAMILY

Film Version: **Recommended**
A faithful and accurate reproduction of the original mountaineering adventure, with notable fine location photography.

Full Film Title
THREE LIVES OF THOMASINA

Release Date
1964

Production Studio
DISNEY

Country of Origin
USA

Running Time (Minutes)
97

Producer
Walt Disney/Hugh Attwooll

Director
Don Chaffey

Principal Performers
Patrick McGoohan, Susan Hampshire, Karen Dotrice, Vincent Winter.

Literary Original and Date of Production
THOMASINA 1957

Author and Biographical Dates
Paul Gallico 1897-

Codings of 16 mm Distribution Agencies
AIM   BUC   CCC   COU   CWF   FNC   MAC
MOD   NAT   NEW   ROA   SWA   TFC   TWY

Recommended Viewing

16 mm Film, Color

SUMMARIES

Literary Original
In rural Scotland, young Mary tends to her ailing cat, Thomasina, while her father, a veterinarian, observes the healing powers of love.

THEME INDICATORS
ADVENTURE
DRAMA
ROMANCE
CHILDREN
CULTURAL
ECOLOGY
ETHICS
FAMILY
FEMINISM
HISTORICAL

Film Version: **Recommended**
In this adaptation, Thomasina the cat becomes narrator and commentator as well as the principal performer, and the original story is further expanded to allow for an other-worldly dream sequence. The end result gives an endearing production that appeals to animal lovers and carries a clear message of the essential value of love.

Full Film Title
THREE MUSKETEERS, THE

Release Date
1949

Production Studio
METRO-GOLDWYN-MAYER

Country of Origin
USA

Running Time (Minutes)
126

Producer
Pandro S. Berman

Director
George Sidney

Principal Performers
Lana Turner, Gene Kelly, Van Heflin, Vincent Price, June Allyson, Frank Morgan, Angela Lansbury, Keenan Wynn, John Sutton, Gig Young.

Literary Original and Date of Production
THREE MUSKETEERS, THE   1844

Author and Biographical Dates
Alexandre Dumas   1802-1870

Codings of 16 mm Distribution Agencies
FNC

Recommended Viewing
Recommended Reading
16 mm Film, Color

SUMMARIES

THEME INDICATORS
ADVENTURE
MILITARY
DRAMA
ROMANCE
CULTURAL
HISTORICAL

Literary Original
D'Artagnan is a young man from the south of France who arrives in Paris in 1625, becomes friends with three soldiers, Athos, Porthos, and Aramis, and is accepted as a recruit into their regiment of musketeers. He is then embroiled in a complicated successions of intrigues and adventures to protect the interests of King Louis XIII against the maneuvers of Cardinal Richelieu.

Film Version: **Highly recommended**
Well-choreographed dueling scenes, high-spirited action, and excellent performances embellish this inventive, energetic remake.

Full Film Title
THREE MUSKETEERS, THE

Release Date
1974

Production Studio
TWENTIETH CENTURY FOX

Country of Origin
USA

Running Time (Minutes)
105

Producer
Michael Alexander/Ilya Salkind

Director
Richard Lester

Principal Performers
Oliver Reed, Charlton Heston, Raquel Welch, Faye Dunaway, Michael York, Richard Chamberlain, Frank Finlay, Geraldine Chaplin, Christopher Lee.

Literary Original and Date of Production
THREE MUSKETEERS, THE   1844

Author and Biographical Dates
Alexandre Dumas   1802-1870

Codings of 16 mm Distribution Agencies
FNC

Recommended Viewing
Recommended Reading
16 mm Film, Color

SUMMARIES

THEME INDICATORS
ADVENTURE
MILITARY
COMEDY
DRAMA
ROMANCE
CULTURAL
HISTORICAL
WAR

Literary Original
D'Artagnan is a young man from the south of France who arrives in Paris in 1625, becomes friends with three soldiers, Athos, Porthos, and Aramis, and is accepted as a recruit into their regiment of musketeers. He is then embroiled in a complicated succession of intrigues and adventures to protect the interests of King Louis XIII against the maneuvers of Cardinal Richelieu.

Film Version: **Recommended**
An entertaining costume spectacular, this version lacks the suspense of plot and sustained action of the original.

Full Film Title
THREE WORLDS OF GULLIVER, THE

Release Date
1960

Production Studio	Country of Origin	Running Time (Minutes)
COLUMBIA	**USA**	**100**

Producer
Charles Schneer

Director
Jack Sher

Principal Performers
Kerwin Matthews, Jo Morrow, June Thorburn, Lee Patterson, Gregoire Aslan, Basil Sydney, Sherri Alberoni, Mary Ellis.

Literary Original and Date of Production
GULLIVER'S TRAVELS 1726

Author and Biographical Dates
Jonathan Swift   1667-1745

Codings of 16 mm Distribution Agencies

ARG	CCC	CHA	CWF	FPC	KER	KPF	MAC	MOD
NAT	NEW	ROA	SEL	SWA	TWY	VCI	WCF	WEL
WHO	WIL							

Recommended Viewing
Recommended Reading
16 mm Film, Color

SUMMARIES

THEME INDICATORS
ADVENTURE
FANTASY
MARINE
COMEDY
DRAMA
CULTURAL
ETHICS

Literary Original
In this fantasy, Swift fires caustic social criticism at England in particular and humanity in general. In the imaginary realms of Lilliput and Brobdingnag, Lemuel Gulliver finds that the scale of things, miniature or gigantic, does little to alter human folly. He begins to hate mankind and upon his return to England is repulsed by the sight of his wife and family. Horses remain his only friends.

Film Version
Excerpts from the original satirical novel are chosen for their potential as incidents using trick photography and special effects, but neither the acting nor the production techniques measure up to the quality of the source material.

Full Film Title
THUNDERHEAD, SON OF FLICKA

Release Date
1954

Production Studio
TWENTIETH CENTURY FOX

Country of Origin
USA

Running Time (Minutes)
78

Producer
Robert Bassler

Director
Louis King

Principal Performers
Roddy McDowall, Preston Foster, Rita Johnson, James Bell, Diana Hale, Carleton Young, Ralph Sanford, Robert Filmer, Alan Bridge.

Literary Original and Date of Production
THUNDERHEAD 1945

Author and Biographical Dates
Mary O'Hara (Mary O'Hara Alsop) 1885-

Codings of 16 mm Distribution Agencies
FNC

Recommended Viewing
Recommended Reading
16 mm Film, Color

SUMMARIES

THEME INDICATORS
ADVENTURE
WESTERN
DRAMA
CHILDREN
CULTURAL
ECOLOGY
FAMILY
HISTORICAL

Literary Original
Son of a famous mother, a white stallion on the McLaughlin ranch responds to the kindness of his young master and is trained as a racehorse. However, he abandons the security of the stable and the corral to succeed his sire as champion of the herd of wild horses on the open range.

Film Version: **Recommended**
Filmed with the same principal actors as *My Friend Flicka*, this sequel follows the story line of the second book in the series by Mary O'Hara and is outstanding in the quality of its location photography.

Full Film Title

TIME MACHINE, THE

Release Date
1960

Production Studio
METRO-GOLDWYN-MAYER

Country of Origin
USA

Running Time (Minutes)
103

Producer
George Pal

Director
George Pal

Principal Performers
Robert Young, Yvette Mimieux, Alan Young, Rod Taylor, Sebastian Cabot, Tom Helmore, Whit Bissell, Doris Lloyd.

Literary Original and Date of Production
TIME MACHINE, THE 1895

Author and Biographical Dates
Herbert George Wells 1866-1946

Codings of 16 mm Distribution Agencies
FNC

Recommended Viewing
Recommended Reading
16 mm Film, Color

SUMMARIES

THEME INDICATORS
ADVENTURE
FANTASY
SCIENCE FICTION
DRAMA
ETHICS
HISTORICAL
WAR

Literary Original
The inventor of a time machine journeys into the future and witnesses the decline of human civilization. In one sequence, the apelike Morlocks, descendants of the industrialized age, are observed living in underground farms. Finally, only giant crabs remain in a world where both sun and earth are dying.

Film Version: **Recommended**
The re-creation of period is carefully handled in the establishment of the Victorian setting, but the suggestion of the remote future is less convincing in the scripted sequences developed from the original science-fiction novel.

Full Film Title
TOBY TYLER

Release Date
1960

Production Studio
DISNEY

Country of Origin
USA

Running Time (Minutes)
96

Producer
Bill Walsh

Director
Charles Barton

Principal Performers
Kevin Corcoran, Henry Calvin, James Drury, Gene Sheldon; with The Flying Viennas, The Jungleland Elephants, The Ringling Brother Clowns.

Literary Original and Date of Production
TOBY TYLER: OR, TEN WEEKS WITH A CIRCUS 1881

Author and Biographical Dates
James Otis Kaler 1848-1912

Codings of 16 mm Distribution Agencies
**CCC CWF DIS FNC MAC
MOD ROA SWA TFC TWY**

Recommended Viewing

16 mm Film, Color

SUMMARIES

THEME INDICATORS
**ADVENTURE
COMEDY
DRAMA
CHILDREN
ECOLOGY
FAMILY**

Literary Original
An American country boy in the 1880s runs away from an unhappy home to join a travelling circus.

Film Version: **Recommended**
The film is a straightforward presentation of the story line, enriched by visual presentation of the details of circus life and appealing in the performances of child and animal characters.

Full Film Title
TO KILL A MOCKINGBIRD

Release Date
1962

Production Studio
UNIVERSAL INTERNATIONAL

Country of Origin
USA

Running Time (Minutes)
129

Producer
Alan J. Pakula

Director
Robert Mulligan

Principal Performers
Gregory Peck, Mary Badham, Philip Alford, Brock Peters, Robert Duvall, John Megna, Frank Overton, Rosemary Murphy, Ruth White, Estelle Evans, Paul Fix.

Literary Original and Date of Production
TO KILL A MOCKINGBIRD   1960

Author and Biographical Dates
Harper Lee   1926-

Codings of 16 mm Distribution Agencies
CWF   SWA   TWY   UNI

Recommended Viewing
Recommended Reading
16 mm Film, B & W

SUMMARIES

Literary Original
The adolescent son of a lawyer describes his school years in a backward small town in southern Alabama and the tensions that divide it when his father arouses the opposition of racists by his successful defense in a criminal trial.

THEME INDICATORS
DRAMA
CHILDREN
CULTURAL
ETHICS
FAMILY
HISTORICAL
RACIAL

Film Version: **Highly recommended**
All the atmosphere, incident, and character of the original novel have been faithfully interpreted in this film, where steady development communicates in itself a feeling of period and setting. The acting performances are noteworthy, and the level of interest well sustained.

Full Film Title
TOM BROWN'S SCHOOLDAYS

Release Date
1940

Production Studio
RKO RADIO

Country of Origin
USA

Running Time (Minutes)
81

Director
Robert Stevenson

Principal Performers
Freddie Bartholomew, Sir Cedric Hardwicke, Billy Halop, Gale Storm, Josephine Hutchinson.

Literary Original and Date of Production
TOM **B**ROWN'S **S**CHOOLDAYS **1857**

Author and Biographical Dates
Thomas Hughes   1822-1896

Codings of 16 mm Distribution Agencies
AIM   BUD   CHA   FCE   IVY
MAC   MOG   TMC   VCI   WHO

Recommended Viewing

16 mm Film, B & W

SUMMARIES

THEME INDICATORS
D**RAMA**
C**HILDREN**
C**ULTURAL**
E**THICS**
H**ISTORICAL**

Literary Original
As a pupil at Rugby, the famous English boarding school, in the nineteenth century, Tom Brown learns the code of behavior in classroom, study, and playing field. He faces up to the school bully, learns to admire the austere standards of the headmaster, Dr. Arnold, and ends up as head pupil, ready to pass on to university.

Film Version: **Recommended**
The rather dull and heavy tone of the Victorian story has been brightened and enlivened in this film adaptation, which stresses the harsher aspects of school life but speeds up the development of the action.

Full Film Title
TOM BROWN'S SCHOOLDAYS

Release Date
1951

Production Studio
UNIVERSAL

Country of Origin
USA

Running Time (Minutes)
94

Producer
Brian Desmond Hurst

Director
Gordon Parry

Principal Performers
John Howard Davies, Robert Newton, James Hayter, Diana Wynyard, Hermione Baddeley, Kathleen Byron, John Charlesworth, John Forrest.

Literary Original and Date of Production
TOM BROWN'S SCHOOLDAYS 1857

Author and Biographical Dates
Thomas Hughes 1822-1896

Codings of 16 mm Distribution Agencies
UNI VCI

Recommended Viewing

16 mm Film, B & W

SUMMARIES

THEME INDICATORS
DRAMA
CHILDREN
ETHICS
HISTORICAL

Literary Original
As a pupil at Rugby, the famous English boarding school, in the nineteenth century, Tom Brown learns the code of behavior in classroom, study, and playing field. He faces up to the school bully, learns to admire the austere standards of the headmaster, Dr. Arnold, and ends up as head pupil, ready to pass on to university.

Film Version
This remake is slower in pace and less interesting in its overall presentation, despite the contributions of a strong acting cast and a careful regard for the detail of the original story.

Full Film Title
TOM SAWYER

Release Date
1973

Production Studio
UNITED ARTISTS

Country of Origin
USA

Running Time (Minutes)
103

Producer
Arthur P. Jacobs

Director
Don Taylor

Principal Performers
Johnnie Whitaker, Celeste Holm, Warren Oates, Jeff East, Jodie Foster.

Literary Original and Date of Production
ADVENTURES OF TOM SAWYER, THE   1876

Author and Biographical Dates
Mark Twain (Samuel Langhorne Clemens)   1835-1910

Codings of 16 mm Distribution Agencies
ROA   UAS   WCF   WHO

Recommended Viewing
Recommended Reading
16 mm Film, Color

SUMMARIES

THEME INDICATORS
ADVENTURE
COMEDY
DRAMA
CHILDREN
CULTURAL
ECOLOGY
ETHICS
FAMILY
HISTORICAL
RACIAL

Literary Original
The setting is a small town along the Mississippi in the mid-1800s. A shrewd youngster, Tom Sawyer, witnesses a murder that occurs in a moonlit cemetery. Revealing his knowledge during the trial of an innocent man, Tom is pursued by the fugitive murderer, Injun Joe.

Film Version: **Recommended**
A carefully scripted version of the novel, with the addition of some musical numbers, this film version conveys a real sense of atmosphere and period by its record of authentic scenes and settings along the Mississippi.

Full Film Title
TONKA

Release Date
1958

Production Studio
DISNEY

Country of Origin
USA

Running Time (Minutes)
97

Producer
James Pratt

Director
Lewis R. Foster

Principal Performers
Sal Mineo, Philip Carey, Jerome Courtland, Rafael Campos, Joy Page.

Literary Original and Date of Production
COMANCHE   1951

Author and Biographical Dates
David Appel

Recommended Viewing

35 mm Film, Color

SUMMARIES

Literary Original
In an episode from the history of the American West, told from the Indian viewpoint, a young Sioux brave tames a splendid wild horse but releases it again. He is reunited with the horse when it becomes a U.S. cavalry mount and survives the defeat of General George Custer at the battle of the Little Big Horn.

THEME INDICATORS
ADVENTURE
MILITARY
WESTERN
DRAMA
CULTURAL
ECOLOGY
ETHICS
HISTORICAL
RACIAL
WAR

Film Version
The story line is repeated fairly literally in a routine and acceptable production that rises to no great heights in recounting a conventional adventure story.

Full Film Title
TREASURE ISLAND

Release Date
1934

Production Studio
METRO-GOLDWYN-MAYER

Country of Origin
USA

Running Time (Minutes)
110

Director
Victor Fleming

Principal Performers
Wallace Beery, Lionel Barrymore, Lewis Stone, Otto Kruger, Douglass Dumbrille, Nigel Bruce, Chic Sale.

Literary Original and Date of Production
TREASURE ISLAND 1883

Author and Biographical Dates
Robert Louis Stevenson 1850-1894

Codings of 16 mm Distribution Agencies
FNC

Recommended Viewing
Recommended Reading
16 mm Film, B & W

SUMMARIES

Literary Original
Young Jim Hawkins gains possession of a pirate map showing the location of a buried hoard of treasure and sails with the local squire and doctor in search of it. The villainous Long John Silver leads the ship's crew in a mutiny. Only after a long and bloody struggle do Jim and his friends succeed in securing the treasure and sailing home.

THEME INDICATORS
ADVENTURE
CRIME
MARINE
DRAMA
CHILDREN
CULTURAL
ETHICS
HISTORICAL

Film Version: **Recommended**
A vintage film version of the story, which captures all the excitement of the action and is rich in detail and well-handled production technique.

Full Film Title
TREASURE ISLAND

Release Date
1950

Production Studio	Country of Origin	Running Time (Minutes)
RKO RADIO PICTURES/DISNEY	**USA**	**96**

Producer
Perce Pearce

Director
Byron Haskin

Principal Performers
Bobby Driscoll, Robert Newton, Basil Sydney, Walter Fitzgerald, Denis O'Dea, Finlay Currie, Ralph Truman, Geoffrey Keen, John Laurie, John Gregson.

Literary Original and Date of Production
TREASURE ISLAND 1883

Author and Biographical Dates
Robert Louis Stevenson 1850-1894

Codings of 16 mm Distribution Agencies
AIM BUC BYU CCC COU CWF DIS FNC
MAC MOD NAT NEW ROA SWA TWY WHO

Recommended Viewing
Recommended Reading
16 mm Film, Color

SUMMARIES

Literary Original
Young Jim Hawkins gains possession of a pirate map showing the location of a buried hoard of treasure and sails with the local squire and doctor in search of it. The villainous Long John Silver leads the ship's crew in a mutiny. Only after a long and bloody struggle do Jim and his friends succeed in securing the treasure and sailing home.

THEME INDICATORS
ADVENTURE
CRIME
MARINE
DRAMA
CHILDREN
CULTURAL
ETHICS
HISTORICAL

Film Version: **Highly recommended**
This Disney remake in color neglects detail for speed of action to make an exciting suspenseful production centering on an exceptional interpretation of the character of the crafty Long John Silver.

Full Film Title
TWENTY THOUSAND LEAGUES UNDER THE SEA

Release Date
1954

Production Studio	Country of Origin	Running Time (Minutes)
DISNEY	**USA**	**127**

Producer
Fred Leahy

Director
Richard Fleischer

Principal Performers
Kirk Douglas, James Mason, Peter Lorre, Paul Lukas, Robert J. Wilke, Carleton Young, Ted De Corsia, Percy Helton, Ted Cooper, Esmeralda.

Literary Original and Date of Production
TWENTY THOUSAND LEAGUES UNDER THE SEA   1870

Author and Biographical Dates
Jules Verne   1828-1905

Codings of 16 mm Distribution Agencies

AIM   CCC   CWF   DIS   FNC   FPC   MAC
MOD   NAT   NEW   ROA   SWA   TFC   TWY

Recommended Viewing
Recommended Reading
16 mm Film, Color

SUMMARIES

THEME INDICATORS
ADVENTURE
CRIME
FANTASY
MARINE
MONSTER
SCIENCE FICTION
DRAMA
ECOLOGY
ETHICS

Literary Original
Two passengers from a U.S. navy ship sent out in 1867 to investigate a mysterious sea monster find themselves captives aboard the Nautilus, a giant submarine designed and built by the brilliant but antisocial Captain Nemo. The strange vessel roams the oceans of the world. The French scientist who is the narrator escapes to tell the secrets of its operations and the plans of its dangerous master.

Film Version: **Highly recommended**
The original story line has been trimmed down to the essentials as the basis for a vivid and fast-paced narrative, with impressive special effects and trick photography supporting good acting performances in a film that communicates all the excitement and suspense intended by the author.

Full Film Title
TWO YEARS BEFORE THE MAST

Release Date
1946

Production Studio
UNIVERSAL/PARAMOUNT

Country of Origin
USA

Running Time (Minutes)
98

Director
John Farrow

Principal Performers
Alan Ladd, Brian Donlevy, Howard Da Silva, William Bendix, Barry Fitzgerald, Albert Dekker, Luis Van Rooten, Darryl Hickman.

Literary Original and Date of Production
TWO YEARS BEFORE THE MAST 1840

Author and Biographical Dates
Richard Henry Dana 1815-1882

Codings of 16 mm Distribution Agencies
UNI

Recommended Viewing

16 mm Film, B & W

SUMMARIES

THEME INDICATORS
ADVENTURE
CRIME
MARINE
DRAMA
ETHICS
HISTORICAL

Literary Original
The book is a log of first-hand observations of the brutal working and living conditions for sailors in the merchant marine, recorded in the 1830s by the author, who signed on as crewman on a Boston ship. The incidents of a trading voyage round Cape Horn to California are recorded with vivid detail of storms, harsh discipline, heavy labor, and soul-destroying callousness of treatment.

Film Version: **Recommended**
The film treatment alters the emphasis of the original by having the central character sign on as a seaman in a deliberate attempt to record and expose brutalities. The resulting melodramatic confrontations weaken the effect of the story, but sufficient detail is preserved to give the production many points of interest.

Full Film Title
VIRGINIAN, THE

Release Date
1946

Production Studio
UNIVERSAL

Country of Origin
USA

Running Time (Minutes)
90

Producer
Paul Jones

Director
Stuart Gilmore

Principal Performers
Joel McCrea, Brian Donlevy, Sonny Tufts, Barbara Britton.

Literary Original and Date of Production
VIRGINIAN, THE   1902

Author and Biographical Dates
Owen Wister   1860-1938

Codings of 16 mm Distribution Agencies
UNI

Recommended Viewing
Recommended Reading
16 mm Film, B & W

SUMMARIES

Literary Original

The Virginian is a young cowboy who brings order and the rule of law to a turbulent community in Wyoming in the early days of the West. After an exciting series of incidents — brawls, shoot-outs, a lynching — he falls in love with the local schoolteacher and is accepted by her as a difficult but dependable husband.

THEME INDICATORS
ADVENTURE
WESTERN
DRAMA
ETHICS
HISTORICAL

Film Version

In this film version, much of the power and the historical validity of the novel have been lost in its conversion into the story line for a western on conventional lines.

Full Film Title
WAR OF THE WORLDS

Release Date
1953

Production Studio
PARAMOUNT

Country of Origin
USA

Running Time (Minutes)
85

Producer
George Pal

Director
Bryon Haskin

Principal Performers
Gene Barry, Ann Robinson, Les Tremayne, Bob Cornthwaite, Sandro Giglio, Lewis Martin, Houseley Stevenson, Paul Frees, Bill Phipps.

Literary Original and Date of Production
WAR OF THE WORLDS, THE   1898

Author and Biographical Dates
Herbert George Wells   1866-1946

Codings of 16 mm Distribution Agencies
PAR

Recommended Viewing

16 mm Film, Color

SUMMARIES

Literary Original
An Englishman describes how hostile Martians descend in spaceships and destroy London with their impregnable machines. Their human opponents are helpless against them, but the invaders succumb to earthly bacteria and die off, leaving the countryside devastated.

THEME INDICATORS
ADVENTURE
FANTASY
MILITARY
MONSTER
SCIENCE FICTION
DRAMA
ECOLOGY
WAR

Film Version: **Recommended**
The location is moved to the U.S.A., and the invaders from outer space modernized into science fiction form in a film adaptation that concentrates on the violence and terrifying events of the original fantasy.

Full Film Title
WATUSI

Release Date
1958

Production Studio
METRO-GOLDWYN-MAYER

Country of Origin
USA

Running Time (Minutes)
85

Producer
Al Zimbalist

Director
Kurt Neumann

Principal Performers
George Montgomery, Taina Elg, David Farrar, Rex Ingram, Dan Seymour.

Literary Original and Date of Production
KING SOLOMON'S MINES   1886

Author and Biographical Dates
H. Rider Haggard   1856-1925

Codings of 16 mm Distribution Agencies
FNC

Recommended Reading
16 mm Film, Color

SUMMARIES

Literary Original
Henry Curtis and Captain John Good enlist the aid of explorer Allan Quatermain in the search for Curtis's brother, not heard from since he departed in quest of the legendary fortunes of King Solomon. In darkest Africa, they survive exposure and bloodthirsty tribesmen before discovering the jewel mines. With a pocketful of diamonds, they escape a death trap and, while returning to civilization, unexpectedly encounter the lost brother.

THEME INDICATORS
ADVENTURE
DRAMA
CULTURAL
ECOLOGY
ETHICS
HISTORICAL
RACIAL

Film Version
This uninspired remake lacks the energy and suspense of Haggard's novel, from which it marginally acquires its plot.

Full Film Title
WEE GEORDIE

Release Date
1955

Production Studio
BRITISH LION FILMS

Country of Origin
Great Britain

Running Time (Minutes)
99

Producer
Frank Launder/Sidney Gilliat

Director
Frank Launder

Principal Performers
Bill Travers, Alastair Sim, Norah Gorsen, Brian Reece, Raymond Huntley, Miles Malleson, Jack Radcliffe, Jameson Clark.

Literary Original and Date of Production
GEORDIE 1950

Author and Biographical Dates
David Walker 1920-

Recommended Viewing

35 mm Film, Color

SUMMARIES

THEME INDICATORS
COMEDY
DRAMA
CHILDREN
CULTURAL
FAMILY

Literary Original
A Scottish gamekeeper's son signs on for a mail-order body-building course. He achieves so much success that he becomes a champion athlete at Olympic Games in Melbourne, Australia.

Film Version
The simple original narrative falls easily into an equally simple and uncomplicated film treatment, in which authentic backgrounds add to the charm of the gently humorous narrative.

Full Film Title
WILLY WONKA AND THE CHOCOLATE FACTORY

Release Date
1971

Production Studio
PARAMOUNT

Country of Origin
USA

Running Time (Minutes)
98

Producer
David Wolper

Director
Mel Stewart

Principal Performers
Gene Wilder, Jack Albertson, Peter Ostrum, Roy Kinnear, Aubrey Woods.

Literary Original and Date of Production
CHARLIE AND THE CHOCOLATE FACTORY   1964

Author and Biographical Dates
Roald Dahl   1916-

Codings of 16 mm Distribution Agencies
FNC

Recommended Viewing
Recommended Reading
16 mm Film, Color

SUMMARIES

Literary Original
A boy finds himself in the spell of a magician when he wins a contest with the prize of a tour of the local chocolate factory.

THEME INDICATORS
ADVENTURE
FANTASY
COMEDY
CHILDREN

Film Version: **Recommended**
The film script was rewritten by the author of the original novel, and the production represents the visualization of a modern fantasy on fairytale lines, with musical interludes and good entertainment values for uncritical viewers.

Full Film Title
WINNIE THE POOH AND THE HONEY TREE

Release Date
1969

Production Studio
DISNEY

Country of Origin
USA

Running Time (Minutes)
84

Director
Wolfgang Reitherman

Principal Performers
Animation

Literary Original and Date of Production
WINNIE-THE-POOH (Series) 1926-1927

Author and Biographical Dates
Alan Alexander Milne 1882-1956

Recommended Viewing
Recommended Reading
35 mm Film, Color

SUMMARIES

THEME INDICATORS
ANIMATION
FANTASY
COMEDY
CHILDREN
CULTURAL
FAMILY

Literary Original
Winnie the Pooh is a teddy bear gifted with all-but-human powers, who is by his own admission not very clever and extremely fond of honey. He has little adventures with his master Christopher Robin and the other characters around his home locality, including a donkey, a piglet, and a pair of kangaroos.

Film Version: **Highly recommended**
Directed by Wolfgang Reitherman, this animated fantasy is considered one of the loveliest works produced by the Disney studios.

Full Film Title
WIZARD OF OZ, THE

Release Date
1939

Production Studio	Country of Origin	Running Time (Minutes)
METRO-GOLDWYN-MAYER	**USA**	**102**

Producer
Mervyn LeRoy

Director
Victor Fleming

Principal Performers
Judy Garland, Ray Bolger, Bert Lahr, Jack Haley, Frank Morgan, Billie Burke, Margaret Hamilton, Charlie Grapewin, The Singer Midgets.

Literary Original and Date of Production
WONDERFUL WIZARD OF OZ, THE   1906

Author and Biographical Dates
Frank Lyman Baum   1856-1919

Codings of 16 mm Distribution Agencies	**Recommended Viewing**
FNC	**Recommended Reading**
	16 mm Film, Color

SUMMARIES

THEME INDICATORS
ADVENTURE
FANTASY
MUSICAL
COMEDY
CHILDREN
FAMILY

Literary Original
Dorothy and her dog Toto find themselves transported, as in a dream, into the wonderful realm of Oz. There the Scarecrow, the Tin Man, the Cowardly Lion, and a host of others befriend them against the sorcery of the Wicked Witch of the West, before they return to the security of their own backyard.

Film Version: **Very highly recommended**
The book blossoms into new life in the screen version, which adds music, special effects and excellent characterizations to make a presentation that is well established as an outstanding classic of children's cinema and a perennial delight to viewers of all ages.

Full Film Title
WONDERFUL WORLD OF THE BROTHERS GRIMM, THE

Release Date
1962

Production Studio
Metro-Goldwyn-Mayer

Country of Origin
USA

Running Time (Minutes)
129

Producer
George Pal

Director
Henry Levin/George Pal

Principal Performers
Laurence Harvey, Claire Bloom, Yvette Mimieux, Russ Tamblyn, Walter Slezak, Barbara Eden, Oscar Homolka, Terry Thomas, Beulah Bondi, Jim Backus.

Literary Original and Date of Production
Grimm's Fairy Tales

Author and Biographical Dates
Jakob Grimm   1785-1863, Wilhelm Grimm   1786-1859

Codings of 16 mm Distribution Agencies
FNC

Recommended Viewing
Recommended Reading
16 mm Film, Color

SUMMARIES

THEME INDICATORS
Fantasy
Comedy

Literary Original
The Rhine Country, the Black Forest, and Bavaria are represented in three stories from the collection of the Brothers Grimm, "The Dancing Princess," "The Cobbler and The Elves," and "The Singing Bone."

Film Version: **Recommended**
A biographical account of the famous collectors of German folktales is illustrated by dramatizations of three of their stories, accurately enough recounted, but undistinguished in execution.

Full Film Title
WUTHERING HEIGHTS

Release Date
1939

Production Studio
METRO-GOLDWYN-MAYER

Country of Origin
USA

Running Time (Minutes)
104

Producer
Samuel Goldwyn

Director
William Wyler

Principal Performers
Laurence Olivier, Merle Oberon, David Niven, Hugh Williams, Flora Robson, Geraldine Fitzgerald, Donald Crisp, Cecil Kellaway.

Literary Original and Date of Production
WUTHERING HEIGHTS   1847

Author and Biographical Dates
Emily Brontë   1818-1848

Codings of 16 mm Distribution Agencies
AIM   BUD   IMA   MAC   ROA   TWY   VCI   WHO

Recommended Viewing
Recommended Reading
16 mm Film, B & W

SUMMARIES

THEME INDICATORS
ROMANCE
TRAGEDY

Literary Original
The daughter of a landed Yorkshire family in the late 1700s falls madly in love with a strange magnetic Gipsy who has been her childhood companion.

ETHICS
FAMILY
FEMINISM
HISTORICAL

Film Version: **Very highly recommended**
The film adaptation loses something of the literary values of the original classic by making dialogue and settings more acceptable to modern audiences. However, the power and sombre tragedy of the work are well preserved, and the acting performances justify the intentions of the production.

Full Film Title
YEARLING, THE

Release Date
1946

Production Studio
METRO-GOLDWYN-MAYER

Country of Origin
USA

Running Time (Minutes)
134

Producer
Sidney Franklin

Director
Clarence Brown

Principal Performers
Gregory Peck, Jane Wyman, Chill Wills, Marjorie Kinnan Rawlings, Clem Bevans, Claude Jarman, Jr., Forrest Tucker, Donn Gift, Daniel White, Matt Willis.

Literary Original and Date of Production
YEARLING, THE   1938

Author and Biographical Dates
Marjorie Kinnan Rawlings   1896-1953

Codings of 16 mm Distribution Agencies
FNC

Recommended Viewing
Recommended Reading
16 mm Film, Color

SUMMARIES

Literary Original
Jody Baxter, the young hero of the Pulitzer Prize-winning novel, is the son of a farmer who struggles to make a marginal living from poor farmland in Florida. He becomes attached to a tame fawn and is heartbroken when his parents are forced to have it killed to protect their scanty crops. The tragedy, however, forces him out of childhood into a deeper vision of life.

THEME INDICATORS
DRAMA
CHILDREN
CULTURAL
ECOLOGY
ETHICS
FAMILY
HISTORICAL

Film Version: **Highly recommended**
The Pulitzer Prize novel is respectfully followed in this visualization, with sensitive and appealing characterizations and an effective communication of the author's feeling for the painful process of growing up.

© Walt Disney Productions

SECTION V
FILM RENTAL INFORMATION

CHAPTER 9

GENERAL FILM RENTAL INFORMATION

LISTED here are some useful and helpful guidelines to follow when renting films for your program. While specifics may vary to some extent between companies, the following are the generally accepted procedures honored by most rental sources.

Who May Rent

Most rental libraries welcome film rental orders from schools, institutions, and organizations, as well as responsible individuals, located throughout the United States.

Restrictions

Generally, the use of the films is restricted to bona fide educational purposes. Under no circumstances may admission be charged directly or indirectly without *prior written permission* from the lending agency. Films may not be used for television purposes, including any form of transmission and videotape copying, unless the user has *obtained prior written permission from the copyright holder*. Contact the appropriate distributor for copyright referral.

How To Order

Films should be ordered by mail at least three weeks in advance of the date desired. Telephone orders are generally accepted only on an emergency basis and are generally limited to a maximum of two films. Films are mailed five days in advance of the utilization dates. Requests that fail to allow adequate time for processing and shipment are generally not processed.

If it becomes necessary to cancel a previously scheduled film booking, notice must be received in writing at least two weeks prior to the scheduled shipping date that appears on the confirmation copy of the rental booking. *Cancellation requests received less than two weeks prior to the scheduled shipping date will not be honored, and the customer is obligated to pay the rental charges.*

Include the following information when you place a film rental order.

    a. Indicate the person and address where the film and confirmation notice should be mailed. If the bill is not to be sent to the same person as the confirmation, be sure to specify to whom it should be sent. Provide a complete billing and mailing address, including zip code. *If your organization requires a purchase order number, submit it with your order.*

    b. Double space between lines. List one title per line. Scheduling clerks need the extra space above each entry for notes about shipping and scheduling.

    c. List the entire title as it appears in the catalog; avoid listing only part of a title. Some of the films are part of a series; be sure to include the series heading also.

    d. Indicate, when there is a choice, whether to ship a color or black and white print. The rental rates will vary accordingly.

    e. Indicate your first and second choice booking dates, or indicate whether the film can be scheduled for the nearest available date. Remember to check vacation and holiday periods before scheduling.

Rental Charges

The listed rental rate for each film generally covers a loan period up to five days, Monday through Friday, if initially requested at the time of the order; otherwise, the loan period is for *one day*. With the continued increased cost of rental library operations, it is essential that you refer to the *most current catalog* for rental rates. If there is doubt about the fee, a phone call will verify current charges.

General Film Rental Information

Penalty Charges

Please make it a practice to return films on the day following use to *avoid* penalty charges.

Damage Charges

The customer is often billed for replacement prints or footage charges covering the loss of, or extensive damage to, a print resulting from careless handling and projection. Extensive damage is interpreted as when the cost of the replacement footage exceeds the rental rates. This charge, in addition to the rental charge, will appear on the rental billing invoice.

Film Repair

Do not attempt to repair damaged film without proper splicing equipment. If the film breaks or an old splice separates, tuck the broken end under several layers of film on the take-up reel and continue projection. Do not attempt to patch with tape, paper clips, or pins. Return all damaged or separated sections for proper splicing. Generally, there is no charge to the customer for minor repairs to films. The customer is responsible for loss of or extensive damage to the films beyond normal wear and minor breaks. See paragraph on damage charges.

Shipping Procedures

Films will be shipped via United States Postal System or United Parcel Service to arrive at least a day before the scheduled show date. Should the preceding user be late in returning the film, every effort will be made to expedite shipping the film to you on time. If a late film cannot possibly reach you in time for the scheduled date, you will be telephoned and a decision reached whether to reschedule or cancel the booking.

The customer is required to return films prepaid on the day following the last day of the scheduled loan period. Return the films on the same reels and in the same cans and shipping cases. Return mailing labels will be provided. Please tape down the end of the films to prevent unraveling during the return shipment. *Insure return shipments for an amount equal to twenty-five (25) times the basic daily rental rate*. Mail the films as "Library Materials," a special low postal rate, or utilize the UPS service for a more rapid, guaranteed return.

Billing Procedures

An invoice for rental services will be submitted to the customer on the first of the month following date of use. *Do not send payment until the invoice statement is received*. Payment should be forwarded within thirty days to the rental agency.

Preview Policy

Most film companies charge the regular rental rate for preview.

General Film Rental Information

SAMPLE FILM RENTAL ORDER

Date: _____

Ship To: _____   Bill to: (if different from address at left)

_____ _____

_____ _____

_____ _____

Customer's Purchase Order No. _____

Confirm to (if different from "Ship To" Address) _____

_____

May films be scheduled to nearest available date?

Yes _____   No _____   Within 2 weeks _____   Within Semester _____

Customer Special Instructions: _____

_____

_____
Signature

List Complete Film Title (Please arrange alphabetically)	B&W or Color	Requested Use Dates		Confirmed Use Date (Leave Blank)
		First	Alternate	

NOTE: *Please observe your vacation schedule when ordering.*

200 Selected Film Classics for Children of All Ages

Customer: _____   Page _____ of _____

Customer Purchase Order No. _____

List Complete Film Title (Please arrange alphabetically)	B&W or Color	Requested Use Dates		Confirmed Use Date (Leave Blank)
		First	Alternate	

© Walt Disney Productions

SECTION VI
FILM DISTRIBUTORS

CHAPTER 10

DIRECTORY OF FILM COMPANIES AND DISTRIBUTORS

Reprinted from *Feature Films on 8mm, 16mm, and Videotape* with permission of the R.R. Bowker Company. Copyright © 1982 by James L. Limbacher.

DIRECTORY OF ADDRESSES AND TELEPHONE NUMBERS

ABC
ABC Wide World of Learning
1330 Ave. of the Americas
New York NY 10019
 (212)581-7777

ABF
ABC Film Library
560 Main St.
Fort Lee NJ 07063

ACT
Action 27 Film Library
Box 315
Franklin Lakes NJ 07417
 (201) 891-8240

ADL
Anti-Defamation League
823 United Nations Plaza
New York NY 10017
 (212)490-2525

AEF
American Educational Films Inc.
162 Fourth Ave. North (Suite 123)
Nashville TN 37219
 (615)242-3330

AFI
The American Film Institute
John F. Kennedy Center
Washington DC 20566
 (202)828-4080

AFL
Asian Film Library
609 Columbus Ave.
New York NY 10024
 (212)877-3732

AIF
America's Films
1735 NW Seventh St.
Miami FL 33125
 (305)643-0250

ALB
Alba House (Don Bosco)
7050 Pinehurst (Box 40)
Dearborn MI 48126
 (313)582-2033

ALD
Alden Films
7820 20th Ave.
Brooklyn NY 11214

AMB
American Mutoscope and Biograph Co.
 of Milwaukee
3802 E. Cudahy Ave.
Cudahy WI 53110

APL
Amerpol Enterprises
11601 Joseph Campeau
Hamtramck MI 48212
 (313)365-6780

APP
Appalshop
Box 743N
Whitesburg KY 41858
 (606)633-5708 and 4811

ARC
Arthur Cantor Inc.
243 W. 44 St.
New York NY 10036
 (212)391-0450

ARG
Arcus Films Inc.
1225 Broadway
New York NY 10001
 (212)686-2216

ASI
The Asia Society
Performing Arts/Film & Broadcasting
725 Park Ave.
New York NY 10021
 (212)288-6400

ATC
Astro Video (Astronics Tele-Cine)
90 Golden Gate Ave.
San Francisco CA 94102
 (800)227-3248 and (415)673-4320

AUB
Audio Brandon Films
34 MacQuesten Pkwy. North
Mt. Vernon NY 10550
 (914)664-5051, (800)742-1889 (NY),
 and (800)431-1994 (outside NY)

AUF
Auteur Films
1042 Wisconsin Ave. NW
Washington DC 20007
 (202)333-6966

AUS
Australian Information Service
636 Fifth Ave.
New York NY 10111
 (212)245-4000

BEN
Benchmark Films
145 Scarborough Rd.
Briarcliff Manor NY 10510
 (914)762-3838

BES
Best Films
Box 725
Del Mar CA 92014
 (714)755-9327

BFC
National Council of Churches of Christ
 in the USA
Communication Commission
475 Riverside Dr. (Rm. 860)
New York NY 10027
 (212)870-2575

BKW
Blackwood Films
251 W. 57 St.
New York NY 10019
 (212)688-0930

Directory of Film Companies and Distributors

BLA
Blackhawk Films
Eastin-Phelan Corp.
Davenport IA 52808
(319)323-9736 and (800)553-1163

BON
Bonaventure Prod.
2 Carlton St. (Suite 715)
Toronto, Ontario M5B 1J3, Canada
(416)366-3057

BRZ
Brazos Films
10341 San Pablo Ave.
El Cerrito CA 94530
(415)525-1494

BUC
Buchan Pictures
254 Delaware Ave.
Buffalo NY 14202
(716)853-1805

BUD
Budget Films
4590 Santa Monica Blvd.
Los Angeles CA 90029
(213)660-0187 and 0800

BUL
Bullfrog Films
Oley PA 19547
(215)779-8226

BYU
Brigham Young University
Ed. Media Services
290 Herald R. Clark Bldg.
Provo UT 84601
(801)374-1211, ext. 2713

CAA
Cinema Arts Associates/Cinema
 Perspectives
200 Park Ave. South (Suite 1319)
New York NY 10003
(212)254-8778

CAL
University of California
Extension Media Center
2223 Fulton St.
Berkeley CA 94720
(415)845-6000

CAM
Cambridge Documentary Films
Box 385
Cambridge MA 02139
(617)354-3677

CAR
Carousel Films
1501 Broadway (Suite 1519)
New York NY 10036
(212)354-0315

CBC
Canadian Broadcasting Corp.
CBC Educational Films
Box 500 (Sta. A)
Toronto, Ontario M5W 1E6, Canada
(416)925-3311

CBS
CBS Inc.
51 W. 52 St.
New York NY 10019
(212)765-4321

CCC
Cine-Craft Co.
1720 W. Marshall
Portland OR 79209
(503)228-7484 and (800)547-4785

CDF
(Merce) Cunningham Dance Foundation
463 West St.
New York NY 10014
(212)691-9751

CDY
Concern for Dying
250 W. 57 St.
New York NY 10019
(212)246-6962

CEA
Carman Educational Assoc.
Box 205
Youngstown NY 14174

CEN
Centron Educational Films
1621 W. Ninth St.
Lawrence KS 66044
(913)843-0400

CES
Cecile Starr
50 W. 96 St.
New York NY 10025
(212)749-1250

CET
Centre Prod.
1327 Spruce St. (Suite 3)
Boulder CO 80302
(303)444-1166

CFM
Classic Film Museum
6 Union Square
Dover-Foxcroft ME 04426
(207)564-8371

CFS
Creative Film Society
7237 Canby Ave.
Reseda CA 91335
(213)881-3887

CHA
Charard Motion Pictures
2110 E. 24 St.
Brooklyn NY 11229
(212)891-4339

CHU
Churchill Films
622 N. Robertson Blvd.
Los Angeles CA 90069

CIE
Cinema Concepts/Cinema Eight
2461 Berlin Turnpike
Newington CT 06111
(203)667-1251

CIN
Hurlock Cine-World
13 Arcadia Rd.
Old Greenwich CT 06870
(203)637-4319

CIV
Cinema 5
1500 Broadway
New York NY 10036
(212)354-5515

CNF
Cine Information
419 Park Ave. South (19th fl.)
New York NY 10016
(212)686-9897

COU
Cousino Visual Ed. Serv.
1945 Franklin Ave.
Toledo OH 43624
(419)246-3691

CPF
US China Peoples Friendship Assoc.
302 Fifth Ave. (10th fl.)
New York NY 10001
(212)736-7355

CRY
Crystal Prod.
Box 12317
Aspen CO 81612

CSF
Center for Southern Folklore
1216 Peabody Ave.
Box 40105
Memphis TN 38104
(901)726-4205

CTH
Corinth Films
410 E. 62 St.
New York NY 10021
(212)421-4770

CTW
Children's Television Workshop
1 Lincoln Plaza
New York NY 10023
(212)595-3456

Directory of Film Companies and Distributors

CWB
Colonial Williamsburg Foundation
Film Distribution Section
Box C
Williamsburg VA 23187
(703)229-1000

CWF
Clem Williams Films
2240 Noblestown Rd.
Pittsburgh PA 15205
(412)921-5810

DBF
Don Bosco Films
48 Main St.
Box T
New Rochelle NY 10802
(914)632-6562

DFA
Dance Film Archive
University of Rochester
Rochester NY 14627

DIS
Walt Disney Prod.
500 S. Buena Vista St.
Burbank CA 91521
(800)423-2555

DOC
Document Associates
211 E. 43 St.
New York NY 10017
(212)682-0730

DRC
Direct Cinema Ltd.
Box 69589
Los Angeles CA 90060
(213)656-4700

DWP
Daniel Wilson Productions
300 W. 55 St.
New York NY 10019
(212)765-7148

EAI
Electronic Arts Intermix
84 Fifth Ave.
New York NY 10011
(212)989-2317

EBE
Encyclopaedia Britannica Ed. Corp.
425 N. Michigan Ave.
Chicago IL 60611
(312)321-6800 and (800)621-3900

EDC
Education Development Center Inc.
39 Chapel St.
Newton MA 02160
(617)969-7100

EDP
Edupac
231 Norfolk St.
Walpole MA 02081
(617)668-7746

ELL
Elliott Film Co.
2635 Nicollet Ave.
Minneapolis MN 55408
(612)870-3750

EMC
Educational Media Corp./UEVA
6930½ Tujunga Ave.
North Hollywood CA 91605
(213)985-3921

EMG
Em Gee Film Library
6924 Canby Ave. (Suite 103)
Reseda CA 91335

EVR
Entertainment Video Releasing
1 E. 57 St.
New York NY 10022
(212)752-2240

FAC
FACSEA (French American Cultural
   Services & Educational Aid)
972 Fifth Ave. (6th fl.)
New York NY 10021
   (212)570-4400

FCE
Film Classic Exchange
1914 S. Vermont Ave.
Los Angeles CA 90007
   (213)731-3854

FES
Festival Films
2841 Irving Ave. South
Minneapolis MN 55408
   (612)822-2680

FFH
Films for the Humanities
Box 2053
Princeton NJ 08540
(201)329-6912

FIN
Edward Finney
1578 Queens Blvd.
Hollywood Ca 90069
   (213)656-0200

FLO
Flower Films/Les Blank
10341 San Pablo Ave.
El Cerrito CA 94530
   (415)525-0942 and 1494

FMC
Canyon Cinema Cooperative
2325 Third St.
San Francisco CA 94107
   (415)626-2255

FML
Film-makers Library
133 E. 58 St. (Suite 703A)
New York NY 10022

FNC
Films Incorporated
733 Green Bay Rd.
Wilmette IL 60091
   (312)256-6600 and (800)323-1406

FPC
Film Presentation Co.
514 Rt. 27 (Box 232)
Iselin NJ 08830
   (201)283-1700

FRE
Fremontia Films
Box 315
Franklin Lakes NJ 07417

FRF
First Run Features
144 Bleecker St.
New York NY 10012
   (212)673-6881 and 6882

FWT
Film Wright
4530 18 St.
San Francisco Ca 94114
   (415)863-6100

GEN
videotapes are generally available
   from local dealers

GKE
Gold Key Entertainment
855 N. Cahuenga Blvd.
Los Angeles CA 90067

GME
Griggs-Moviedrome
263 Harrison St.
Nutley NJ 07110

Directory of Film Companies and Distributors

GMP
Green Mountain Post Films
Box 229
Turners Falls MA 01376
(413)863-4754

GOL
Golden Tapes Videotape Library
336 Foothill Rd.
Beverly Hills CA 90213
(213)550-8156

GOS
Gospel Films
Box 455
Muskegon MI 49443
(616)773-3361
or
2735 E. Apple Ave.
Muskegon MI 49442

GPN
Great Plains National ITV Library
Box 80669
Lincoln NE 68501
(402)472-2007

GPS
Glenn Photo Supply
6924 Canby Ave. (Suite 103)
Reseda CA 91335

GRA
Graphic Curriculum
699 Madison Ave.
New York NY 10021
(212)688-0033

GRE
Joseph Green Pictures Co.
200 W. 58 St.
New York NY 10019
(212)246-9343 and 9344

GRO
Grove Press Film Div.
196 W. Houston St.
New York NY 10014
(212)242-4900

HER
Gary L. Herne Sales
910 Hilton Rd.
Ferndale MI 48220
(313)398-4144

HOL
Theodore Holcomb
11 E. 90 St.
New York NY 10028
(212)861-6293

ICA
Icarus Films/Cinema Perspectives
200 Park Ave. South (Suite 1319)
New York NY 10003
(212)674-3375

ICS
Institutional Cinema Inc.
10 First St.
Saugerties NY 12477
(914)246-2848

IFB
International Film Bureau
332 S. Michigan Ave.
Chicago IL 60604
(312)427-4545

ILL
University of Illinois
Film Center
1325 S. Oak St.
Champaign IL 61820
(217)333-1360

IMA
Images Film Archive
300 Phillips Park Rd.
Mamaroneck NY 10543
(914)381-2993

IND
Indiana University
Audio-Visual Center
Bloomington IN 47405
(812)332-0211

IQF
I. Q. Films
Box 326
Wappingers Falls NY 12590
(914)297-0070

IRE
Embassy of Ireland
2234 Massachusetts Ave. NW
Washington DC 20008
(202)483-7639

ISH
Institute for the Study of Human Issues
3401 Market St. (Suite 252)
Philadelphia PA 19104

IVY
Ivy Films
165 W. 46 St.
New York NY 10036
(212)765-3940

JAN
Janus Films
c/o Films Inc.
733 Green Bay Rd.
Wilmette IL 60091
(312)256-6600 and (800)323-1406

JAP
The Japan Society
NHK Films
333 E. 47 St.
New York NY 10017
(212)832-1155

JER
JER Pictures
165 W. 46 St.
New York NY 10036
(212)247-4220

JNP
Jeffrey Norton Publishers
Audio Division
145 E. 49 St.
New York NY 10017
(212)753-1783

KEN
Kent State University
Film Rental Center
Audio Visual Services
Kent OH 44242
(216)672-3456

KER
Kerr Film Exchange
3034 Canon St.
San Diego CA 92106
(714)224-2406

KIL
The Killiam Collection
Rental Division
6 E. 39 St.
New York NY 10016
(212)684-3920

KIN
King Features Prod.
235 E. 45 St.
New York NY 10017
(212)682-5600

KPF
Kit Parker Films
1245 Tenth St.
Monterey CA 93940
(403)649-5573

LAF
Latin-American Film Project
c/o Unifilm
419 Park Ave. South (19th fl.)
New York NY 10016
(212)686-9897

LCA
Learning Corp. of America
1350 Ave. of the Americas
New York NY 10019
(212)397-9330

LEA
Pennebaker Associates
21 W. 86 St.
New York NY 10024
(212)469-9195

LEW
Lewis Film Serv.
1425 E. Central
Witchita KS 67214
(316)263-6991

LFA
Lutheran Film Associates
1 Main Pl.
Dallas TX 75250
(214)747-8048

LSU
Louisiana State University
Instructional Resources Center
Himes Hall (Rm. 118)
Baton Rouge LA 70803
(504)388-1135

LUC
Lucerne Films
37 Ground Pine Rd.
Morris Plains NJ 07950

MAC
Macmillan Films
34 MacQuestern Pkwy. South
Mount Vernon NY 10550
(914)664-5051

MAG
Magnetic Video Corp.
23705 Industrial Park Dr.
Farmington Hills MI 48018
(313)477-6066

MAL
Embassy of Malaysia
2401 Massachusetts Ave. NW
Washington DC 20008
(202)234-7600

MAS
Master & Masterworks
1431 Ocean Ave. (Suite 1400)
Santa Monica CA 90401
(213)393-8337

MAY
Maysles Films
250 W. 54 St.
New York NY 10019
(212)582-6050

MER
Merco International Films
Box B
Somis CA 93066
(805)484-2213

MHF
CRM/McGraw-Hill Films
110 Fifteenth St.
Del Mar CA 92014
(714)453-5000

MIC
University of Michigan
Media Resources Center
416 Fourth St.
Ann Arbor MI 48109
(313)764-5360

MJK
Maljack Productions VCI
Box 153
Tinley Park IL 60477
(312)687-7881

MMA
Museum of Modern Art
Department of Film
11 W. 53 St.
New York NY 10019
(212)956-4204 and 4205

MMM
Mass Media Associates
2116 N. Charles St.
Baltimore MD 21218
(301)727-3270

MOD
Modern Sound Pictures
1402 Howard St.
Omaha NE 68102
(402)341-8476

MOG
Mogull's Films
1280 North Ave.
Plainfield NJ 07062
   (201)753-6004

MOK
Arthur Mokin Prod.
17 W. 60 St.
New York NY 10023
   (212)757-4868

MOM
Modern Mass Media
Box 950
Chatham NJ 07928
   (201)635-6000

MTI
MTI Teleprograms
3710 Commercial Ave.
Northbrook IL 60062
   (312)291-9400 and (800)323-5343

MTP
Modern Talking Pictures
(check local area for nearest office)

NAC
National Audio-Visual Center
General Services Administration
Washington DC 20409
   (301)763-1896

NAT
National Film Serv.
14 Glenwood Ave.
Raleigh NC 27602
   (919)832-3901

NCE
New Cinema Ltd.
35 Britain St.
Toronto, Ontario M5A 1R7, Canada
   (416)862-1674

NCS
National Cinema Service
Box 43
Ho-Ho-Kus NJ 07423
   (201)445-0776

NDF
New Day Films
7 Harvard St.
Brookline MA 02145
   (617)566-5914

NEW
Newman Film Library
1444 Michigan Ave.
Grand Rapids MI 49503
   (616)454-8157

NFB
National Film Board of Canada
1251 Ave. of the Americas
New York NY 10020
   (212)586-5131

NFV
National Film and Video Center
7566 Main St.
Sykesville MD 21784
   (800)638-1688

NGE
National Geographic Society
Educational Serv., Dept. 78
Washington DC 20036

NLC
New Line Cinema
853 Broadway (16th fl.)
New York NY 10003
   (212)674-7460 and (800)221-5150

NSR
California Newsreel/Media at
   Work/Resolution
630 Natoma
San Francisco CA 94103
   (415)621-6196

NTA
National Telefilm Associates
12636 Beatrice St.
Los Angeles CA 90066
   (213)390-3663

NWU
Northwestern University
Film Library
Box 1665
Evanston IL 60204
   (312)869-0600

NYF
New Yorker Films
16 W. 61 St.
New York NY 10023
(212)247-6110

NYU
New York University
Film Library
26 Washington Pl.
New York NY 10003
(212)777-2000

ODE
Odeon Films
Box 315
Franklin Lakes NJ 07417

OKS
Oklahoma State University
Audio-Visual Center
Stillwater OK 74078
(405)372-6211

OPC
Open Circle Cinema
Box 315
Franklin Lakes NJ 07417
(201)891-8240

PBS
PBS Video
475 L'Enfant Plaza SW
Washington DC 20024
(202)488-5220 and (800)424-7963

PEN
Pennsylvania State University
Audio-Visual Services
Special Services Bldg.
University Park PA 16802
(814)865-6314

PER
Perspective Films
369 W. Erie St.
Chicago IL 60610
(312)977-4100 and (800)621-2131

PNX
Phoenix/BFA Films and Video
470 Park Ave. South
New York NY 10016
(212)684-5910

POL
Embassy of the Polish People's Republic
2640 16 St. NW
Washington DC 20009
(202)234-3800

PYR
Pyramid Films
Box 1048
Santa Monica CA 90406
(213)828-7577

QUA
Quality X Video Cassette Co.
356 W. 44 St.
New York NY 10036
(212)541-7860

RAD
Film Images/Radim Films
1034 Lake St.
Oak Park IL 60301
(312)386-4826

RAY
Bruce A. Raymond Prod.
353 St. Clair Ave. East
Toronto, Ontario M4T 1P3, Canada
(416)485-3406

RBF
Red Ball Films
41 Union Square
New York NY 10003
(212)924-4368

RED
Red Fox Enterprises
Rt. 209 East
Elizabethville PA 17023

REE
Reel Images
456 Monroe Turnpike
Monroe CT 06468
　(203)261-5022 and (800)243-9289

RKO
RKO Radio Pictures
1440 Broadway
New York NY 10018
　(212)764-7108

ROA
Roa's Films
1696 N. Astor St.
Milwaukee WI 53202
　(414)271-0861 and (800)558-9015

SAF
Step Ahead Films
1800 Ave. of the Stars (Suite 900)
Los Angeles CA 90067

SBC
Serious Business Co.
1145 Mandana Blvd.
Oakland CA 94610
　(415)832-5600

SDS
South Dakota State University
Audio-Visual Center
University Station
Brookings SD 57006
　(605)688-5115
　and
University of South Dakota
Film Library
Educational Media Center
Vermillion SD 57069
　(605)677-5411

SEE
See-Art Films
Box 638
Ardsley-on-Hudson NY 10503
　(914)591-9207

SEI
Salzburg Enterprises
Atrium Bldg.
98 Cutter Mill Rd.
Great Neck NY 11201
　(516)487-4515

SEL
Select Film/Video
115 W. 31 St.
New York NY 10001
　(212)594-4450

SIX
Distribution 16
32 W. 40 ST. (#2-L)
New York NY 10018
　(212)730-0280

SOU
Southern Chroniclers
Box 9925
Savannah GA 31412
　(912)236-7757

SPE
Special Purpose Films
26740 Latigo Shore Dr.
Malibu CA 90265

SPF
Specialty Films
911 NE 50th
Seattle WA 98105
　(206)634-3834

STA
Standard Film Service
Box 52
Frankenmuth MI 48734
　(517)652-8881

STE
Sterling Educational Films
241 E. 34 St.
New York NY 10016
　(212)683-6300

Directory of Film Companies and Distributors

STO
Stouffer Enterprises
Box 4740
Aspen CO 81611
(303)925-9227

SWA
Swank Motion Pictures
201 S. Jefferson Ave.
St. Louis MO 63166
(314)534-6300

SYR
Syracuse University
Film Rental Center
1455 E. Colvin St.
Syracuse NY 13210
(315)423-2452 and 479-6631

TAM
Tamarelle's French Film House
110 Cohasset Stage Rd.
Chico Ca 95925
(916)895-3429

TEX
Texture Films
1600 Broadway
New York NY 10019
(212)586-6960

TFC
"The" Film Center
938 K St. NW
Washington DC 20001
(202)393-1205

THR
Threshold Films
2025 N. Highland Ave.
Hollywood Ca 90068
(213)874-8413

THU
Thunderbird Films
3500 Verdugo Rd.
Los Angeles CA 90065
(213)256-6566

TIM
Time-Life Multimedia
Time & Life Bldg.
New York NY 10020
(212)664-0408

TLC
The Liberty Co.
695 W. Seventh St.
Plainfield NJ 07060
(201)757-1450

TNM
The Nostalgia Merchant
6255 Sunset Blvd. (Suite 1019)
Hollywood CA 90028
(800)421-4495

TRI
Tricontinental Film Center/Unifilm
419 Park Ave. South
New York NY 10016
(212)686-9897

TVG
TVG Documentary Arts Project
Box 315
Franklin Lakes NJ 07417
(201)891-8240

TVL
The Video Library
2 Union Hill Industrial Park
West Conshohocken PA 19428
(215)825-7080

TWF
Trans-World Films
332 S. Michigan Ave.
Chicago IL 60604
(312)922-1530

TWY
Twyman Films
4700 Wadsworth Rd.
Dayton OH 45414
(513)222-4014 and (800)543-9594

UAS
United Artists 16
729 Seventh Ave.
New York NY 10019
  (212)575-4715 and (800)223-0933

UCV
University Community Video
Studio A, Rarig Center
University of Minnesota
Minneapolis MN 55455
  (612)373-9838

UFM
Unifilm
419 Park Ave. South
New York NY 10016
  (212)686-9897

UMC
United Methodist Communications
810 Twelfth Ave. South
Nashville TN 37203
  (615)256-0530 and (800)251-4091

UND
United Documentary Films
Box 315
Franklin Lakes NJ 07417
  (201)891-8240

UOC
University of Colorado
Educational Media Center
Bureau of Audio-Visual Instruction
Box 379
Boulder CO 80309
  (303)443-2211

UON
University of Nevada
Audio-Visual Center
Education Bldg.
Reno NV 89507

UTA
University of Utah
Educational Media Center
Milton Bennion Hall 207
Salt Lake City UT 84110
  (801)322-6112

VCA
Video Corp. of America
Home Video Corp.
231 E. 55 St.
New York NY 10022
  (212)355-1600 and (800)223-1318

VCI
Video Communications Inc.
6555 E. Skelly Dr.
Tulsa OK 74145
  (618)583-2681

VIE
Viewfinders
Box 1665
Evanston IL 60204
  (312)869-0600

VIX
Videx Home Library
Box G (Madison Square Sta.)
New York NY 10010
  (212)925-7744 and (800)221-5480

VSQ
Vision Quest
Box 206
Lawenceville NJ 08648
  (609)896-1359

VTN
Video Tape Network
115 E. 62 St.
New York NY 10021
  (212)759-8735

VYD
Vydio Philms
Box 6586
Surfside FL 33154

WCF
Westcoast Films
25 Lusk St.
San Francisco CA 94107
  (415)227-3058

Directory of Film Companies and Distributors

WEF
Wayne Ewing Films
Box 32269
Washington DC 2007

WEL
Welling Motion Pictures
454 Meacham Ave.
Elmont NY 11003
 (516)354-1066, 1067, and 1068

WES
Weston Woods Studio
Weston CT 06680
 (203)226-0600 and (800)243-5020

WGP
William Greaves Prod.
1776 Broadway (Suite 1802)
New York NY 10019
 (212)586-7710 and (516)775-1285

WHO
Wholesome Film Center
20 Melrose St.
Boston MA 02116
 (617)426-0155

WIL
Willoughby-Peerless
115 W. 31 St.
New York NY 10001
 (212)594-4450

WMM
Women Make Movies
100 Fifth Ave. (Rm. 1208)
New York NY 10011
 (212)929-6477

WNC
World Northal Corp.
1 Dag Hammarskjold Plaza
New York NY 10017
 (212)223-8181

WNE
WNET/13 Media Serv.
356 W. 58 St.
New York NY 10019
 (212)262-4940

WOM
Wombat Productions Inc.
Little Lake, Glendale Rd.
Box 70
Ossining NY 10562
 (914)762-0011

WRS
Walter Reade 16
241 E. 34 St.
New York NY 10016
 (212)683-6300

WWP
Wade William Prod.
5500 Ward Pkwy.
Kansas City MO 64113
 (816)523-2699

XEX
Xerox Films
Communications Park
Video and Film
Box 4000
Mt. Kisco NY 10549
 (914)666-4100

YPS
Young People's Specials
Multimedia Program Prod.
140 W. Ninth St.
Cincinnati OH 45202

ZPH
Zippoah Films
54 Lewis Wharf
Boston MA 02110
 (617)742-6680

© Walt Disney Productions

SECTION VII
HOW TO USE AND CARE FOR FILMS

CHAPTER 11

FILM CARE AND PROJECTION GUIDES

A Few Words on Film

A THIN sheet of flexible cellulose or polyester is used for the *film base*, or support. The *base* is coated with a light-sensitive *emulsion* in which the photographic image is formed.

Motion picture film is commonly available in three sizes: 8 mm*, 16 mm, and 35 mm (Fig. 1). The measurement, in millimeters, describes the width of the film, not the size of the frame. Sound is recorded on an optical sound track or a magnetic sound stripe.

Both the emulsion and the base of the film are subject to damage from improper handling or storage.

Film Maintenance

A consistent, thorough maintenance program is important to any film library, regardless of size. The time and expenditure are worthwhile investments; it usually takes less time to prevent a problem than it does to solve it.

Preventive Measures
1. Clean and lubricate library films regularly. Circulated films should be cleaned after every use.

The authors wish to thank William N. Stelcher, President, Kinetronics for providing material from *Handbook of Motion Picture Film Care*, © 1978 by Kinetronics Corporation, Lake Bluff, Illinois, for use in this chapter.

*Note: Super 8 mm and 8 mm film are the same width. Super 8 mm film, though, has a larger frame area and is perforated differently than regular 8 mm film. Not all projectors are designed to accept both types; check the manufacturer's instructions in regard to compatibility.

2. Review the quality of films during projection or inspect after use by other persons.

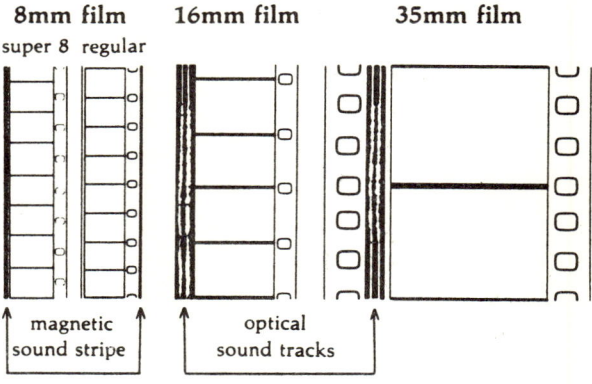

Figure 1.

3. Store films properly. Review or check films that have been stored or unused for one to three years. Look for dust and dirt, mold, mildew, and signs of brittleness such as splices beginning to open at the corners.
4. Handle films carefully. Avoid the following:
    a. Touching film surface with fingers.
    b. Letting loose film fall on tables, floors, and so forth.
    c. Placing anything on top of films.
    d. Stepping on films.
5. Wear film gloves whenever handling films.
6. Make splices and other repairs carefully.
7. Discard bent or damaged reels or cartridges.
8. When mailing films, use standard plastic or fiber shipping cases. These have been specially designed to protect films from most damage.
9. Do not pull the end of a wound reel of film to tighten it.
10. Do not overfill reels; allow ¼ to ½ inch of space to the rim.
11. It is recommended that smoking, drinking, or eating not be permitted in areas where film is handled or stored.
12. Use a film *leader* (2 to 3 feet is recommended) to protect the *head* of

the film from damage caused by improper threading. A 2 to 3 foot *trailer* is also used to identify the *tail* end of the film. Green is most often used for the head, and red for the tail.
13. Provide general maintenance and servicing for projectors according to the manufacturer's recommendations.
14. Keep projectors covered when not in use.
15. Project films with care.
    a. Follow projector manufacturer's instructions for threading, operating, and rewinding.
    b. Clean the film path on the projector (Fig. 2) before each film use or at least daily. A cotton swab or small brush can be used.

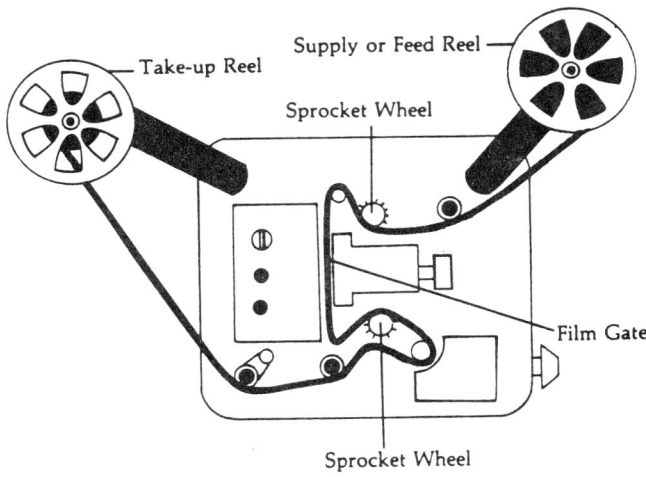

Figure 2. A generalized view of a 16 mm motion picture projector, illustrating the film path. The projector parts, particularly the film gate, should be cleaned regularly.

    c. Use a *take-up reel* that is as large as the film's reel and be sure both are securely situated or latched on the reel spindles.
    d. Before starting the projector, check that the film is threaded correctly and the sprocket teeth and film sprocket holes are properly engaged.

e. Stay nearby when operating a projector. If the film begins to jump and *chatter* or other problems develop, stop the projector first; then try to find the source of the problem.
f. If a film breaks, stop the projector immediately. Overlap the free end onto the *take-up reel*, rotate the reel to secure the end, and mark the break with a slip of paper. Never use adhesive tape, staples, paper clips, or other objects to temporarily mend broken film — such materials may permanently damage that part of the film.
g. When using film *cartridges*, wait until the film has stopped before removing the cartridge.
h. Always report any problems with films or projectors to the person responsible for them; this helps prevent further damage to the materials and inconvenience to other users. If you cannot directly report the difficulties, write them down and include the note with the film or tape it to the projector.

© Walt Disney Productions

SECTION VIII
INDEX

AUTHOR INDEX

A

Aberson, Helen (coauthor) (dates not available)
Dumbo, 96
Adamson, Joy (1910-   )
Born Free, 69
Living Free, 156
Alcott, Louisa May (1832-1888)
Little Men, 151
Little Women, 154, 155
Appel, David (dates not available)
Tonka, 239
Atkinson, Eleanor (1863-1942)
Greyfriars Bobby, 110
Austen, Jane (1775-1817)
Pride and Prejudice, 192

B

Bach, Richard (1936-   )
Jonathan Livingston Seagull, 128
Bagnold, Enid (1889-   )
National Velvet, 179
Barrie, Sir James Matthew (1860-1937)
Peter Pan, 187
Baum, Frank Lyman (1856-1919)
Wizard of Oz, The, 250
Benson, Sally (1900-1972)
Meet Me in St. Louis, 169
Blackmore, Richard Dodridge, (1825-1900)
Lorna Doone, 157, 158

Bolt, Robert (1924-   )
Man for All Seasons, A, 164
Bonnet, Theodore (1865-1920)
Mudlark, The, 175
Boulle, Pierre (1912-   )
Planet of the Apes, 190
Brontë, Emily (1818-1848)
Wuthering Heights, 252
Buck, Pearl S. (1892-1973)
Good Earth, The, 107
Bulwer-Lytton, Sir Edward (1803-1873)
Last Days of Pompeii, 144
Burnett, Frances Hodgson (1849-1924)
Little Lord Fauntleroy, 150
Little Princess, The, 153
Secret Garden, The, 211
Burnford, Sheila (1918-   )
Incredible Journey, The, 124
Burroughs, Edgar Rice (1875-1950)
Tarzan the Ape Man, 225

C

Carroll, Lewis (Charles Lutwidge Dodgson) (1832-1898)
Alice in Wonderland, 56
Alice's Adventures in Wonderland, 57
Collodi, Carlo (Carlo Lorenzini) (1892-1890)
Pinocchio, 189
Cooper, James Fenimore (1798-1851)
Last of the Mohicans, 145
Last of the Redmen, 146

Note: Titles of works listed under authors' names are film titles, not necessarily the authors' book titles.

Crane, Stephen (1871-1900)
  Red Badge of Courage, The, 199
Curie, Eve (1904-   )
  Madame Curie, 163

D

Dahl, Roald (1916-   )
  Willy Wonka and the Chocolate Factory, 248
Dana, Richard Henry (1815-1882)
  Two Years Before the Mast, 243
Defoe Daniel (1660-1731)
  Adventures of Robinson Crusoe, The, 54
Dickens, Charles (1812-1870)
  Christmas Carol, A, 80, 81
  David Copperfield, 88, 89
  Great Expectations, 109
  Nicholas Nickleby, 180
  Oliver Twist, 183
  Pickwick Papers, The, 188
  Scrooge, 208
  Tale of Two Cities, A, 222, 223
Douglas, Lloyd Cassel (1877-1951)
  Big Fisherman, The, 65
  Robe, The, 202
Doyle, Sir Arthur Conan (1859-1930)
  Hound of the Baskervilles, The, 119, 120
  Lost World, The, 160
Dumas, Alexandre (1802-1870)
  Count of Monte Cristo, The, 84
  Man in the Iron Mask, The, 165
  Three Musketeers, The, 229, 230

E

Edmonds, Walter D. (1903-   )
  Drums Along the Mohawk, 95

F

Fleming, Ian (1908-1964)
  Chitty Chitty Bang Bang, 79
Forester, Cecil Scott (1899-1966)
  Captain Horatio Hornblower, R.N., 75

G

Gallico, Paul (1897-   )
  Three Lives of Thomasina, 228
George, Jean Graighead (1919-   )
  My Side of the Mountain, 177
Gipson, Fred (1908-1973)
  Old Yeller, 182
  Savage Sam, 205
Gordon, Gordon and Mildred (1912-   )
  That Darn Cat, 226
Greene, Ward (1892-1956)
  Lady and the Tramp, The, 142
Grimm Brothers (Jakob 1785-1863 and Wilhelm 1786-1859)
  Wonderful World of the Brothers Grimm, The, 251

H

Haggard, H. Rider (1856-1925)
  King Solomon's Mines, 139
  She, 213
  Watusi, 246
Heyerdahl, Thor (1914-   )
  Kon-Tiki, 141
Hilton, James (1900-1954)
  Goodbye Mr. Chips, 106
  Lost Horizon, 159
Hope, Anthony (1863-1933)
  Prisoner of Zenda, 193, 194
Hughes, Richard (1900-   )
  High Wind in Jamaica, A, 118
Hughes, Thomas (1822-1896)
  Tom Brown's Schooldays, 236, 237
Hugo, Victor (1802-1885)
  Hunchback of Notre Dame, The, 122

I

Irving, Washington (1783-1859)
  Ichabod and Mr. Toad, 123

K

Kaler, James Otis (1848-1912)
  Toby Tyler, 234
Kastner, Erich (1899-1974)
  Emil and the Detectives, 99
Kavanagh, Herminie Templeton (dates not available)
  Darby O'Gill and the Little People, 87
Kipling, Rudyard (1865-1936)
  Captains Courageous 76
  Elephant Boy, 97
  Gunga Din, 112
  Jungle Book, The, 132
  Kim, 134

Author Index

Kjelgaard, Jim (1910-1959)
Big Red, 66
Knight, Eric (1897-1943)
Lassie Come Home, 143

L

Lee, Harper (1926-   )
To Kill a Mockingbird, 235
Lofting, Hugh (1886-1947)
Doctor Dolittle, 90
London, Jack (1876-1916)
Call of the Wild, The, 71, 72
Sea Wolf, The, 210

M

McCulley, Johnston (1883-1958)
Mark of Zorro, The, 166
Malory, Sir Thomas (1400-1471)
Knights of the Round Table, The, 140
Mason, Alfred Edward Woodley (1865-1948)
Four Feathers, The, 103
Storm over the Nile, 217
Maxwell, Gavin (1914-1969)
Ring of Bright Water, 201
Melville, Herman (1819-1941)
Moby Dick, 172
Milne, Alan Alexander (1882-1956)
Winnie the Pooh and the Honey Tree, 249
Montgomery, Lucy Maud (1874-1942)
Anne of Green Gables, 58

N

Nesbit, Edith (1858-1924)
Railway Children, The, 197
North, Sterling (1906-1974)
So Dear to My Heart, 214

O

O'Hara, Mary (Mary O'Hara Alsop) (1885-   )
My Friend Flicka, 176
Thunderhead, Son of Flicka, 232
Orczy, Baroness Emma Magdalena (1865-1947)
Elusive Pimpernel, The, 98
Scarlet Pimpernel, The, 207

Oursler, Fulton (1893-1952)
Greatest Story Ever Told, The, 108

P

Pearl, Harold (coauthor) (dates not available)
Dumbo, 96
Perreault, Charles (1628-1703)
Cinderella, 82
Podhajsky, Alois (dates not available)
Miracle of the White Stallions, The, 171
Porter, Eleanor Hodgman (1868-1920)
Pollyanna, 191

R

Rawlings, Marjorie Kinnan (1896-1953)
Yearling, The, 253
Rice, Alice Hegan (1870-1942)
Mrs. Wiggs of the Cabbage Patch, 173, 174
Richter, Conrad (1890-1968)
Light in the Forest, The, 149
Roberts, Kenneth (1885-1957)
Northwest Passage, 181
Rostand, Edmond (1868-1918)
Cyrano de Bergerac, 85

S

Sabatini, Rafael (1875-1950)
Black Swan, The, 68
Captain Blood, 74
Fortunes of Captain Blood, The, 102
Scaramouche, 206
Sea Hawk, The, 209
Saint-Exupéry, Antoine de (1900-1944)
Little Prince, The, 152
Salten, Felix (1869-1945)
Bambi, 61
Schaefer, Jack (1907-   )
Shane, 212
Scott, Sir Walter (1771-1832)
Ivanhoe, 127
King Richard and the Crusaders, 138
Quentin Durward, 195
Seton, Ernest Thompson (1860-1946)
King of the Grizzlies, 137
Legend of Lobo, The, 147
Sewell, Anna (1820-1878)
Black Beauty, 67

Shakespeare, William (1564-1616)
 As You Like It, 60
 Chimes at Midnight, 78
 Hamlet, 113, 114
 Henry V, 117
 Julius Caesar, 130, 131
 King Lear, 136
 Macbeth, 161, 162
 Midsummer Night's Dream, A, 170
 Othello, 185, 186
 Richard III, 200
 Romeo and Juliet, 203, 204
 Taming of the Shrew, The, 224
Shelley, Mary (1791-1851)
 Frankenstein, 104
Sherwood, Robert E. (1896-1955)
 Abe Lincoln in Illinois, 50
Sienkewicz, Henry (1846-1916)
 Quo Vadis?, 196
Smith, Dodie (1896-)
 One Hundred and One Dalmatians, 184
Spyri, Johanna Hauser (1827-1901)
 Heidi, 115, 116
Stevenson, Robert Louis (1850-1894)
 Dr. Jekyll and Mr. Hyde, 91, 92
 Kidnapped, 133
 Master of Ballantrae, The, 168
 Treasure Island, 240, 241
Swift, Jonathan (1667-1745)
 Gulliver's Travels, 111
 Three Worlds of Gulliver, The, 231

T
Thorndike, Arthur Russell (1885-1972)
 Dr. Syn, 93
 Doctor Syn Alias the Scarecrow, 94
Trapp, Maria Augusta (1905-)
 Sound of Music, The, 216
Travers, Pamela Lyndon (1906-)
 Mary Poppins, 167
Twain, Mark (Samuel Langhorne Clemens) (1835-1910)
 Adventures of Huckleberry Finn, 51, 52
 Adventures of Tom Sawyer, 238
 Connecticut Yankee, A, 83
 Huckleberry Finn, 121
 Tom Sawyer, 55

U
Ullman, James Ramsay (1907-1971)
 Third Man on the Mountain, 227

V
Verne, Jules (1828-1905)
 Around the World in Eighty Days, 59
 Five Weeks in a Balloon, 101
 From the Earth to the Moon, 105
 In Search of the Castaways, 125
 Journey to the Centre of the Earth, A, 129
 Light at the Edge of the World, The, 148
 Mysterious Island, The, 178
 Twenty Thousand Leagues Under the Sea, 242

W
Walker, David (1920-)
 Wee Geordie 247
Wallace, Edgar (1875-1932)
 King Kong, 135
Wallace, Lew (1827-1905)
 Ben Hur, 64
Webster, Jean (1876-1916)
 Daddy Long Legs, 86
Wells, Herbert George (1866-1946)
 First Men in the Moon, The, 100
 Invisible Man, The, 126
 Time Machine, The, 233
 War of the Worlds, The, 245
Werfel, Franz (1890-1945)
 Song of Bernadette, The, 215
White, Elwyn Brooks (1899-)
 Charlotte's Web, 77
White, Terence Hanbury (1906-1964)
 Sword in the Stone, The, 221
Wiggin, Kate Douglas (1856-1923)
 Rebecca of Sunnybrook Farm, 198
 Summer Magic, 218
Wilde, Oscar (1856-1900)
 Canterville Ghost, The, 73
Wister, Owen (1860-1938)
 Virginian, The, 244
Wouk, Herman (1915-)
 Caine Mutiny, The, 70
Wren, Percival Christopher (1885-1941)
 Beau Geste, 62, 63
Wyss, Johann (1781-1830)
 Swiss Family Robinson, The, 219, 220